# TRAVELS WITH RACHEL

## *In Search of South America*

George Mahood

*To our kind and generous friends and family for
making this adventure possible – thank you*

www.facebook.com/georgemahood

www.twitter.com/georgemahood

www.instagram.com/georgemahood

www.georgemahood.com

# ONE

The U.S. customs officer eyeballed me, his stony face devoid of any emotion. I was in deep trouble. I had not set foot in America since overstaying my visa by two months, during an eight–month road trip around the United States a few years earlier. There had been no problems passing through customs when I left the country, my passport glanced at only briefly on the way out, but the world had changed since then and airport security across the globe had tightened considerably. It hadn't even crossed my mind when my wife Rachel and I booked our flights to South America that I would once again have to pass through U.S. security. We were in Houston, Texas for a matter of minutes before catching a connecting flight to Quito.

The officer looked down at the passport again and back up at me, his eyes now cold and menacing. Surely this was it? Reinforcements would be called, I would be marched away by armed guards, interrogated for hours in a small cramped holding cell, stripped naked, given a full body cavity search, and then – if I was lucky – put on the first plane back to England. Our travels would be over before we had even reached the South American continent.

He looked down at my passport once more. This time studying it for a few seconds longer. He shook his head a little and raised his eyes towards mine. The edges of his mouth twitched very slightly and then stretched slowly into a smile, which turned swiftly into a grin that spread across his entire face. He let out a booming laugh that echoed around the terminal and caused those in the adjacent queues to turn and look our way. Just when I thought things couldn't get any worse, I now had a large audience to witness my humiliation.

He laughed again, this time trying to disguise it with a cough, and a globule of snot rocketed from his nose onto the passport in his hand. He quickly wiped it off, and it was at this point I realised he hadn't even been looking at my expired visa. He was looking at my passport photo.

It was a photo taken at the age of 17 during the year of my life that I had frizzy, shoulder-length hair. Shortly after the photo was taken I had my hair cut short, but had suffered the passport photo ever since. It was taken nine years previously. I was just a boy. A boy with really stupid hair. On every holiday since, I had been quizzed or laughed at by officials who didn't believe that I was the same person pictured. It wasn't due to expire for another year. I had been so preoccupied with worrying about my visa that I had completely forgotten about the damn photo.

'You have a nice day now!' said the officer, finally pulling himself together and handing me my passport.

'Let me guess, your hair?' said Rachel, as we hurried to catch our connecting flight.

'Every bloody time! At least he didn't look at the visa. I can't wait until this passport expires.'

It was midnight when we landed in Quito, Ecuador's capital city. Travelling with only hand luggage, Rachel and I were the first into the arrivals hall – after only a brief snigger at my passport photo from the Ecuadorian officials. We had expected the airport to be deserted in the middle of the night, but the small terminal was bustling with taxi drivers and tour operators fighting for our custom. From our limited research before coming to South America, it appeared that rule number one when travelling in the continent was: *DO NOT get into any random cars.* We had a room booked at a hostel but had not arranged any means of getting there, so pushed dismissively through the haggling taxi drivers to a small information desk at the far end of the building.

'Taxi? Por favor,' I said, in my basic Spanish.

'Si. Taxis!' said the lady, gesturing to the huddle of drivers who had followed us to the information desk.

'Ah, no. Telephonio taxi?' I tried, with my thumb and little finger extended into the international sign language for telephone. Probably.

The lady shook her head and looked at me as though I had made the stupidest request in the world. I wanted to whip out my Lonely Planet and show her the bit about being wary of unlicensed cabs. Who was I kidding? This was South America. We weren't going to get very far if we stuck to the rules.

'I guess we just pick one of these guys,' I said to Rachel. 'Who shall we go with?'

'Er... I don't know. What does a trustworthy taxi driver look like?'

There was a smiling man to my right whose smile got even bigger when I pointed at him.

'Yeah, he looks trustworthy,' said Rachel as we followed him outside to his cab. 'Good choice.'

'And he's small and old,' I said. 'I reckon I could take him down if it came to it.'

Rachel gave me a look that suggested she thought otherwise.

'Hostal L'Auberge Inn, por favor,' I said to the driver.

'Bueno,' he said.


Ecuador was the first of three countries Rachel and I would be visiting in South America, the other two being Peru and Bolivia. We had our first night's accommodation booked, but nothing arranged from that point onwards. No accommodation, no tours and no transport, except our return flight back to the UK from Peru's capital Lima in six weeks' time.


Rachel and I became friends at school. We remained close and saw each other regularly during our three years at different universities a few hours apart. We finally became a couple towards the end of our final year of university, after I had already made plans to travel across America with my friend Mark. Mark and I travelled the southern United States together for three months, he returned home, and I worked at a ski resort in Colorado for a few months, all the while trying to persuade Rachel to come to America to join me for the rest of the road trip. She eventually agreed, and we had an incredible few months exploring the back roads of the northern United States together, sleeping in the back of our rusty shitmobile named Josephine.

Being apart for almost six months and then travelling together in such a confined space had made our relationship stronger. A few months after we came home, we moved into a damp and mouldy one bedroom flat in downtown Northampton. A year later, we bought our first house together, and 18 months after that we were married.

I had been working in charity fundraising, which sounds far more exciting and altruistic than it was. My job title was Data Information Officer, which combined three dull words together to make for one exceedingly dull job. I was responsible for the accuracy of the names and the addresses of all those on the charity's database.

There were two clocks on the wall in the communal office in which I worked. One was five minutes slow, the other five minutes fast. I timed my arrival to work by the slow clock, and when I left at the end of the day I went by the fast one. I effectively shaved 10 minutes off every working day. Once 5 pm came around (or 4.55 pm), I would leave work, walk the 1.5 miles home, and then not have to think about my job until 9am (or 9.05am) the following morning.

I was good at the job (a five–year–old could have been good at my job), and I tried to make the most of the role. I produced some phenomenal analytical reports about the average donations received from different demographics in the East Midlands area, and the accuracy of my database's postcodes for supporters aged

65 and over in North Yorkshire is still talked about by Data Information Officers around the world.

The job was fine. It paid the bills. It wasn't in the least bit stressful or difficult. But there is only so much fulfilment you can get from a database full of names and addresses, and being a Data Information Officer gave me absolutely zero job satisfaction.

It's not as if I hadn't been warned. When I went for my job interview, the head of department – who would later become my boss – told me she didn't think I was suited to the role and even suggested I was perhaps overqualified (the only time in my life anyone has ever told me that), and that I would find the job unfulfilling and boring. I told her that I didn't mind and that I wasn't hugely ambitious in terms of a career. I just wanted a job.

I knew my job as Data Information Officer was not going to be my career forever. It was just a temporary thing to pay the bills. Only, that temporary position had stretched to over four years, and I had done absolutely nothing to try and change it.

Rachel had lacked any career aspirations too, and had worked in a series of equally tedious admin jobs for three of those four years. She then realised that something needed to change. She left her job and enrolled on a teacher training course at the local college to qualify as a primary school teacher. She spent the year before we came to South America studying hard and teaching in several school placements around the county. It was extremely challenging, she worked long hours, had lots of studying and lesson preparation to do, but there was a spark in her I had not seen before. Teaching had energised her and given her a new zest for life.

I was envious. Not envious enough to want to train to be a primary school teacher, but Rachel's career change made me realise that I didn't have to plod through life, working in a job that gave me nothing in the way of enjoyment. I didn't know what it was I wanted to do. But I knew it didn't involve staring at a database all day long.

Life had become too easy. I needed risk. I needed fun. I needed an adventure. While Rachel did her teacher training course, I saved up all my annual leave, booked a couple of months off with this accrued holiday, and told my boss I would not be returning to work. She couldn't believe it had taken me over four years. Rachel and I booked flights to South America that departed a couple of days after she qualified. She already had a permanent teaching position lined up at a school for when she returned at the end of the summer. I had nothing.

Rachel and I had married a year earlier. We asked our wedding guests not to bring us presents – we had lived together for three years and had accumulated a house full of crap. Instead, we set up an account with a travel agent and any guests who wanted to buy us a present had the option of contributing to our honeymoon fund. This fund paid for our tickets to South America. We did have a short, cheap package holiday to Corfu immediately after our wedding – where we rarely ventured further afield than the hotel's swimming pool and restaurant – but South America was always going to be our proper honeymoon.

I had travelled fairly extensively all over Europe, the United States and Canada. But every one of my trips had been to a country where I either shared a common language or was in an environment not too dissimilar to the UK. South America represented a different kind of travelling and a different kind of challenge.

There are a lot of risks associated with travelling in South America. According to media reports, bus hijackings, street robberies, and kidnappings are not uncommon. Not to mention the thousands of deadly animals in the Amazon rainforest. A close friend of my sister was hit by a stray bullet during a raid on a bus in Peru only weeks before we flew to South America, and was lucky to escape with non–life–threatening injuries. Another friend of a friend spent weeks in a Bolivian hospital after contracting malaria.

Despite the potential dangers, South America offered so much more as a travel destination than anywhere we had ever been. It was a continent full of excitement and experiences that we would not be able to have in other parts of the world. It was because of this that it became our honeymoon destination of choice. Rachel and I were both apprehensive about the trip, and had genuine concerns about safety, security, disease and illness. Rachel was also deeply worried she might not see a pair of hair straighteners, and I feared that it would be impossible to check the football results from the middle of the Amazon jungle. But we knew that this fear could be used as a positive, and channelled into ensuring we had the holiday of a lifetime.

And so we found ourselves in a taxi, circling the dark streets of Quito for many miles before we reached the hostel. There was one building I swear we passed three times. But we made it to our accommodation without incident, and collapsed into a deep sleep.

# TWO

We woke early on our first morning in Ecuador, partly due to jetlag, but mostly because of excitement. We could hear the city streets bursting to life outside our window. Quito was wide awake, and so were we. We threw on some clothes, packed a small daysack, and headed out the door.

Quito sits at the foot of the Pichincha volcano, and the city is split quite distinctly into two halves. The southern part is the original 'old town', with its narrow streets lined with imposing colonial buildings painted in every shade of pink and orange imaginable. The 'new town' to the north is more developed, with shops, banks, office buildings and city parks. Our hostel was positioned conveniently between the two.

We walked north along Avenue Gran Columbia, passing the pretty Parque El Arbolito – where office workers were enjoying a morning coffee before work – and into the new town.

At 9,350 ft, Quito is the second highest capital city in the world. La Paz, Bolivia's capital, is the runaway winner. To ease ourselves into life at high–altitude in the Andes, and reduce the risk of altitude sickness, we ate a lavish breakfast of omelette, pancakes, fruit salad and coffee. We phoned our parents to let them know we had arrived safely, emailed friends from an internet café, and leisurely wandered the streets. We were well aware that this was as civilised as life was going to be for the next six weeks. Quito's 'new town' feels a lot like any other commercial city centre, and is far removed from the rest of Ecuador, Peru and Bolivia.

Any possible altitude sickness we might have felt had been counteracted by the feeling of excitement at being in a continent neither of us had visited before. Mid–morning, we got a series of buses to The Mitad del Mundo – the 'Middle of the World' – which lies about 23km north of Quito. Considering it is one of Quito's biggest tourist attractions, it was surprisingly difficult to find.

'I think this is where we have to change buses,' I said, glancing out of the window and matching a street sign to one on my map.

'Really? Are you sure?' said Rachel.

'Yes. Quick, let's get off.'

The bus had slowed to a crawl but showed no signs of coming to a complete standstill. A couple of passengers stepped off the moving vehicle without a second thought.

'I guess we just jump,' I said to Rachel, as I stepped from the bus onto the road. I turned, expecting to see Rachel following behind, but she stood frozen in the doorway.

'Come on,' I said.

'Is it not going to stop? Surely it's going to stop.'

'I don't think it is. Quickly. Just step off.'

She hesitated a moment longer and then the doors of the bus swung closed and she was left squashed against the other side of it.

Her eyes widened, and I could see the panic fill her face. She shouted something through the glass, but I couldn't hear anything over the rumble of the traffic. And then the bus engine growled, it spat out a cloud of black smoke from its exhaust pipe and accelerated up the street. Rachel's helpless eyes followed mine and I pointed frantically in the direction of the bus, not quite sure what I meant by my own gesticulation.

Moments later, the bus was gone, and we were separated in a continent we had been in for less than 12 hours. We had mobile phones, but both were out of service until we bought new SIM cards – a job which we had planned to do later that day. Rachel didn't have a map or any money, or any idea where we were, or even where we were staying.

I decided to follow the bus in the hope that it stuck to the main road and that Rachel would have the common sense to successfully disembark at the next stop. I dodged in and out of market traders, hordes of people heavily laden with sacks of vegetables, old men on bikes, and several dogs. After about half a mile, I eventually caught sight of Rachel. She was standing at the side of the road staring at a lamppost.

'Oh, thank god you're here,' she said, throwing her arms around me. 'I didn't know what to do. I was looking at this bus timetable but then I realised I had no idea where I am or where we were going.'

'Let's not get separated again, ok? Oh, and that's not a bus timetable, it's a list of church services.'

'Oh. I thought it looked a bit weird.'

We caught another bus and arrived at the Mitad del Mundo just before midday. Rachel disembarked first this time. The Mitad del Mundo is a fairly tacky and incredibly touristy monument that marks the line of the equator. It serves no real purpose other than for people to go and stand with a foot either side of the equator and pose for a photo. So that's what we did. It was surprisingly enjoyable and made the journey well worthwhile.

The location of the Mitad del Mundo was calculated during the Franco–Spanish Geodesic Mission in 1736. We were busy marvelling at the achievement of this study when we read in our guidebook that these calculations have since proved to be inaccurate. After the introduction of GPS, the true equator was shown to be a couple of hundred metres further away. Spotting an amazing business opportunity, the owners of the land where the correct middle of the world was recorded, promptly opened their own rival attraction just next to the large Mitad del Mundo complex.

The Intiñan museum is a completely different spectacle to the official site. It is quirkier, crappier, and far more low–key, but infinitely more enjoyable. Members of staff demonstrated how water goes down a plughole anticlockwise on one side of the equator, yet clockwise only a few metres away. They also performed an illusion that involved balancing eggs on nails. Both tricks were extremely dubious, but they were performed so quickly and enthusiastically (not to mention the added confusion of the language barrier), that we couldn't help but be impressed, even if it was all an elaborate scam.

In order to further enhance the museum (pad it out a bit), visitors get to walk through gardens of cacti and totem poles and look at exhibits of traditional Ecuadorian life. It was a fun way to spend an hour and it contrasted perfectly to the grandeur of the main monument next door.

There has been further controversy in recent years, after arguments and debate began about the variations between the data of military and commercial GPS systems. It is now suggested that neither site marks the correct middle of the world. It is claimed that the nearby peak of Catequilla marks the true centre. Atop this hill, a stone circle sits, built over a thousand years ago by pre–Inca inhabitants of the area. Without any optical instruments, computers or GPS, it turns out these early settlers had already calculated the true middle of the world, simply by observing the sun, shadows and the stars.

Even with the help of a map, bus timetable, guide book, signposts and an imposing 30-meter-tall monument, Rachel and I still struggled to find it. Mankind is doomed.

Rachel and I knew no Spanish when we booked our flights to South America. We could probably have survived with a phrasebook and a smile, but we wanted to at least make an effort with the language. Spanish is the main language of Ecuador, Peru and Bolivia. 36 different indigenous languages are also spoken in Bolivia, but we thought it might perhaps be a little ambitious to try and learn those too.

Before the summer, we booked onto an adult education Spanish language course in Northampton. It was one hour a week for 12 weeks. The course was taught by a Spanish woman called Pillar. Pillar was in her sixties and a lovely person but a terrible teacher. She spoke in a mixture of English, Spanish and Catalan, and during the whole 12 weeks I don't think she finished a single sentence in any language. She would start explaining something to us in English, then get confused and finish the sentence using Spanish words that she had not yet taught us, mixed up with a bit of her native Catalan. The lessons were very enjoyable, though, despite the fact we had no idea what was going on. It felt like we were back at school and we were even set homework assignments each week.

What made our lessons particularly memorable was another of the pupils – Marjorie. Marjorie was also in her sixties and keen to learn Spanish as she had just bought a holiday flat in Tenerife. It became clear early on that Marjorie was not best suited to learning a foreign language. Our group would take it in turns to read a simple line of English from our textbook and try to translate it into Spanish. When asked, Marjorie just read the words in English, but said them slowly and with a slight Spanish accent. Pillar would reiterate that she wanted Marjorie to at least try to speak in Spanish. So Marjorie would just repeat the English even slower with a slightly thicker Spanish accent. Pillar would then look a bit flustered and explain to Marjorie that she was still speaking English, but Marjorie seemed to think she was speaking Spanish fluently. Pillar looked so perplexed that she started to doubt her own language skills. Because she taught in a random blend of English, Spanish and Catalan, Pillar began to question whether it was Marjorie that was speaking incorrectly or in fact her.

During the twelve weeks of lessons, we never heard Marjorie utter a single word of Spanish. That was, until we had our graduation party at the end of the last lesson. Pillar had prepared a traditional Spanish tortilla for us, and as she handed Marjorie a slice, Marjorie instinctively said 'gracias'. Pillar froze in astonishment and the rest of the group applauded, much to Marjorie's confusion. I think I saw a tear in Pillar's eye as she realised her 12 weeks of teaching had not been completely wasted.

'De nada,' smiled Pillar. 'It's nothing.'

I have no doubt Marjorie converses in English with her Spanish neighbours in Tenerife, truly believing she is fluent in their language.

Our Spanish did improve. Not as much as we hoped, but we had developed a basic vocabulary and learned enough to get by, or at least show that we were making an effort. Like Marjorie, I have a false confidence with foreign languages and believe I am much better than I actually am. I will happily string a sentence together using a combination of the few foreign words I know, and connect them together with English words that I don't know the translation for.

We caught a bus back into Quito's old town and had a late lunch of chicken and rice at a café just off Plaza de San Francisco in the shadows of the imposing church. Late afternoon we took a taxi up to El Panecillo (the little bread loaf), which is a prominent hill to the southern end of the city. At the top, sits the magnificent statue of Le Virgen de Quito with her stunning vantage point over the city.

On the way up, our taxi was stopped by a police officer and our angry driver was taken across the road to a police vehicle where he was questioned for 15 minutes. Rachel and I sat in the back of the taxi, realising it would have been much quicker to walk. We watched some money change hands and the driver returned looking mightily fed up with his ordeal and I'm certain our fare increased to compensate for the notes he slipped the police officer.

We spent half an hour admiring the views of Quito as the evening light began to fade. The old town below us, with its pastel–coloured buildings and prominent white churches every few blocks, gave way to the steel and glass of the new town in the distance. To our left, the rugged Pichincha volcano, and looming on the horizon behind us, the ominous and permanently snow–covered cone of the volcano Cotopaxi, both making Quito look small in comparison. We caught another taxi back uptown to our hostel. This driver was waved at cheerily by the police officers on our way down.

Back at the hostel we played pool and drank beer with a Danish guy called Henrik. Beer was payed for by an honesty box next to a small fridge in the corner. Henrik didn't have any money with him, and as the beers were so cheap, I bought him beer after beer until he was dancing around the pool table swinging his pool cue like a baton twirler.

'I never been this drunk,' he slurred, as he stooped to try and pot a yellow.

'You do seem a little merry, Henrik,' I said.

'I never been drunk… EVER!' he shouted.

'Huh? Never?'

'Tonight was FIRST TIME I drink beer.'

'Wait? What? The first time you've drunk beer? How old are you, Henrik?'

'14,' he said.

'Wh…? Did you say 14?'

I could hear Rachel sniggering behind me.

'Yep. Fourteen.'

'And are you here on your own? Where are your parents?'

'My parents? They have gone for dinner. They'll be back soon.'

'Oh shit. I think we need to get you to bed.'

'Bed?' he said. 'I like bed.'

We helped Henrik up the stairs and back to his room, bouncing off the corridor walls as he went.

'Right, you need to go to bed now, Henrik. If your mum and dad ask, tell them you are not feeling well and that it must have been something you ate.'

'Ok,' he smiled.

'Goodnight, Henrik. It was nice to meet you.'

'Nice to meet you too, George and Rachel. You English are a lot of fun.'

And with that he swung the door closed in our face.

'Quick,' I said to Rachel, 'let's get out of here before his parents get back.'

'I can't believe you got a 14–year–old boy drunk,' laughed Rachel, as we walked out into the street.

'How was I supposed to know he was 14? He looked much older.'

'That's what they all say.'

We got a table at a nearby pizzeria where we were seated with three other young–looking European tourists. I resisted engaging in conversation in case Rachel accused me of grooming them.

# THREE

We skipped the hostel's breakfast the following morning, in case we bumped into Henrik or his parents. We checked out of L'Auberge Inn and grabbed our first of many weird–looking and even weirder–tasting South American pastries at a nearby bakery instead.

A misty haze had hung over Quito since our arrival, giving everything a slightly grey hue. We rode a trolley towards the main bus station. Trolley, by the way, is what South Americans (and Americans) call trams. We didn't ride a supermarket trolley (or cart or basket, as they are called in America) into town. Although that would have been a lot more fun. The trolley we did ride was very enjoyable. So enjoyable in fact that we missed our stop. We were so paranoid about being separated again, that we both hesitated a split second too long and failed to get off in time.

When we eventually did disembark, we found ourselves in a heavily militarised area, with armed soldiers guarding every imposing building. There was no indication of how long we would have to wait for a return trolley, and neither of us wanted to linger for too long in the gaze of the frightening looking guards with assault rifles, so we followed the trolley line in the direction we had come, back towards the bus station.

Our very brief stay in Quito was over. The city still had so much more to offer, but it was only ever going to be our access point for exploring other parts of South America.

A three–hour bus journey took us to the town of Latacunga, or 'Latacunga Latacunga Latacunga', as Rachel and I started calling it, after the bus driver repeatedly shouted the phrase out the open door to waiting passengers at every stop. Latacunga Latacunga Latacunga – so good they named it thrice.

Despite our inability to successfully disembark the buses and trolleys in Quito at our desired stops, the public transport we had used so far had been very straightforward and nowhere near as chaotic and scary as we had been warned. Our journey to Latacunga Latacunga Latacunga was our first experience of a rural South American bus journey, and a real eye–opener of what we would come to expect from the rest of our trip. Despite all the horror stories we had heard about public transport in South America, we were not prepared for the experience.

The rules of the road in rural South America differ very slightly from other more developed places, in that they don't seem to exist. At one point on our way to Latacunga Latacunga Latacunga, we were hurtling up a mountain road with a sheer drop to our left, all the way down to the valley floor below. A blind right–hand bend was fast approaching, when the bus driver decided to overtake the van that was chugging up the same hill. Although dangerous, this was not particularly unusual. What made it even more terrifying, however, was that the van we were overtaking was already in the process of overtaking a slow–moving tractor. So there we were, three vehicles wide, navigating a blind corner on a treacherous mountain road with only inches between the bus wheels and certain death. Rachel and I were the only tourists on a bus full of completely unflinching Ecuadorians. Rachel was dozing at the time and I decided not to alert her to our predicament. My heart rate quickened, and I felt my stomach do somersaults. It was a situation

25

completely out of my control and the lives of an entire bus full of passengers rested solely in the hands of our idiotic driver. I closed my eyes and hoped for the best. It was scarier than any rollercoaster I have ever been on.

Fortunately, we didn't meet any oncoming vehicles, and the driver eventually pulled back over to the right side of the road. There were plenty of other incidents during this and our many other journeys when we did meet oncoming vehicles. On those occasions, there would be a loud angry blast of the horn from the approaching vehicle, followed by an even louder one from our bus in retaliation. The oncoming vehicle would then be forced to either slam on the brakes or, more likely, swerve out of the way, as braking seemed to be a considered a sign of weakness in South America. The bus driver would act like it was the most natural thing in the world, and judging by the lack of reaction from the passengers, it was.

The white crosses that littered the roadside of these rural roads suggested that the outcome was not always so lucky.


A woman resplendent in a series of brightly coloured shawls and a black panama hat popular in the area, boarded the bus in one of the many villages we stopped in. She walked down the aisle selling small plastic bags of boiled sweets. We bought a bag and she continued down the bus. Ten minutes later, another similarly–dressed woman boarded at a different stop and offered identical bags of sweets.

'No gracias,' I said, holding up the bag I had already purchased.

'Más?' she said. 'More?'

'No gracias,' I repeated. Even with continuous sucking, the bag was big enough to last us for several days.

She smiled wider, which was the Spanish for, *go on, go on, go on.*

'No gracias,' I said, and I even patted my stomach to demonstrate how I couldn't possibly find room for any more boiled sweets.

She smiled and eventually continued on her way.

Ten minutes later, a third woman boarded the bus and began walking up and down the aisle selling bags of the same sweets. Again, because we already had sweets, she targeted us, thinking we would want more, despite none of the other passengers having bought any sweets.

It was unclear where these women were coming from, or when and where they disembarked, but it seemed that they would have had more success if they had diversified what they were selling. Not once during the three–hour journey did anyone try to sell us anything other than boiled sweets.

It was mid–July when we arrived in Ecuador. As we were in the Southern Hemisphere (apart from the brief moment when we stepped over the equatorial line at the Midad del Mundo), it was the middle of winter. It had been fairly mild so far, but it would get colder the further south we headed. We would be spending a lot of time high up in the Andes where the nights would be particularly cold. We also hoped to spend some time in the Amazon jungle, where temperatures remain hot and humid throughout the year. Packing our hand–luggage–sized rucksacks with clothes to cater for all climates had been a struggle, but we hoped we had everything we would need.

We definitely only had room for one bag of boiled sweets.

Latacunga (I'm bored of writing it three times) was a lively looking town, sitting directly below the slopes of the Cotopaxi volcano, but we didn't have time to appreciate it as I spent our brief visit there fearing I was going to wet myself while we hunted frantically for a toilet.

After successfully loitering in a café long enough to look like a customer, I made it to their toilet just in time, and we had a quick browse of the town's market before returning to the bus station to wait for a connecting bus to the village of Quilotoa, where we would be spending the night.

As a dilapidated bus spluttered into Latacunga's bus station, what seemed like hundreds of Ecuadorians, all heavily laden with bags of food from the market, swarmed around it. The roof of the bus was piled high with people's belongings, and, judging by the countless faces we could see at the window, it appeared to already be full.

The doors opened, and half a dozen people disembarked. Then the assembled masses aggressively fought their way onto the bus to try and get the last few remaining seats. Rachel and I stood patiently at the back, resigned to the fact that we weren't going to be getting on this bus. The bus door stayed open and the people kept on squeezing through, until eventually, Rachel and I were the only two left standing on the tarmac.

The driver looked over to us and shouted 'Vamos!' – 'let's go.'

I pointed to Rachel and me, to ask whether he was including us in his declaration.

'Si!' he said. 'Vamos!'

Rachel and I squeezed our way up the steps, where two other passengers were already standing. We looked down to our left and every inch of space was filled with bodies or bags. The aisle was packed solidly all the way from the back, right up to the driver's seat, and Rachel and I were the only gringos on the bus.

'Aquí,' said the driver, banging his hand on the dashboard to his right. 'Here.'

'Here?' I said. 'Really?'

'Si, si!'

'Does he want us to sit on the dashboard?' asked Rachel.

'Yes, it looks that way.'

We perched nervously on the dashboard with our rucksacks on our laps and our backs against the windscreen. There aren't many bus rides that require you to sit closer to the front of the vehicle than the driver.

'What's that?' asked Rachel, pointing to a suspicious hole in the windscreen just next to us.

'Err… it looks like a bullet hole,' I said. 'I'm sure it's nothing to worry about. Maybe don't lean against it though, just in case.'

The road from Latacunga began to climb past fields of crops and livestock, higher into the Andes. Compared to our death–defying ride earlier in the day, this second leg of the journey was thankfully far more sedate, as we had to stop regularly for obstacles in the road, such as herds of sheep, stray dogs and even more women selling boiled sweets.

Occasionally on the roadside, we would pass Ecuadorian families, standing with what looked like their entire worldly possessions piled up on the ground beside them: bags, animals, furniture, mattresses. Those going in the same direction as us would flag the bus down, and somehow – with the help of the driver – load all their belongings onto the roof and squash themselves into the bus too. South American local buses, as we quickly learned, are never full. We were soon sharing the dashboard with four others.

An hour into the journey, the driver shouted something frantically to the rest of the passengers, which we assumed must have translated as 'Duck! Duck!' because everyone bowed their heads in what was reminiscent of the world's most rubbish game of hide–and–seek. I glanced out the window and saw we were approaching a police checkpoint. Rachel and I instinctively ducked our heads as requested, in the hope that two white gringos with rucksacks sitting on a bus dashboard next to four others would look a little less conspicuous.

Somehow, the eagle–eyed policeman spotted us and signalled the driver to stop.

A no–nonsense officer approached the bus and stood at the bottom of the steps. He couldn't board the vehicle, as even the lowest step was occupied by a couple of passengers. He glanced up at the heaving bus and then over to us pathetic specimens on the dashboard and gave a brief laugh and a shake of his head. He signalled through the bodies to the driver to step off the bus, and a mass of passengers climbed down the steps to allow him space to exit.

We watched from the window as angry words were exchanged between the driver and the police officer. A few notes were passed between the two, which was either a fine, or more likely a bribe, and the driver was allowed to continue his journey with all of his passengers. He didn't seem in the least bit aggrieved when he took his place back in the driver's seat, almost as though he had expected to have to pay a fee. The additional passenger fares from his heavily overloaded bus would have more than compensated.

# FOUR

It was mid-afternoon when we arrived in the small village of Quilotoa. Rachel and I were the only passengers to disembark at this tourist stop, and the bus continued onwards to the next town.

The settlement of Quilotoa, consisting of a small handful of buildings, sits high in the Ecuadorian Andes. The village had sprung up in recent years to cater to the growing number of tourists coming to the area. The main draw to the region is Laguna Quilotoa – a volcanic lake formed after a mighty eruption in 1280, that left behind a 3km wide crater now filled with a beautiful (and probably highly toxic) emerald green water.

Our accommodation for the night was a basic hostel – that appeared to be only partially complete – with an outside toilet a short walk from the main building. But at only $8 for dinner, bed and breakfast, it felt like the greatest place in the world.

After dumping our bags in our room, we followed the dusty, winding path down the inside of the rocky crater to the water's edge. We sat and skimmed stones across the glasslike surface in the eerie silence, before tackling the exhausting climb back to the crater rim, just as the sun was beginning to set. It had taken us half an hour to reach the bottom and an hour and a half to get back up. We didn't pass another person in either direction, and had an entire volcanic crater to ourselves. Apparently a 'growing number of tourists' in Ecuador is two.

Once we had reached the top, I took a dramatic self–timer photograph of Rachel and me standing on the crater rim, looking down over the lake below us. It wasn't until we were back in England that I looked at our photos and realised we were standing next to an almighty dog turd, which slightly detracts from the image. Still, it was definitely a keeper.

During dinner, we were joined by four other tourists. These were the first fellow travellers we had spoken to – apart from Henrik, the 14–year–old Danish boy, who I had tried to erase all memory of.

Chris and Isla were a lovely Scottish couple, following a similar route to Rachel and me. They had already been to Peru and Bolivia, and gave us a rundown of some of their highlights. The others were Tabitha and Chloe, a couple of slightly annoying girls from London. There was a somewhat awkward atmosphere around them, and they gave the impression that the presence of other British people was spoiling their experience of Ecuador. It was almost as though Laguna Quilotoa had been their little secret and how dare we have heard about it too.

It's a complicated dynamic when fellow backpackers get together. Each wants to appear confident as a traveller, but without coming across as a knobbish know–it–all. Just because you are united by a common language, doesn't automatically mean you have to be friends, but travelling is all about interactions, even if it is with people from your home country. It is a wonderful opportunity to learn from others, with advice and stories readily exchanged. Most conversations with fellow travellers are extremely positive. Tabitha and Chloe were thankfully in the minority.

As we lay in bed that night, wearing almost all of our clothes to keep warm – including a pair of sexy thermal long johns that ripped at the crotch the first time I put them on – the noise of the hustle and bustle of the Quito streets had been replaced with the sound of the wind whistling through the gaps around our window frame. We couldn't stop smiling. We were sleeping in a hostel on the edge of a volcano in the middle of who–knows–where in South America. Life was pretty bloody good.

And then I woke in the night, desperate for a wee, and had to venture to the outside toilet in the icy darkness. I cursed South America and its stupid lack of modern facilities.

We woke at 6.30am with the intention of watching the sunrise over the laguna. We hurriedly got dressed and walked up to the crater rim.

'You just missed it,' said Tabitha and Chloe smugly in unison.

'Missed what?' I said.

'The sunrise. I assume that's why you are out here so early? It was spectacular.'

'Sunrise? No, we're not bothered about the sunrise. We like to go on a morning walk, just AFTER sunrise every morning.'

'Whatever,' they both said, and wandered back towards the hostel.

Chris and Isla were also sitting at the crater's edge and we walked over to say hello.

'Don't listen to them,' said Isla. 'You couldn't even see the sun because of the cloud. You didn't miss a thing.'

After a decent breakfast, the six of us were given a lift from the hostel to the village's bus stop in the back of a pickup truck where we waited for a bus to the village of Chugchilán. When the bus arrived, the driver tried to charge us $5 each, which was an unreasonably high fare for a local bus in Ecuador. It was clear he was charging tourist prices.

'Doesn't look like we have much choice,' said Tabitha, boarding the bus with Chloe and handing over their fare. Chris and Isla refused to pay, so Rachel and I decided to make alternative travel plans with them, and we waved a fond farewell to the two London girls.

The man with the pickup truck who had dropped us off was still loitering, and we asked if he would be prepared to match the bus fare of $5 per person to give us a ride into town. He gladly agreed and drove the four of us into Chugchilán in the back of his truck. Standing up in the back of a flatbed, with the wind in your hair, is surely one of the greatest ways to travel. The incredulous look on Tabitha and Chloe's faces as our truck overtook their bus was one of the highlights of the day.

Chugchilán is a small and authentic farming village in central Ecuador. It has become a popular stop on the Quilotoa Circuit, which is a recognised route through towns and villages in the hilly Cotopaxi Province. We said *goodbye* to Chris and Isla and then said *hello* a few minutes later as we checked in to the same hostel together. Hostal Mama Hilda was a huge step up from our previous night's accommodation: hot showers, comfy beds and extravagant hammocks strung up outside our rooms.

Rachel and I spent most of the day lazing around, reading our books, writing our journals and doing very little else. We took a couple of short hikes around the lush green countryside, but after a few days of an intense introduction to South America, we felt we needed time to recharge. We were on our honeymoon, after all.

We went to bed that night with the intention of waking up at 3 am to catch a bus to Sasquili market with Chris and Isla. It was supposedly legendary. However, when our alarm sounded at 3am the next morning, we realised that no market in the world can possibly be legendary enough to warrant getting up at 3 am for. We had a backup plan that was potentially far more exciting anyway. And it would allow us another six hours of sleep.

# FIVE

Rachel and I had read stories about the Chugchilán milk truck, but we didn't know if it was real or a travellers' myth. Legend claimed that if you waited by the side of the road at a certain spot in the small village of Chugchilán, a pickup truck would pass through at about 9.30am delivering the milk to the villagers. For a small fee, it was possible to hitch a ride on the back of this milk truck, all the way to the town of Sigchos.

We checked out of Mama Hilda's and waited patiently with our rucksacks by the roadside. At 9.25am we heard English voices behind us. It was Tabitha and Chloe, the London girls, who had been staying at a neighbouring guesthouse. Their faces fell when they saw us waiting by the side of the road.

'Are you waiting for a bus?' asked Tabitha.

'No,' said Rachel. 'We're waiting for a milk truck.'

'Oh,' said Chloe. 'The milk truck? You've heard about that too?'

'Yes,' said Rachel. 'Does it definitely exist?'

'I hope so,' said Tabitha. 'We heard about it from Rob's brother who used to go out with a Norwegian girl called Ria, who had this friend who worked as a waitress in Quito and knew loads of ultra–cool stuff about Ecuador that very few tourists know about. How did you guys hear about it?'

'Lonely Planet,' I said.

'Oh, right. We don't do guide books. We just go with the flow.'

It was clear that both Tabitha and Chloe were mightily disappointed to be in the company of other Brits again. And on this particular occasion, so were we.

Sure enough, after a short wait, a battered old blue and white pickup truck pulled up alongside us. There was an elderly man driving and boy of about 16 in the passenger seat, but no passengers in the back.

The boy jumped out of the truck and ran to the back and dropped the tailgate. We exchanged looks, seeking permission to board, and he nodded enthusiastically. The back of the truck was already filled with several urns of milk (it was a milk truck, after all), as well as a few boxes covered in blankets and half a dozen crates of assorted vegetables.

The four of us piled our rucksacks into a small gap and squashed ourselves onto the truck, perching on crates and urns. The boy closed the tailgate and we were off.

What followed was one and a half of the most memorable hours of the trip. The pickup truck wound its way along dusty country roads, pulling up outside each dwelling that we passed. At each house, the residents would appear right on cue, with an assortment of vessels to hold their milk. The boy would fill the various containers from the milk urns and the customer would either hand over some money, or make payment by way of an exchange of goods.

I soon discovered that the boxes at our feet covered in blankets contained live chickens. Some people paid for their milk with a chicken or some vegetables, which were then added to the boxes or crates. Other people bought chickens or vegetables with money. Some people even paid for chickens or vegetables with their own milk. I mean, milk they had obtained from their own animals, not their own breasts. At least, I don't think it was. The milk that people paid with was added to a different urn than the other.

It was a fascinating system to watch. Strangely, no real bartering seemed to take place. Everyone knew the value of each other's goods and the system worked flawlessly.

To begin with we were just observers, witnessing a unique slice of Ecuadorian life. But it was difficult not to feel like we were getting in the way, when we were clearly getting in the way. So, we offered to help, and for the remainder of the journey we assisted the boy with filling pots of milk, stacking vegetables and passing live chickens backwards and forwards. Our poor Spanish didn't cause too many problems, and with a lot of pointing and holding up of fingers, we became a highly proficient team. Even Tabitha and Chloe had embraced the situation and I think I caught them smiling at one point.

We left the milk truck in the small town of Sigchos. Tabitha and Chloe were off to find a vegan café that was recommended to them by Tabitha's yoga teacher's cousin's ex–boyfriend who once stumbled upon this place when he was off his face on some hallucinogenic Ecuadorian drug. They invited us along. We wouldn't find it on our own as it was ultra–cool and didn't have a sign outside and very few people knew where it was or that it even existed. It was one of those places that definitely wouldn't be in any guide book. We politely declined and said our goodbyes. Part of me felt honoured that they had considered us worthy to impart their secret information to, but the other part of me was desperate to see the back of them.

We had a three hour wait in Sigchos for our connecting bus, so we had a look around the town – it didn't take very long – and then sat in the main square and ate a bowl of fried potatoes and onions bought from a street vendor. We saw Tabitha and Chloe pass a few times, trying not to look like they were still looking for the café, but clearly still looking for the café. Part of me hopes they still are.

Following a predictably scary bus journey back to Latacunga, we boarded another bus to Ambato and then another to the city of Baños, which we eventually reached at 7.30 pm; a journey of ten hours, three bus rides, and a milk truck.


Baños is known as the Adventure Capital of Ecuador. It is a popular destination for mountain biking, hiking, kayaking and horse riding in the spectacular foothills of the imposing Tungurahua – an active volcano that has experienced lots of partial eruptions in recent years. The word Tungurahua is from indigenous Quichua words meaning 'Throat of Fire' making it the world's most excellently named volcano.

We checked into Plantas Y Blanco – a fairly classy hostel that boasted a beautiful roof terrace with stunning views of the surrounding countryside.

'What do we do if it erupts?' asked Rachel, as we had a beer on the roof terrace under the intimidating presence of the Throat of Fire.

'Run, I guess.'

'Seriously, what would happen?'

'I think there is usually some advance warning and then the authorities would evacuate the town.'

'What if we don't get any warning and it just erupts in the middle of the night and we don't have time to escape?'

'Then at least we will die together. Me and you. Together in the Throat of Hell.'

'That's not even remotely funny. And I thought you said Tungurahua means Throat of Fire?'

'It does. But Throat of Hell sounds way better.'

Rachel didn't respond to this. She just gave me a stare that was more terrifying than any volcano.

'Let's go out for dinner,' I said. 'Forget about the volcano.'

'Dinner sounds good. Where shall we go?'

'I don't know. Let's find somewhere nice. It might be our last supper.'

'You can be a real dick sometimes.'

'I know. I'm sorry.'

We had a couple of delicious steaks at a nearby restaurant called Marianne. If it was to be our last supper, then it was a damn good one. After a few cocktails back at the hostel bar, even Rachel admitted that if tonight was going to be our last night then it wouldn't be a bad way to go.

As we sat chatting with full stomachs, we felt acutely aware of the strange and slightly uncomfortable dichotomy of being first world travellers in a less developed country. In the morning, we had been helping locals swap chickens for milk from the back of a rusty pickup truck, in the evening we were sipping mojitos on a roof terrace.

# SIX

Spoiler Alert - we survived the night and ate breakfast on the roof terrace surrounded by lush tropical views. It was a fantastic way to begin the day, and the fact that the pancakes didn't taste nearly as good as they looked didn't dampen our enthusiasm. #firstworldproblems

'What's the plan for today?' asked Rachel.

'I was thinking we should hire bikes and go for a bike ride.'

'Isn't it all mountains around here?'

'There's a road that we can follow that just goes downhill all the way to the jungle.'

'But then surely it's uphill all the way back?'

'It would be a one–way trip. Apparently it's easy to get a lift back to Baños on a bus.'

'Sounds like my kind of bike ride.'

Rachel's experience of cycling was somewhat limited. She could ride a bike, just about, but cycling didn't come naturally to her. We had been out for the occasional short bike ride together at home, where she would ride the 15–year–old mountain bike that she had owned since she was a child. It had slightly squeaky brakes. This squeaking annoyed Rachel so much that she refused to use the brakes, instead choosing to stop the bike by dragging her feet along the ground. During a family holiday, we hired bikes and made sure to pick one for Rachel without squeaky brakes so that she could learn that brakes can in fact be quite useful. This bike had 18 gears, which was 17 more than she had ever had need for before. She refused to use the gears, thinking it constituted cheating, and preferred to push her bike up the steep hills rather than resort to changing gear.

There wouldn't be much need for gears for our bike ride from Baños. Rachel wouldn't even have much need for pedals, as we would be mostly freewheeling. She would, however, have need for brakes, seeing as we were going to be descending a mountainous valley for the entire day. We found a bike rental shop and hired a couple of fairly decent looking mountain bikes for the day.

'See,' I said, 'this is a squeak–free bike. Are you happy?'

'Very. Thanks.'

'Do you promise to use the brakes?'

'I promise.'


Baños is a small and compact town, and it wasn't long before we had passed through its suburbs and were out in the open countryside. The views down into the vibrant green valley to our right were magnificent and the road descended at a perfect cycle friendly gradient – just steep enough to be able to freewheel at a decent speed, but not steep enough to require excessive braking.

What made the ride even more pleasant was the road surface. Many of the roads we had travelled on in Ecuador had been dirt roads, rutted and rocky or dusty and crumbling. The few that were tarmacked were littered with potholes and cracks. The road from Baños to Puyo was one of the best I had ever cycled on. We stopped at a roadside viewpoint and I started chatting to an American who was also on a bike. I began singing the praises of Ecuadorians for providing such an amazing resource for cyclists.

'It ain't done for cyclists,' he said. 'This road was mostly funded by big multi–nationals.'

'Wow. How come?' I asked, impressed that big multi–national companies were helping to provide quality roads in rural Ecuador.

'This is one of the main roads in and out of the Amazon for all the logging trucks and the tanker trucks for the oil and gas companies.'

'Oh.'

Our enjoyment of such an incredible road was now tainted with the guilt that it was only made possible by those responsible for destroying the rainforest. Still, it was a damn fine road.


The road from Baños to Puyo passes through several tunnels. We had been told that the first one was permitted for cyclists, and cycle paths were in place to skirt around the others. We had already passed through the first and had reached another much bigger one, with heavy traffic moving in both directions. There were signs of a cycle path around to the right, but a recent landslide had made it impassable and a fence was in place to block access. Despite the *no cycling* sign, we were left with no choice but to go through the tunnel.

We had no lights and the tunnel was poorly lit, so we waited for a lull in the traffic before making a break for it. The tunnel was 300m long and Rachel set off first, pedalling as fast as her legs would allow. Seeing as she was in her lowest gear and refusing to change, they were spinning pretty fucking fast. I followed closely after, keeping an eye out for vehicles approaching from behind.

Water poured through the roof of the tunnel at regular intervals. Not just the odd drip that you might expect in a tunnel, but huge gushing streams, so it felt like we were cycling through a waterfall.

We passed the halfway point without incident but then the roar of an engine echoed down the tunnel behind us. I turned to see a pair of blinding headlights bearing down on us.

'Oh shiiiit, we are going to die!' shouted Rachel.

'No we aren't. Just stay calm.'

'This is terrifying! Should we stop?'

'There's not enough space to stop. Just keep pedalling.'

Rachel's legs span faster than I thought physically possible. I was worried she was going to snap the pedals clean off her bike from metal fatigue. There was a loud blast of a horn behind that echoed and filled the tunnel, making it sound more like a dozen vehicles.

By this point I could make out that it was a large bus. The horn blasted again, so at least the driver was aware of us. There was no room for us to pull over, and no room for him to safely overtake as there was a steady stream of vehicles coming the other way (not that this had deterred most of our other bus drivers in Ecuador). The end of the tunnel was only a hundred metres away, so I decided to stand my ground and positioned myself away from the edge of the road to prevent any urge of the bus driver to overtake.

Once we had made it back into the daylight, we pulled over to a safe spot on the side of the road and breathed a sigh of relief. The bus driver blasted his horn again and waved his fist and shouted something to us out of the open window as he passed, which I presume was Spanish for 'Hey, gringos, I hope you have a wonderful time in Ecuador.'

We stopped off at the access point to El Paílón del Diablo – the Devil's Cauldron – a waterfall on the Rio Verde. We bought a drink from a snack bar and the owner agreed to keep an eye on our bikes for us while we hiked down to the river. We followed a steep and slippery set of steps down to the impressive waterfall, where we crossed a dramatic suspension bridge over the Rio Verde for even better views. The waterfall was even more notable because it was called Devil's Cauldron. If it had simply been called Rio Verde Waterfall, we probably wouldn't have bothered stopping.

After a long slog back up the path to the road, we continued onwards on our bikes. This section of road was still busy, but there was a decent hard shoulder and plenty of room on the road. We could feel the humidity changing as we neared the rainforest, and the vegetation on both sides of us grew thicker, taller and greener the lower we went. Even the smell was noticeable; a deep earthiness that teased our senses.

We reached another tunnel, and Rachel and I agreed that no matter what, we would not be cycling through it. Our map showed an alternative route up to the left along the old road which bypassed the tunnel.

I'm not convinced we took the correct turn, because within minutes we were heaving our bikes up an incredibly steep dirt track, deeper and deeper into the wilderness. The muddy trail was devoid of traffic or any other people. We would occasionally pass a homestead in the forest, and this would fill us with hope that we were still going the right way, but whenever we tried to stop to ask for directions, an angry dog would take a dislike to us and ensure we hurried on past.

After a detour of what seemed like hours, we made it back to the main road and once again were able to appreciate the incredibly smooth and beautiful road surface that those bastard rainforest destroyers had built.

The road slowly levelled out, as the foothills of the Andes gave way to the Amazon river basin. It was late afternoon when we reached the small settlement of Mera and decided to call it a day. There was a police checkpoint to negotiate if we travelled further, and although we had our passports and nothing to hide, we were ready to finish. We had cycled about 45km, which was further than either of us had ever cycled before. Admittedly there were only a few sections where we had to pedal – most notably the thousands of revolutions Rachel managed in the tunnel – but it was still a very respectable day on the bike.

'That was amazing. Who knew cycling could be so much fun?' said Rachel.

'It was brilliant. Well done for using your brakes. Did I even see you change gear towards the end there too?'

'That was an accident. I changed it straight back. So how do we get a bus back to Baños?' asked Rachel. 'Where is the bus stop?'

'I don't think there are any bus stops. I guess we just flag down a bus and see what happens.'

'What about our bikes?'

'Who knows?'

We didn't have to wait long for a bus. As it approached, it appeared to already be full. But as we had learned from our time in

South America, there is always room for more passengers. I held out my arm and the bus came to a stop alongside us.

'Baños?' I asked through the open door.

'Si,' said the driver.

'Bicicletas?' I said again.

'Si, si. Paolo!' he shouted.

A man, presumably Paolo, came down the steps, took both bikes off us and then one at a time flung them up onto the roof of the bus, which was already heavily laden with bags and the contents of people's houses.

'Ok?' I asked, pointing to the bikes.

'Si. Ok,' said Paolo, with a look as if to say, *'why wouldn't they be ok?'*

I shrugged to Rachel and we boarded the bus. As it trudged back up the road that we had just cycled down, I kept looking out the back window, expecting to see our bikes bouncing down the road and off into Devil's Cauldron. Miraculously, they were still on the roof when we got back to Baños. We gave the driver and Paolo a few dollars (even though they hadn't asked for a fare), and took our bikes back to the rental shop.

Baños's full name is Baños de Agua Santa – Baths of Holy Water – and the town is famous for its hot springs with supposedly magical healing properties. After a long day in the saddle, our evening was spent soothing our aching limbs in this holy water, which is basically a big brown swimming pool with a dramatic waterfall as a backdrop. We did feel remarkably healed, though, and treated ourselves to a lovely dinner at a little French restaurant (when in Ecuador...), imaginatively called 'Le Petit Restaurante'.

# SEVEN

The following morning, we set off on another expedition – this time not on two wheels but on four legs. We hired horses. I am even worse at riding horses than Rachel is at riding bicycles, which is really saying something.

I have always been nervous around horses. As an eight–year–old boy, I was once coerced by my parents to take part in a horse race while on holiday in Somerset. It wasn't actually a horse race, as such, it was a donkey derby. But when you are an eight–year–old child, it is basically the same thing. A group of six or seven of us children were assigned a donkey each and we lined up at the starting line. The donkeys were to race around a short track marked out on a village field to the makeshift finish line, and spectators could bet real money on the outcome of the race.

My horse was called Buckaroo. It wasn't. But it might as well have been. Because, as soon as the starting pistol fired, my donkey bolted up the field like I was in a rodeo. I gripped the reins tightly and hung on for dear life. The first half of the race was petrifying as I thought my life was about to end, and I wouldn't even get the ice–cream we had been promised afterwards. But then, as the finish line approached, and I realised that victory was inevitable, I started to revel in the glory. I had asked my dad to bet £1 of my holiday money on Buckaroo, and if I won, I stood to win about £3. Being bucked around like a ragdoll was no hardship if it meant winning £3. I could see the faces in the crowd watching, a mixture of fear and happiness in their eyes as my rabid donkey approached the line. With only a couple of strides left before the finishing tape, my senseless steed came to a complete standstill and began chewing the grass. I gave the reins a tug and offered the donkey a little gentle encouragement with my heels. He refused to budge and continued to munch the grass. The rest of the donkeys all crossed the line before me and a marshal came and helped me dismount Buckaroo, still having not even completed the course.

I have ridden horses on a couple of occasions since and each time, after a catalogue of mishaps, I have vowed I would never ride one again. Rachel had riding lessons as a child so is very competent, and she had been looking forward to this opportunity in Baños for some time.

'You realise we will be riding up the slopes of the volcano?' I said, trying to put her off the idea.

'It's not going to erupt,' said Rachel. 'You said we will get a warning.'

'Well what if the warning happens when we are up on the slopes?'

'Then I'll have my horse to escape on.'

'What about me? I can't ride horses properly. You know that.'

'You will be left alone in the Throat of Hell.'

'It's the Throat of Fire!'

'No, you were right. Throat of Hell sounds much better.'


Ivan, our guide for the day, drove us in his jeep from the centre of Baños to his horses' field in the hills above the town, ready for the start of our four–hour trek up the volcano. Envisaging the slopes of a volcano, we imagined a dark, scorched earth, with the remains of hardened lava piled up after recent eruptions. The grassy lower slopes of Tungurahua are in fact beautiful. The area is thick with dense green foliage and a network of cobbled tracks and footpaths.

Ivan looked slightly intimidating when we first met him. He was a well–built man wearing a bandana and a cowboy hat, with a pair of wraparound sunglasses and a goatee beard. If you were going to a fancy–dress party as the leader of a South American drug cartel, you would dress exactly like Ivan.

Minutes after he had introduced himself, this illusion was shattered by his continuous smile, infectious laugh and warm personality. Even though he spoke absolutely no English and our Spanish was limited, we had some hysterical conversations using a mixture of pointing, miming, Spanglish, and interpretive dance. A young foal came along with us too for some exercise. It was a genuinely brilliant few hours and changed my opinion of horse-riding dramatically. As it was only Ivan, Rachel and me, I felt no shame at being so incompetent on a horse. Yes, I was the worst rider in the group by a long way, but I was also the third best. Ivan had offered me the most docile of horses after realising my inexperience, and it was friendly and compliant throughout.

Ivan kept pointing up to the Throat of Fire above us and then shouting 'BOOM' and miming a huge eruption with his arms. Rachel burst into laughter every time.

'BOOM!' Ivan said again.

Again, Rachel chuckled.

'Why is it funny if Ivan pretends the volcano is going to erupt, but if I do it I am being a dick?'

'I don't know. But it is.'

'BOOM!' said Ivan.

Again, Rachel laughed, and this time I couldn't help but join in.

'See,' said Rachel. 'It's the way you say it.'

Ivan's small tour company – Ringo Horses – had been mentioned in our guide book. When we returned to his jeep, I tore out the listing from my book and gave it to him. He had no idea that his little business was featured in a book published in the UK, and stood and stared in amazement at the article for some time, despite not being able to understand a word of it. All that was written was the address and the words *'nice horses, very well looked after'*. They were indeed, and I tried my best to translate this into Spanish for Ivan. It seemed to work because Ivan gave each of his horses a kiss on the nose before ushering them back into their field.

'I need a haircut,' I said, looking at my scruffy face in the mirror after we had returned to the hostel for a shower and a change of clothes.

Days of inadequate sleep, infrequent showering and laziness at shaving had made me look like a different person. It was something I naively thought I could fix with a haircut.

'I'll do it,' said Rachel eagerly.

'Er… thanks, but unfortunately we don't have any scissors.'

'We could buy some?'

'Nah, it would probably be easier and cheaper for me to just go to a hairdresser.'

'Please let me cut it. I let you cut my hair in America. It would be nice to return the favour.'

'You mean get revenge?'

'Well, maybe.'

'Thanks, but no thanks.'

I had offered to cut Rachel's hair a few years previously when we were travelling together in America. It had not gone quite to plan. The fact that we were both inebriated at the time probably didn't help. I knew she was looking for an opportunity to get her own back.

'I'll go and see if I can find somewhere in town,' I said. 'See you in a bit.'

I found a hair salon that was adorned with posters of western men in the window, all with haircuts that were trendy in the 1980s. The posters were faded and crinkled and had obviously been there since the haircuts were still in fashion. I hadn't seen any other hairdressers in Baños, so stepped inside.

There was one other customer present; a large jovial lady who sat having her hair braided at the seat nearest the door. *Perhaps I should go for braids? Then I wouldn't even need to ask for anything, I could just point.*

A lady of indeterminable age pointed to an empty chair and I took a seat. She looked at me in the mirror and presumably asked what I would like. Things suddenly seemed a lot more complicated than I had anticipated. I had hoped that I could just point to a photo on the wall or a picture in a magazine, and ask for the same. But there were no magazines, and I certainly didn't want to look like any of the men in the posters.

It was at this point that I realised I hadn't seen a single decent haircut during our whole time in Ecuador. Not one. This is obviously the reason why the majority of South Americans wear hats.

I started to mime a scissor cutting motion to the top part of my head with my fingers, and then made a buzzing sound to mimic a set of electric clippers on the sides and back. The lady having her hair braided next to me began chuckling, as did the braider.

I knew I would be leaving with either a mullet, a perm, rat's tail, tramlines or a unique combination of all four. My hairdresser stared at my reflection in the mirror, shrugged her shoulders and said 'No entiendo' – 'I don't understand'.

'Oh well. Shave it all,' I said, mimicking the clippers all over, deciding that this was the safest option. I then held up my thumb and forefinger a little over an inch apart to show her to not cut it too short and to leave a bit of length.

'Si, bueno,' she said, reaching for the clippers.

Rather than starting with the side of my head to check I was happy with the length, she did her first stroke straight down the middle of my head from my forehead all the way to the back.

It was cropped shorter than I had ever had it cut before, but it was too late to say anything. She had given me an exceptional inverse mohawk, with a tightly shaved strip down the middle, and the remains of my big bouffant puffed up either side.

'Ok?' she asked.

What could I say? There was no way to correct it now and there was no going back.

'Perfecto!' I said, in that polite British way we respond to all bad haircuts while we quietly sob inside.

The haircut was over minutes later and she paused only slightly when trying to decide what to do to about my neck. She was so used to leaving the hair hanging long in a mullet or rat's tail that the sight of an exposed hairy neck perplexed her. So she just left it as it was and I had to shave it myself later.

'Oh god, what have you done?' asked Rachel when I returned to the hostel.

'It's not THAT bad, is it?'

'It's hideous. I can't even look at you.'

She shielded her eyes theatrically for at least an hour and wouldn't make eye contact with me. To be honest, I think that if I hadn't told her I was going to the hairdresser, she probably wouldn't even have noticed.

Rachel is not the most observant person, particularly when it comes to me. I once shaved off my beard with a razor on only half of my face, leaving a distinct dividing line that ran from the middle of my top lip all the way down my chin and neck. I'm not quite sure why I did it, and I didn't plan to exhibit it in public. I spent two hours with Rachel after shaving, even having long face–to–face conversations with her and she still didn't even notice. I eventually had to point it out to her, at which point she decided she couldn't look at me again until I shaved it all off.

I told this anecdote to Rachel's sister and she responded by telling me a story about when they were teenagers and their dad shaved off his moustache that he had sported for ALL OF RACHEL'S LIFE. She didn't notice that either until it was pointed out to her.

'Is it really that bad?' I asked, as we sat having a beer on the roof terrace later that evening.

'It's just, well, it's just…'

'What?'

'I don't know. It's so short. And it makes your eyebrows look so prominent.'

'My eyebrows, sorry eyebrow, IS prominent. It always has been.'

'Yes, but now it's longer than your actual hair.'

'Boy, you sure know how to knock a man's self–confidence.'

'Sorry.'

I looked up at the Throat of Fire high above us, and with a big theatrical arm gesture shouted 'BOOM' in my best Ivan impression, hoping to lighten the mood.

'Grow up, George,' she said.

# EIGHT

It was the morning of our first wedding anniversary. Married life had been brilliant so far and I felt incredibly lucky to be with Rachel. I hoped she felt the same about me, even with my new haircut. There we were, a year on, enjoying our delayed honeymoon immensely. So how did we mark this momentous milestone in our married life? With a day of bus journeys, of course.

We did have time for a delicious breakfast burrito at Casa Hood before catching a bus to Ambato and then a connecting bus to Cuenca which we didn't reach until late evening.

Cuenca is the third largest city in Ecuador, behind Guayaquil and Quito, and is considered by most Ecuadorians to be its finest. It became a designated UNESCO World Heritage Site in 1999, due to its beautiful maze of cobbled streets and its striking Spanish colonial architecture.

Rachel had been keen to stay in Baños another night, but as a surprise I had made a reservation for us in Cuenca. Apart from our first night in Quito, all of our accommodation so far had been booked when we arrived at our destinations. We had not had any trouble finding places to stay, but as it was going to be our wedding anniversary, I had thoughtfully planned a few days ahead and booked us a room, so that we weren't left homeless on our special day. And it wasn't just any old room in a hostel. I booked us a room in an actual hotel, which by Ecuadorian standards, looked pretty damn swanky… on the internet at least.

It was dark when we got off the bus in Cuenca.

'Any idea where we are going to stay?' asked Rachel.

'As a matter of fact, yes I do! Follow me!' I said.

'Where?'

'You'll see.'

We followed my map through winding streets for ten minutes until we reached an ugly building which disappointingly had a sign that bore the name of the hotel I'd booked.

'What is this place?' said Rachel.

'This,' I said, 'Is one of Cuenca's finest establishments. I've booked us a room for a couple of nights.'

'Really? That's very sweet of you. It looks… well… it looks… er… lovely.'

'I'm sure it's much nicer inside.'

Thankfully, the hotel was much nicer inside. We walked up to the front desk and I showed the lady my passport. She snorted at my long–haired photo, then confirmed my booking. She handed me the key and directed us down a corridor to our room.

At the end of the corridor we reached a set of double doors that opened into a large dining area, half–filled with people eating their dinner.

'Did we already walk past our room?' asked Rachel.

'No. I think that's it over there,' I said, spotting a door in the opposite wall of the dining room.

I tentatively unlocked the door and opened it to reveal a small plain room with two single beds a few feet apart. Slightly disconcertingly, there was a huge window on the wall between the bedroom and the dining room. An elderly couple sat eating their dinner only inches away from the window on the other side.

'We can't stay here,' I said. 'This is not what the room looked like on the internet.'

'Oh, it'll be fine,' said Rachel, trying to stifle a giggle. 'Look, we can close the curtain.'

She pulled at the scraggy curtain, and it hung limply over some of the window, still leaving huge gaps revealing the dining room.

'I love it. Thank you,' she said, giving me a hug. 'Happy anniversary!'

'I'm so sorry. This place looked really posh online. It's not even as nice as some of the hostels we've stayed in. I'll go and see if they have a different room.'

'Don't worry. It's fine. It's only for a couple of nights. We can just move these beds together.' Rachel tried to drag one of the beds towards the other, but they were both bolted to the floor.

The man sitting at the table looked up from his meal and peered through our window to see what the commotion was about. I gave him a cheery wave and he immediately looked down at his meal again.

'I'll go and speak to reception,' I said. 'I'll be back soon.'

After a lengthy discussion using a combination of my poor Spanish and my phrasebook (which unfortunately didn't have the Spanish for *our bedroom appears to be part of the dining room, you moron* in it), I established that they didn't have any other rooms available.

After a bit more persuading, and some sterner words spoken, I explained that the room was not what I had requested, and I would like a refund so that we could go somewhere else. After this was eventually issued, Rachel and I left the hotel to find another.

Fortunately, the nearby Hostal Chordeleg on Columbia and Torres had a private room, which, although a hostel, was a penthouse compared to the previous place. Rather than head out again to find somewhere to eat, I went and bought a huge takeaway pizza from a nearby restaurant and a bottle of wine, and we ate dinner in our room. It was not the most romantic of wedding anniversaries, but it seemed to be quite fitting for our time in South America.

We spent the following day exploring Cuenca. The Pumapungo Museum was an eclectic mix of Inca ruins, an aviary of random birds, a museum of artefacts, and a botanical garden all rolled into one. It was an enjoyable way to spend a morning, but Cuenca was already making us feel a little claustrophobic. Our bike ride, horse ride, and hikes had by far been the highlights of our time so far in Ecuador, and we craved more adventures out in the countryside.

We had an early dinner at an energetic restaurant next to the cathedral and went to sleep, with plans to leave Cuenca first thing the following morning.

What better way to cure our claustrophobia than a cramped five–hour bus journey to Loja, where we caught a ride in a minibus to the village of Vilcabamba in southern Ecuador.

For decades the small village of Vilcabamba has had a reputation for having one of the oldest living populations in the world. It claimed to have many residents over the age of 100, with some reaching 120, and one even recorded as being 135. After a National Geographic story about the town's people by Dr Alexander Leaf of Harvard Medical School in 1973, the village's status as a haven for longevity grew. Scientists and tourists flocked to the area, searching for the secret to their long life. It was concluded that a combination of factors, including diet, climate, air and the relaxed way of life all contributed to this active aging population.

The population increased as Ecuadorians and tourists wanted to reap the benefits of Vilcabamba's lifestyle. Products even appeared on supermarket shelves, promising to replicate the secrets of Vilcabamba in a tablet or drink form.

This fame lasted for many years until researchers and scientists became slightly suspicious of Vilcabamba's claims. Even Dr Leaf, who published the original article, became sceptical. One of the men he interviewed in 1973 had claimed to be 122. Two years later when interviewed again he was 134. Further delving now suggests that the original reports of Vilcabamba's aging population came about due to an error in the reporting. It is common in many small communities for identical names to be passed on through generations, and birth records of fathers or uncles were mistakenly being used to verify the birthdays of the individuals being studied. This never would have happened if I had been Vilcabamba's Data Information Officer. The elderly population seemed to enjoy the attention they were getting and the status that they gained by their perceived old age, so took some liberties when keeping track of the years. Basically, Vilcabamba is a town full of fucking liars.

We were met at the bus stop by a rep from Hosteria Las Ruinas De Quinara. We instinctively said 'no' to him, as we had grown accustomed to people trying to sell us tours, transport or accommodation. But as we were walking away, we heard the words '*swimming pool*', '*jacuzzi*', '*table tennis*', '*sauna*', '*breakfast*' and '*$7*'.

'Did he say table tennis?' said Rachel.

'Yes, I think so. Shall we go?'

'Definitely.'

Rachel is a little bit obsessed with table tennis. She had a table tennis table in her garage as a child. Her sister wasn't keen on playing, and her parents were often busy, so Rachel would spend many hours playing table tennis on her own in the garage with half of the table folded up. She claims Forrest Gump learned his technique from her. With this devotion to the sport, you would expect Rachel to be some sort of elite player. She is, like me, distinctly average. But her competitive nature has made for some fierce battles between the two of us over the years.

Years later when we were planning a holiday to Dorset, we had no idea where in the county we should base ourselves. To narrow our search down, we googled '*holiday houses in Dorset with table tennis*' and booked the first place that came up. We had a fantastic week, despite seeing hardly anything of Dorset.

The hostel in Vilcabamba lived up to its billing. We spent our evening drinking cold beer and playing table tennis outside in the hostel's courtyard. If this was the lifestyle of most Vilcabambians then it's no wonder they live so long. Table tennis was given an added edge by the fact that the table was surrounded by bushes, and the ball would often have to be retrieved cautiously from amongst them, so as not to disturb the lizards, spiders, bees and who knows what else lurked in there.

I won the series 5–4. Get in!

# NINE

After moaning about the claustrophobia of Cuenca, followed by a day of buses, we set off after breakfast the following morning for a hike up to the prominent peak of Mandango that overlooks Vilcabamba. I picked up a hand drawn map from the hostel reception detailing a four–hour walk called the Mandango Trail. It was described as *moderate difficulty* on the piece of paper. Tourist guides always exaggerate these things, so if something was described as *moderate*, we assumed it would mean it was easy.

It turned out to be one of the scariest experiences of our lives.

The first section of the route meandered gently through some woodland, before beginning a steep and strenuous climb up to the first peak which was marked by a white cross. We were hot and sweaty, but the views down into Vilcabamba made it worth the effort. Rachel, who is not known for her uphill hiking abilities, felt particularly proud of her achievement upon reaching the top.

We sat and ate a couple of empanadas we had brought with us, removed a few layers, and assumed by reaching the peak we had done the worst of it.

Little did we know, we had not even got started.

Many hikers climb up to this peak and then return the same way. I say 'many', but we didn't see another person during the whole morning. The route we had set out to follow was circular and descended the mountain from the other end of the ridge from where we were standing.

We set out to traverse the ridge, and the path became narrower and narrower, with the grass slopes to either side becoming more and more precipitous, until it felt like we were walking along a balance beam. A balance beam that was high up in the Andes.

Having hiked Angel's Landing in America's Zion National Park, I was convinced that it would be the scariest walk I would ever do. The Mandango Trail probably trumped it. Not necessarily because it was more dangerous, but because this time I had Rachel with me.

'I can't do this,' she said, sitting down on her bottom, the ground disappearing to the valley floor on either side of her.

'Yes you can! Let's just take it nice and slowly and we'll make it down.'

'I can't. I really can't.'

She started sobbing uncontrollably. I walked back the few steps along the ridge towards her and noticed that my legs had turned to jelly too.

'It's going to be ok, I promise. It's just like walking along a narrow pavement. You've never fallen off a pavement, have you?'

'Yes, I have. Plenty of times.'

'Oh. Ok, look, hold my hand. We'll just take it slowly.'

'No. I can't do it, George. I can't stand up. My legs will give way.'

'Well what are you going to do? Climb the whole way along the ridge on your arse?'

'Yes!'

So she did.

And I did too.

After I had sat down near her in solidarity, I decided that if she was going to shuffle along on her backside then I might as well do the same. Also, I realised that her fear had transferred over to me and my legs were refusing to support my weight too. I don't think I could have walked off that mountain if I had tried.

The wind picked up and it took us a long while to shuffle along that ridge on our bottoms. Rachel's sobbing had quietened to a gentle murmur.

Eventually the path began to descend, and we were both able to return to our feet to walk the last section down to the foot of the ridge.

We followed what we thought was the path back down into town, which then petered out into nothing. We spent 40 minutes on a detour trying to find our way, before retracing our steps to the foot of the ridge where we eventually found the correct path. An encounter with some angry dogs on the way back into Vilcabamba secured the Mandango Trail's place in Rachel's top five worst experiences of all time.

As we walked through the town towards the hostel, an elderly Ecuadorian man outside a bar, who possessed more gold chains than teeth, collared us.

'San Pedrillo?' he said, in a slightly hushed and shady tone.

'Qué?' I said.

'You want San Pedrillo?' he said again, this time even shadier.

'Isn't that a make of bottled water?' I said.

'No. Sanpellegrino is water. San Pedrillo is cactus juice.'

'Ah, yes. I remember. I read about it.'

'Come in. You should try it?'

'Do you want to?' asked Rachel. 'You're always keen to try the local food and drink.'

'Not this time. It said in the guidebook that's it is a hallucinogenic and can cause flashbacks for many years.'

'Oh.'

'Come in,' said the man. 'It's great shit.'

'No thanks,' I said. 'We've got to go and play table tennis.'

'Maybe we should have had some of that cactus juice,' said Rachel, back at the hostel.

'Why?'

'I'm going to be having flashbacks about that Mandango Trail for the rest of my life. Perhaps hallucinogenic flashbacks would have been preferable.'

Strange feelings of elation come from conquering something seemingly unachievable. Despite her continued protestations about how much she had hated the Mandango Trail, there was definitely something in Rachel's manner that afternoon that showed that she was secretly delighted she had done it.

We spent the afternoon at the hostel, swimming in the pool and playing table tennis (Rachel beat me 3–2, but I'm claiming I let her win after her morning's trauma. And my table tennis bat had an annoying flappy bit of rubber on it that put me off my game). Later that evening we got the minibus to Loja where we would catch a night bus to Piura, Peru, and then onwards to the coastal town of Huanchaco. It would be a long and tedious journey of over 500 miles.

Before coming to South America, many people had suggested that we shouldn't eat street food because of the risk to our delicate Western stomachs. Rachel had been more cautious than me. I had ignored this advice and only showed restraint when offered hallucinogenic cactus juice with life–altering side–effects. I don't think you can fully embrace a country unless you eat its street food.

We were almost two weeks into our trip, and I hadn't experienced even so much as a stomach grumble. I felt indestructible. So when we arrived in Loja with a couple of hours to kill before our night bus, I went off in search of something to eat. The only food available in Loja's bus station was a suspect meat and onion concoction, served with some rice that looked suitable for building roads with, cooked by a man in a dark corner. I was very hungry so devoured a huge portion in minutes. It was a meal I would later regret enormously.

The 10.30 pm bus didn't arrive. It turned out it didn't even exist. After a confusing conversation with an official (well, I assumed he was an official. He was wearing a high–vis waistcoat. Perhaps he was just a normal man on his way home from work, which would explain the confusion), we boarded a bus soon after 11 pm, which we hoped would take us to Piura in Peru by the morning.

# TEN

'Rachel, wake up. We're crossing the border,' I said.

'Huh? What? Which border?'

'The border into Peru. I think we have to get off.'

We shuffled half–asleep from the bus, holding our passports, and spent a perplexing hour being directed back and forth over a bridge between the Ecuadorian and Peruvian control points, getting a series of exit stamps and entry stamps and visas. Both sets of officials laughed at my passport photo each time they saw it. When we eventually got back on the bus, which had thankfully waited for us, all of the other Peruvian and Ecuadorian passengers – who had a far more straightforward border crossing – were fast asleep.

We arrived in Piura at 7am. Our connecting bus to Trujillo didn't leave for a few hours, but after our restless night crossing the border, we didn't feel much like venturing further than the streets surrounding Piura's bus station.

Very few of the places we had been to had banks or cash machines. The currency of Ecuador is the US Dollar, but Peru and Bolivia both have their own currencies. US Dollars are sought after across the whole of South America, so Rachel and I had various stashes hidden in pockets, money belts and our backpacks.

Since our arrival in Peru, several men had approached us offering to exchange US Dollars for Peruvian Sol. I knew it was inevitable that I would have to change money on the street, but I was a little apprehensive doing it for the first time. As we waited for the bus in Piura, I decided to give it a try on a busy nearby street. I was approached straightaway by a street cashier (I don't think that's their official title), and a few minutes later I had a wad of Peruvian Sol.

Over the next few weeks I learned to really enjoy the bartering. The scene always played out exactly the same each time. I would be approached by a street cashier and I would ask in my Spanglish what the exchange rate was, 'Qué es the exchange rate?' The street cashier would give me their first offer, and I would take a sharp intake of breath through my teeth and begin to walk away. They would then call after me, the rate miraculously changing in my favour, and I would look a little more interested. At this point, another street cashier from across the road would get wind of the deal and rush over to offer an even better deal. The two men would then start bartering with each other to fight for my custom. I would eventually offer a deal, which one of them would accept, and I would walk away with my new currency, making sure to check the notes for any noticeable fakes first. It is possible the two street cashiers were working together, but the exchange rate was always far better than any bank or ATM, and the experience infinitely more enjoyable, so I never bothered changing money through the official channels during the rest of our time in South America.

We dozed in and out of sleep on the yellow plastic chairs for four hours in Piura bus station. We were routinely woken by large Peruvian ladies selling 'chipas', which were basically transparent plastic bags full of tortilla chips. They carried trays stacked with about 30 of these bags piled on top of each other. There were three women, and they all did circumnavigations of the small waiting room, calling 'cheeepas… cheeeeepas' at regular intervals. Nobody was offering anything else for sale. Just chipas. Nobody wanted chipas. Ironically, I was now craving some of those boiled sweets offered by the continuous stream of Ecuadorian ladies on the bus during our first week. Back then I had been craving chipas.

I eventually relented to the repetitive chanting and bought a bag of chipas in the hope that it would ward off future flybys and allow us some peace and quiet. The lady who I bought it off smiled gratefully and then concentrated her sales efforts on the other side of the room. Not so, with the other two sellers. They now saw me as even more of a potential customer, despite the fact that I was holding a bag of chipas that would last me several hours.

'Chipas?' they said.

'No gracias,' I replied, with my mouth full of chipas. 'Tengo chipas already' – 'I have tortilla chips already', probably.

Then the next lady would arrive, and I would have to go through the motions again. After a while I foolishly bought another bag, and so the third seller was offended that she was the only person I hadn't bought a bag from. So I bought a third and final bag and hid behind them for the remainder of our time in Piura's bus station. They continued to pester me, assuming me to be some wealthy chipas addict. Rachel sat next to me engrossed in her book, seemingly oblivious to the chipas harassment that was taking place. Nobody else in the bus station bought any at all.

The bus from Piura to Trujillo, where we would get our connection to Huanchaco, was long and monotonous. Either side of us the Sechura desert stretched to the horizon. This section of

Peru must be one of the most desolate landscapes on earth. It was crazy to think that just over the horizon to the west of us were the crashing waves of the South Pacific Ocean. And just over the horizon to the east were the dramatic peaks of the Andes mountains, and beyond that the Amazon rainforest. But here, in this vast strip of land in between, there was absolutely nothing but dry and dusty desert. Occasionally we would pass a clumsily assembled roadside café, built from random sections of chipboard, but these structures looked as transient as the grains of sand they were built on.

Despite its perceived dryness, these lowlands can be prone to flooding in El Niño years. In 1998, runoff from flooded rivers led to the formation of a three–metre–deep puddle here that stretched for 90 miles. It temporarily became the second largest lake in the whole of Peru.

We arrived in Trujillo in the early evening and got a taxi to the town of Huanchaco, which we had heard wonderful things about from Chris and Isla, the Scottish couple we had met at Laguna Quilotoa. We found a room at a hostel and went out for dinner.

Huanchaco is credited as being where the Peruvian dish ceviche originated. Ceviche is a dish consisting of raw fish with lemon juice and often chili. My stomach was feeling a little delicate for the first time, so we played it safe and ordered two of the biggest burgers we had ever seen from a café with outdoor seating in a pleasant central square.

My body started doing horrible things in the night. Perhaps it was punishment for not ordering ceviche. I was forced to dash from the room to the small communal toilet across the hallway. I made this trip countless times throughout the night, my body exploding from both ends. I spent far more time sitting on and kneeling by that toilet than I did in bed. I didn't get a moment's sleep, and poor Rachel slept only intermittently between my sprints back and forth across the bedroom to the door.

It could have been the burgers, or the three bags of chipas, but Rachel had eaten both of those too. The more likely culprit was the questionable looking bowl of rice and meat I had eaten in Loja bus station the night before.

'I feel very sorry for you,' said Rachel. 'Is there anything I can get you?'

'No thanks. There's nothing you can do. Roll on, death.'

# ELEVEN

Morning couldn't come soon enough. At first light, we headed outside to explore Huanchaco, and the fresh air made me feel considerably better. I was no longer yearning for death.

Huanchaco is a pretty little seaside town, but a thick grey cloud lingered in the sky, and we realised we hadn't seen the sun since entering Peru. Due to the vast differences in atmospherics (look at me, pretending to know what I'm talking about), with the sea, desert and mountains all in close proximity to one another, it is apparently not uncommon for Peru's coastline to be shrouded in cloud for weeks at a time.

As well as ceviche, Huanchaco is also famous for its 'caballitos de totora', which are unique wicker fishing boats. The boats are a cross between a canoe and a surfboard, constructed out of tightly woven reeds, and measuring about five meters long. Fisherman have been using them in Huanchaco for 3,000 years, and some historians claim that these fishermen and their caballitos de totora were the very first surfers. These types of boat are still used today, and you can see them lined up along the waterfront, drying in the sun. If the sun ever makes an appearance.

At the end of the promenade we passed a little stall selling freshly squeezed fruit juices.

'Shall we have one?' I asked Rachel.

'Are you having one?'

'Yeah, why not?'

'Are you sure that's wise? I thought your stomach was a little delicate at the moment?'

'It's only fruit juice. Surely it will be good for me? I need to get my energy back somehow.'

'Alright then,' she said. 'Thanks.'

'Dos fruit smoothies, por favor,' I said to the man, holding up two fingers to prove that I knew the Spanish word for the number two.

He then gestured to all the fruit with his hands and said something which I interpreted as '*which of these fine fruits would you like included in your fruit juice, young sir?*'

I responded with the same gesture accompanied by a slight shrug of the shoulders, which he correctly interpreted as '*I don't really know. What would you recommend, my good man? How about a bit of everything?*'

A minute later he presented us with two huge plastic cups filled to the brim with a vibrant red concoction. This was going to be the magic medicine that would make me feel human again.

I tentatively took a sip. It tasted even better than it looked. Fresh, cold and zingy.

Rachel and I strolled back along the promenade hand in hand, sipping on our fruit smoothies, enjoying a rare moment of tranquillity on our frenetic tour of South America.

Five minutes later my stomach gave a slight gurgle that was audible to Rachel. She looked at me.

'George, are you ok?' she asked, a look of deep concern on her face. 'You look, err, you look… green.'

'I feel…' I started to say, before an uncontrollable torrent of bright red fruit juice gushed from my gaping mouth. I have never projectile vomited in such spectacular fashion, and hope never to do so again. It was like a horizontal version of Old Faithful, as the liquid blasted several feet across the pavement and continued for quite some time. Thankfully, the waterfront was relatively quiet so early in the morning, but a few bystanders shrieked and scattered at the sight of me spewing my guts across the concrete. Rachel had retreated a few paces and stood there in awe as the display continued.

Eventually, after the episode finished, and presumably every drop of fluid from my stomach had been expended, I was able to assess the situation.

'Oh. My. God,' said Rachel, with a mixture of concern and amusement. 'I have never seen anything like that before. Are you alright?'

'Er… wow… I feel a bit better now thanks. Do you want the rest of my smoothie? I don't think I'm quite ready for it yet.'

We walked quickly away from the trail of devastation I had left across the Huanchaco waterfront, repainting the sidewalk with the bright red contents of my stomach. To passers-by, it would have looked like a murder scene, and we hoped for a high tide to come and wash away the evidence.

'Do you want to go back to the hotel?' said Rachel. 'Should you go and see a doctor?'

'No thanks. I'll be fine. I think I'll just avoid any fruit smoothies, or any food for a little while.'

'I think that's a good idea.'

The town of Huanchaco became forever referred to between the two of us as HuanChucko from then on.

Our next planned destination was Arequipa in the south of Peru. It was almost 1,000 miles away from HuanChucko, and the thought of spending a couple of days on buses did not appeal.

It was time to get out the credit card.

It was time to book a flight.

The day didn't improve much after my projectile vomiting incident. We went to an internet café to try and book flights to Arequipa, but my credit card was declined, and a message told me to phone my bank in the UK. I then ran out of phone credit midway through the conversation to try and resolve it, which wasn't helped by my frequent dashes between the payphone and the toilet. We decided to cancel the rest of the day and have an early night.

My stomach was still a little uneasy the following morning, but I had improved significantly since the previous day. We took a taxi to Chan Chan, which is the oldest adobe city in the world, don't you know. The archaeological site was once the capital of the Chimú empire, before they were defeated by the Incas in the second half of the 15th century.

The entrance to Chan Chan was deserted when we arrived, apart from two women at the ticket desk. We paid our entry fee and were asked if we would like to pay an additional charge for a guided tour.

'Si, por favor,' I said.

One of the women then asked if we would like a private tour, or the cheaper group tour option. I looked back at the empty car park.

'Cuando does the group tour leave?' I asked.

'Ahora mismo,' she said. 'Right now.'

'Ok, dos boletos for the group tour, por favor.'

Sure enough, one of the women became our tour guide and our 'group', consisting of just me and Rachel, departed immediately. I gave the extra money we would have had to pay for a private tour directly to our guide as a tip at the end, and I went from being a tight selfish gringo to a wise and generous man in a split second.

The archaeological ruins of Chan Chan are vast and impressive. They extend for over 20 square kilometres. Fortunately, our tour only covered the best bits in the centre. I was still feeling sorry for myself, so was more than happy with a 'best of' tour. We walked through the remains of courtyards, storerooms, temples and gardens. As the city was built from mud and sand, centuries of deterioration from rain, wind, flood and looters had eroded the huge structures into low walls that ended below our waists. Either that or the Chimú people were extremely small. The incredibly intricate detail on the walls remains, though, with animals, faces and elaborate patterns etched into every surface.

From Chan Chan we went to the archaeological sites of Huaca del Sol and Huaca de la Luna. These two temples were built by the Moche civilisation, which predates the Chimú by a few hundred years. This site was more popular than the other, and our group tour even included three other tourists. It was led by a student who was using tour–guiding to improve her English. She was very knowledgeable and extremely funny.

Parts of the temples were very well preserved with brightly coloured murals featuring engraved pictures of deities forming the centrepieces. It was spectacular to look at, but there was one particular attraction that caught our eye.

'Oh my god. What's that?' said Rachel, pointing to a strange creature curled up asleep in the middle of one of the courtyards.

'It's a dog,' said the tour guide.

'But it's… it's…' said Rachel.

'Ugly?'

'No, I wasn't going to say that.'

'You can say that,' said the tour guide.

'Ok. It is ugly,' said Rachel. 'But I was going to say, it doesn't have any hair.'

'That's right. It's a Peruvian hairless dog.'

'A hairless dog? Has it been shaved to look like that?'

'No. They are born like that. People in this area, including the Moche, Chimú and Inca people all kept Peruvian Hairless Dogs.'

'It has a blond mohawk!' I said.

'Yes, that one is not a complete hairless. I like its hair though. He looks like that evil leader gremlin in the film Gremlins. What was his name?'

'Stripe!' I shouted.

'That's it! Stripe. Well done. He looks just like Stripe.'

He did look just like Stripe from Gremlins – ugly and evil, but you sort of wanted to give him a cuddle at the same time. All day, our tour guides had asked us questions to assess our knowledge of ancient history. Neither Rachel nor I had known the answer to a single question, and we had been ashamed of our ignorance; Rachel more so, considering she studied History and Ancient History at university. I was proud to finally know the answer to a history question, even if it was one concerning 80s movie trivia.

We stood around marvelling at Stripe the Peruvian Hairless Dog for a while and then booked a taxi to Trujillo airport.

We arrived at the airport way too early, and still unsure whether we had tickets following my credit card problems the previous day. Once the check–in desk opened, we were able to resolve the situation, and bought tickets to Lima and then a connecting flight to Arequipa.

I tentatively ate a toasted cheese sandwich at an airport cafe, which was the first solid food I had eaten since the burgers in HuanChucko 48 hours previously. Rachel kept her distance, half expecting me to violently launch the contents of my stomach across the departure lounge. Fortunately, my body was feeling a lot more stable and I managed to keep the toastie down.

# TWELVE

Our house and cats in Northampton had been left in the hands of Graeme. Graeme has been one of my closest friends since school, but he is not the most reliable or responsible person in the world.

I once lent Graeme an electric guitar and a small amplifier of mine, and when I asked him about it a year later, he admitted he had sold it to either pay to have his electricity reconnected, or to buy a bag of weed. He couldn't remember which, therefore making the latter seem more likely. He promised to pay me back one day.

A couple of months before coming to South America, Rachel and I heard a knock on the door one morning. I opened it to find two large men in black leather jackets, shaven heads, and very stern faces standing on our doorstep. One of the men thrust a piece of paper towards me.

'What's this?' I said.

'A repossession notice.'

'What do you mean?'

'We are here to take your possessions.'

'What are you talking about?'

'Read the letter,' he said, and tried to step inside. I went to close the door but he stuck his huge black steel toe–capped boot in the door frame.

'Hold on just a minute,' I said, skim reading the letter. It said that despite several attempts to get me to make adequate repayments of my debt, the collection company were left with no alternative but to take our possessions.

'There must be some mistake.'

'Are you not in debt?'

'Well, yes, a bit. But not like this. I haven't received any warnings, I just…' and then I saw the name at the top of the letter. It was addressed to Graeme.

'Ah, this letter isn't even addressed to me. It's a friend of mine.'

'Does he live here?'

'No. Leave it with me. I will sort this out straight away.'

'You've got two hours,' he said. 'If the boss doesn't tell us it's resolved in two hours then we will be back.'

I closed the door and immediately phoned Graeme and calmly and politely asked WHY THE FUCK TWO FUCKING BAILIFFS were on our doorstep trying to take our possessions.

'I don't know why they came to your house,' said Graeme.

'Well, did you give your debt collection company our address?'

'Err… yeah, I might have.'

'Why would you do that?'

'I don't know. I didn't want them to go to my flat and take all my stuff.'

'But… you… oh never mind. You need to get this sorted… IMMEDIATELY!'

'It's already sorted. There must be a mistake. I'm up to date with all my payments.'

'Well can you phone them now and tell them to stop these blokes coming back?'

'Can you call them for me please?' said Graeme. 'My phone is out of credit.'

'Fine!'

I tried several times to phone the debt collection agency but got an engaged tone each time. An hour had passed since the men's visit and Rachel was looking mightily pissed off.

'It's not my fault,' I said, as she continued to glare at me.

'Graeme is YOUR friend,' she said.

'He is OUR friend. And I didn't give him permission to use our address.'

Thankfully the agency's office was located only a mile from our house so I jumped on my bike and headed down there. Eventually, the staff agreed that Graeme had an adequate repayment plan in place and they phoned the heavies to call off their return.

Despite all this, Graeme is still a close and loyal friend.

Rachel, quite understandably, wasn't too keen on the idea of him housesitting while we were away. But she didn't want to put the cats into a cattery for six weeks, and we couldn't find anyone who would be happy to come and feed them every day, so she agreed that Graeme was our only option.

As we waited for our flight, I left Rachel in the café and found a payphone to give him a call. He hadn't responded to any of my emails, texts, or answered his phone on my previous attempts to call him, but that wasn't too unusual.

I dialled his number. It went straight to voicemail.

'Hi Graeme. It's George. Just calling to say hi. We are at an airport in Trujillo, Peru. I think it's probably pronounced Tru–he–oh, rather than Tru–Jillo, but I'm not sure. Anyway, just phoning to see how everything is back home? I hope everything is ok. Maybe send me a text or drop me an email sometime? Rachel and I are a little worried about you because we haven't heard from you. Speak soon, buddy.'

'Any luck?' said Rachel, when I returned to the café.

'No answer.'

'Where is he? I knew it was a bad idea letting Graeme housesit.'

'I'm sure it will be fine. He won't let us down.'


The Andes mountains looked stunning from the aeroplane window, their snow–capped peaks visible in the distance, and the mystery of the Amazon rainforest that lay hidden behind them. It increased our excitement about what still lay ahead of us during our time in South America. It was an even better feeling to see the distance we were covering in a matter of minutes on an aeroplane. Buses had been a memorable experience so far, and we would be spending plenty more time on them, but by flying we had effectively gained at least a day of our holiday.


Arequipa is the main gateway town to Colca Canyon, where we hoped to go and see the mighty Andean condors. But Peru's second biggest city also had a lot to offer, so we decided to spend a day or two there either side of our canyon trip.

We landed in Arequipa at 9 pm and got a taxi to a hostel recommended in our guide book. It was full, so we tried all the neighbouring hostels, but they were all fully booked too. This was the first time in South America we had struggled to find a place to stay. We eventually got a seedy and overpriced bedroom with retro neon lighting at the Posada De Sancho.


I was feeling a little more human by the following morning. The seedy overpriced bedroom was more than made up for by the view from the hostel's roof terrace where we ate breakfast. Like Baños, Arequipa sits at the foot of an active volcano. This one is the tamely named El Misti.

'Are you not worried about that volcano erupting?' I said.

'Nah,' said Rachel. 'El Misti doesn't sound nearly as scary as the throat of fire. What does it mean?'

'I don't know. The Misti, presumably.'

'See, not scary at all.'

'So it's all in the name?'

'Maybe. Also, it looks too far away to cause any harm.'

'I think that Mandango Trail has toughened you up.'

'Ha, maybe you're right.'


We spent our morning exploring one of Arequipa's most popular attractions. Built in 1579, the Santa Catalina Monastery in the centre of the city was entirely closed to the public until 1970. At its peak, it housed 450 people (nuns and servants). Nowadays, about 20 nuns live in one corner of the huge walled mini–town, and the rest of it is open to the public. The complex is strikingly beautiful, with dozens of courtyards, and warrens of cobbled streets and staircases, all painted in beautiful blues and reds. There were well stocked kitchens, rooms decked out with fine furniture, and hundreds of expensive looking paintings and artefacts. The nuns who entered here had all supposedly taken vows of poverty. It is a gorgeous and opulent mini–city within a city, and it is no wonder the nuns kept their little secret closed to the public for 400 years.

After a lunch of crepes (when in Peru…), we spent a couple of hours exploring the streets of Arequipa, and a couple more hours visiting the various travel agencies that organised tours to nearby Colca Canyon. After visiting our tenth agency, we realised they were all pretty much identical, and so picked one at random and booked a two–day tour beginning the following morning.

We enjoyed a nice evening meal at a small restaurant on one of Arequipa's back streets, and I even felt brave enough to have some wine. Things were definitely improving.

# THIRTEEN

We woke early and packed one small rucksack between us for our Colca Canyon trip. The hostel kindly agreed to look after our other bag for us while we were away and would reserve a room for our return. At least, at the time that is what I thought my conversation with the owner communicated.

The bus arrived at the expected time of 8.30am, which was a little surprising, as our experience with transport in South America was that it never ever arrived on time, and often didn't arrive at all.

Our guide was a smiley man named Juan Pablo, who had a number of jokes that didn't really make sense after he had translated them from Spanish into broken English. But we laughed a lot, because he did, and it was impossible not to be amused by his infectious enthusiasm.

Arequipa sits at 2,335m, which is already 1,000m higher than any mountain in the UK. But nothing about the city feels like you are high up, as it is surrounded by even higher peaks. As the bus began to ascend from Arequipa, higher onto the Andean plateau, I did briefly wonder whether the altitude had perhaps caused my illness. I then remembered that the one time I had projectile vomited was when I was standing at sea level, literally right next to the sea. It wasn't until reaching the mountains that I started to feel human again. Perhaps I was suffering from low–altitude sickness, which it turns out, is actually a thing.

Our visit to Colca Canyon was not scheduled until the following morning. Our tour included a stopover in the town of Chivay, before an early start on the second day to see the condors.

On the way to Chivay, our bus stopped at Patapampa mountain pass which sits at 4,910 metres above sea level. This is higher than any mountain in the Alps and the Rockies. Yet the Peruvians think nothing of building a road that passes directly across it. This viewpoint is also known as the Mirador de los Volcanes, because of the eight remarkable volcanos visible from the site. It was staggering to think that each of those peaks were thousands of metres higher than the point in which we were standing.

The effect of the altitude was quickly noticeable as we took a short walk. Our breathing became laboured and we felt light–headed and slightly dizzy. Some other members of the group climbed back onto the bus straightaway, but Rachel and I had a stroll around the hundreds of stone cairns built by tourists, and the occasional stubborn green shrub that refused to accept that the top of a mountain is a ridiculous place to try to survive.

Juan Pablo made us all a cup of mate de coca – a tea made from coca leaves and sweetened with shit-loads of sugar. Locals use coca tea to help cope with altitude sickness, although no scientific studies have ever proved its effectiveness. It is more likely that it acts as a stimulant because of its mind–altering qualities. The leaves of the coca plant are the base ingredient for cocaine, and although considered mild in its dosage, one cup of mate de coca is enough to test positive for a cocaine drug test.

'This is delicious,' said Rachel. 'I could definitely get used to this. It's much nicer than tea and coffee. I'm going to have to take some home.'

Later that day, Rachel did buy a couple of bags of coca leaves to take home. Luckily, we found out just before flying back to the UK that coca leaves are illegal in most countries outside of the Andes.

Strangely, the countless traders chose not to impart this information when readily selling the leaves to tourists.

We arrived in the small town of Chivay just after midday. Our entire tour group of about 20 people were ushered from the bus into a restaurant called Casa Blanca for their 'menu turistico' (that's Spanish for 'tourist menu', in case you were confused). This included an alpaca steak that had been cooked for so long it was impossible to identify it as meat, let alone alpaca. We were then all checked into a functional but featureless hostel before boarding the bus again to some nearby hot springs.

The hot springs were crowded but quite enjoyable. For about 10 minutes. Only the bus was not due to pick us up for two hours. By the time it came, we all had skin like shrivelled testicles.

After a quick change back at the hostel, we boarded the bus again, to be driven no more than 20 metres up the road to a restaurant.

'Are we there already?' I asked Juan Pablo.

'Si!' he said, pointing to the restaurant, which was just there.

'Ok. Would it not have been easier to walk?'

'No, no, you have paid for the bus with your tour.'

The restaurant had been described as a 'traditional local restaurant', and we realised now that 'local' in this case referred to its proximity to the hostel, rather than its authenticity of rural South America. The place was packed from wall to wall with other tour groups all shouting to each other over the noise of an energetic South American band playing at the far end of the room.

It was an enjoyable evening and the menu turistico (tourist menu, remember?) was surprisingly good. We spoke to an English couple who were on the final leg of a year–long round the world trip, and a Portuguese lookalike of the magician David Blaine. He was travelling alone and latched onto us because he seemed to have a bit of a thing for Rachel.

Just as it seemed the evening was drawing to a close, a troupe of 'traditional' dancers all pranced into the room and assembled in a line near the end of our table. They launched into an exuberant dance, and – having consumed a fair bit of wine – we all enthusiastically tapped in time to the music and smiled politely. I perhaps tapped and smiled too enthusiastically and politely, as one of the male dancers ushered for me to get up and join them. I laughed and politely declined, which I hoped would be the end of it, but he then walked over and took hold of my arm and forcibly removed me from my chair.

Before I knew it, I was one of the dancers.

I tried to encourage Rachel to join me, but she just laughed and resolutely folded her arms. I then tried to encourage Portuguese David Blaine, but he seemed to be excited about spending time alone with Rachel.

I wildly flailed my arms and legs around, mimicking the other dancers as best as I could. Each time I thought I had it nailed, they changed their style and moves. I couldn't keep up. It was mildly amusing for the first minute or so, but the song went on for bloody ages. Rachel kept smiling for a lot longer than I did, but then even she got bored and looked more than ready for the song to finish. It eventually did, and the novelty had worn off completely by then, so we didn't even mention it once I returned to the table.

After the meal, in an act of rebellion – and much to Juan Pablo's disgust – Rachel, Portuguese David Blaine and I declined the offer of the bus and walked the 20 metres back to our hostel.

We were woken by Juan Pablo at 5am the following morning. After a quick breakfast, we boarded our bus to Cruz del Condor. Portuguese David Blaine had overslept and sheepishly climbed onto the bus after we had all been sitting waiting for him for ten minutes. Juan Pablo and the bus driver chuffed something angrily at him which we interpreted as '*now we are going to miss the condors, you useless shit–for–brains*'.

It transpired that it wasn't the condors that Juan Pablo and our driver were in a rush for. We had a couple of other planned detours along the way.

The first was quite bizarre. We were all shepherded off the bus at a small village called Yanque a few miles from Chivay, where a group of about 20 children, all in traditional costume, performed a dance for us. Thankfully this time I was not required to join them.

It was a surreal experience. It was 6am and I think we were half expected to believe these children just happened to be standing there so early in the morning as they presumably were at villages across South America every day before school. We gave a small donation and climbed back onto the bus, hoping that our next stop would be the condors. The condors had been the focus of the Colca Canyon tour. In fact, they were the sole reason that people book the tour, yet the previous 24 hours had been padded out with hot springs, meals, musicians, and far too many dancers. We were, however, reassured to see how so many different sections of the community were benefitting from tourism in the area.

The bus continued for another ten minutes and then pulled over again.

'Are we at the canyon now?' said Rachel.

I looked out of the window, where a Peruvian family dressed in traditional dress (of course) just happened to be standing by the roadside with a llama and a baby alpaca. What were the chances?

'Er, no,' I said. 'It looks like it's another chance for us to meet the locals.'

'Oh great,' said Rachel.

We reluctantly climbed off the bus. Portuguese David Blaine didn't even bother this time. We made all the right noises of appreciation to the family, contributed to the collection, and then went to board the bus.

'Er, George!' said Rachel. 'Wait a minute.'

I turned around to see Rachel standing there with a giant eagle–like bird on her head and a look of terror on her face. A man standing next to her wearing a large leather glove was pointing at Rachel and then to me saying, 'foto, foto, foto.'

'What is it?' I asked Juan Pablo.

'Bird,' he said.

'Si, I know it's a bird. Qué type of bird?'

'Big bird,' he laughed, before climbing back onto the bus.

'It looks like a black–chested buzzard eagle,' said Portuguese David Blaine, who had stepped off the bus, eager to take a photo of Rachel. I mean, to take a photo of the black–chested buzzard eagle, of course.

'Thanks. That's what I thought,' I coughed.

I took a photo, knowing that it was going to cost me, and gave the man a tip. It is not every day you get to take a photo of a black–chested buzzard eagle on your wife's head. It was far more entertaining than my dancing.

The condors were well worth the wait and all the detours and distractions along the way. Due to our delayed start (thanks a lot, Portuguese David Blaine, you useless shit–for–brains), and our various stops en route, the condors were already in flight when we arrived.

The Cruz del Condor viewpoint at Colca Canyon is considered the best, and most reliable, place in South America for viewing these magnificent birds. There were several other tour groups already parked up, but it didn't feel in the least bit crowded and there was plenty of room to walk about and marvel at both the canyon and the condors.

The Andean condor has one of the largest wingspans of any bird in the world. The largest is the wandering albatross, which is basically just a big fat seagull that looks far less impressive than the condor, so it doesn't really count. The Andean condor is by far the greatest bird I have ever seen. They were majestic and serene and so much more remarkable than I thought a bird could be. Despite their size, they flew silently and effortlessly, their feathered wing tips out–stretched like fingers as they danced on the rising thermals.

Colca Canyon itself was a sight to behold. It is one of the deepest in the world, and Juan Pablo was proud to tell us frequently that it is 'two altitude of Grand Canyon' which loosely translates that it is twice as deep as The Grand Canyon.

Due to the viewpoint's location midway down the canyon's side, the condors were gliding directly above us, out in the canyon at the same level as us, and directly below us. We were able to see them closely from all angles.

After about 40 minutes, all the condors swooped one by one down into the canyon, presumably to hunt for their breakfast. It was like one of them had checked their watch and said, '*Right, the show's over, kids. Hasta la vista!* ' We didn't even get a chance to tip them.

Juan Pablo rounded us all up and we started to make our way back to the bus. There were shouts from a couple of stragglers from our group to say that another five condors had arrived (it's possible it was the same birds, to be fair. They all looked very similar). They hung around for a twenty–minute encore (in the air, not at the viewpoint chatting to visitors), and then dispersed. In total we were able to watch the condors for an hour. It is an hour we will certainly never forget.

After a quick cup of mate de coca back at the bus, Juan Pablo took us on an hour–long walking tour along the canyon edge. He told us lots of facts about the canyon, most of which got lost in translation. For example, he told us that Colca Canyon is big enough to hold the water of four swimming pools. That makes the Grand Canyon big enough to hold the water of two.

The bus took us back towards Chivay, stopping briefly on the way to look at some impressive Inca terraces in the valley below. Not terraces of the patio or decking variety – Incas weren't into those. An Inca terrace is a piece of sloped ground that has been landscaped into a flat surface, to make for easier farming. I looked around, eagerly expecting a group of traditionally dressed school children to serenade us, or somebody to wrap a baby alpaca around my shoulders to pose for a photo, but the place was eerily deserted. I was almost disappointed.

After a quick and tasty empanada from the market in Chivay containing an unidentified filling (hopefully not condor), our group had a long and bumpy bus ride back to Arequipa where we arrived in the evening. We said goodbye and thank you to Juan Pablo, Portuguese David Blaine and the rest of the group, and went our separate ways.


The hostel where we had left our bag and reserved a room had not reserved us a room. It was full and there were no rooms available.

'Can we have our bag por favor' I said to the lady at reception.

She grumbled something and disappeared into the back office.

'Eight dollars,' she said, passing us our bag, but not letting go of it.

'Qué? You said you would look after it because we were going to book a room for the night.'

'No rooms,' she said. 'Eight dollars.'

'But that's not our fault. You said you would reserve us a room. We are not paying for a room we don't have.'

'We wash clothes,' she said.

'What clothes?'

'Here clothes,' she said, holding up a separate carrier bag full of neatly folded laundry. 'Eight dollars.'

'Is that our clothes? We didn't ask for them to be washed.'

'Eight dollars,' she said again.

'Did… is… what… qué…?' I said to Rachel, who seemed to be very amused by the conversation.

'Just pay her the eight dollars,' said Rachel.

'What for? They didn't keep a room for us, and we didn't ask them to wash our clothes.'

'Just pay her.'

'Fine! But I'm not happy about this,' I said, slamming eight dollars on the desk before retrieving our rucksack and freshly laundered clothes and stomping off out of the hostel.

'Why the hell are they going through our rucksack?' I said to Rachel outside.

'I don't know. Maybe she thought that's what we wanted.'

'How can asking for a room to be reserved be mis–translated as *please wash our dirty clothes*?'

'I don't know. Your Spanish is a bit dodgy.'

'Thanks a lot. You can do all the negotiating from now on.'

'No, it's ok. Sorry, you're doing an excellent job, really. Well, look on the bright side, at least we have a bag full of freshly washed clothes.'

'That's true. But we still don't have anywhere to sleep tonight.'


That hostel had taken us a long time to find when we first arrived in Arequipa, so finding an alternative took even longer. All the surrounding hostels were full, and we started thinking about the prospect of spending the night on the street, or worse still, having to pay for an expensive hotel. We did eventually find a suitably cheap and cheerful place called Hostal Rivero, which was confusingly nowhere near a river. The room was the size of a shoebox, and there was only room for one of us to get dressed at a time, but it was perfectly adequate, and we dumped our bags and had a delicious kebab at El Turko (when in Peru…) before having an early night.

# FOURTEEN

Bolivia was the next stop on our trip. We were far from done with Peru, but as our return flight was from Lima, it made sense to spend some time in Bolivia before travelling back through Peru on our return to Lima.

I left Rachel in bed and set off first thing to try and book bus tickets to Puno, where we would get a connection to Bolivia's capital La Paz. Most of the buses we had got so far in South America had been local buses that didn't require tickets to be bought in advance. Even our bus across the border from Ecuador to Peru was paid for as we boarded it. For the more popular long–distance routes, it was advised to buy tickets beforehand to guarantee a space.

It was a long walk to the ticket office and when I arrived I was told there were no tickets available for the next two days. The following day was Peruvian Independence Day and families were all heading home for the occasion, so tickets were in high demand.

Another tourist advised me to go to the bus terminal on the edge of town where I might have success getting tickets through an agency. After a taxi ride, I managed to purchase a couple of tickets for the 10.30 pm bus to Puno later that day. By the time my taxi arrived back at the hostel it was midday. Rachel had assumed something terrible had happened to me. She had been on the verge of contacting the hospital and police stations, but realised she didn't speak much Spanish, so decided to just read her book instead.

'My stomach is going crazy. I feel awful,' she said.

'I'm so sorry. I didn't mean to be gone that long.'

'No, not because of you! I think I've come down with food poisoning now.'

'Oh no!'


Our bus journey to Puno was not for another ten hours, which was probably for the best as we now had another day to explore Arequipa some more, and hopefully allow time for Rachel to recover.

I ate a huge bowl of noodles for lunch and Rachel opted to play it safe with a fruit salad. I reminded her about what happened when I had fruit with my dodgy stomach in HuanChucko.

'I'll be fine,' she said. 'I'm not going to power hose the surrounding area like you did.'

She cautiously ate a chunk of watermelon and then a look of queasiness passed over her face.

'Are you ok?' I asked.

'Yes,' she said, putting down her spoon. 'I don't think I'll risk eating any more though.'


When American anthropologist Johan Reinhard and Miguel Zárate, his Peruvian climbing partner, set off on a scientific expedition up Mount Ambato in 1995, they didn't expect to make one of the most important archaeological discoveries of all time. As they neared the summit, Reinhard and Zárate uncovered the perfectly preserved body of an Inca girl wrapped in a blanket. She was surrounded by other artefacts like food and statues, suggesting that Juanita – as she later became known – had been killed as part of some ritual sacrifice and an offering to the gods, sometime between the years of 1450 and 1480. She was thought to be as young as 12.

Juanita has been on display in Arequipa's Museo Santuarios Andinos ever since (apart from when she occasionally jets off on her world tours).

We had a fascinating, and slightly macabre, tour of the museum, marvelling at Juanita and several other ice mummies. Many rural Peruvians still make sacrifices to the gods in return for water and good harvests, but these days the sacrifice tends to be beer (specifically Chicha), rather than children.


We spent a couple of hours playing pool in a bar later that afternoon. While Rachel was racking up the balls, I tried calling Graeme again from a payphone in the corner. I knew it would be about 10 pm in Northampton, which was the perfect time to catch him. This time he answered.

'Graeme!' I said. 'You're alive.'

'George, man, how are you? Where are you?'

'We are in Arequipa.'

'What country is that in? You guys having a good time?'

'It's in Peru. Yeah, we are having an awesome time thanks. You're a difficult man to get hold of. Did you get my messages and emails?'

'Sorry, I've got no phone credit. I could see the answerphone message thingy on my phone but haven't been able to check it.'

'What about the emails?'

'Nah, I'm trying to have a bit of a break from all that internety stuff.'

'Oh. Ok. Well I'm glad you're ok. We were worried about you.'

'You mean Rachel was worried I'd burned your house down?'

'Well… yeah, basically. So… how is the house? Are the cats still alive?'

'Yep, the cats are both still alive. The house is fine. I haven't burned it down, yet. Everything is just as you left it. Father Dougal is curled up on my lap here in the garden.'

'You're in the garden? At 10 o'clock?'

'Yep. Just chilling in the garden. It's a nice warm evening.'

'Cool, sounds good. Are you just sitting there in the dark?'

'Er… yeah, kind of. And… er…you know… reading.'

'In the dark? I didn't even know you could read in the light.'

'Very funny.'

'Is that the TV I can hear in the background?'

'What?'

'You said you were outside. But I can hear the TV.'

'Nope. No TV.'

'I'm sure I can hear a TV in the background.'

'Must be interference on the line,' he said, sounding as though he was frantically searching for the TV remote control, in the dark.

'Graeme, what the hell is going on?'

'Nothing. Don't be cross. I've just rearranged things a little.'

'What do you mean you've rearranged things? Have you put the TV outside?'

'No! Don't be ridiculous. I would never take the TV outside.'

'What have you done then?'

'I am outside, but I moved the TV unit up to the patio doors so that I can watch it from the garden.'

'Ah, I see,' I said, suddenly understanding what he was up to. Graeme is a heavy smoker but has never smoked inside our house. Even though he was going to be living at our house for six weeks, we told him the rule still applied and he could only smoke in the garden. He didn't protest. 'Is it so that you can smoke and watch TV at the same time?'

'Exactly!'

'Ok, that's fair enough, I suppose. Good ingenuity. Is it not a bit uncomfortable sitting on those metal chairs to watch TV?'

'What?'

'Those metal chairs in the garden. I assume that's what you are sitting on?'

'Er… yeah.'

'Graeme! What are you not telling me?'

'Don't be mad!'

'I will be mad if you don't tell me what the fuck you've done.'

'I did try and sit on those metal chairs, but you're right, they are really uncomfortable.'

'Sooooo?'

'So, I sort of dragged the sofa outside instead.'

'You have put our sofa in the bloody garden?'

'Not the garden. It's on the patio. You told me I couldn't smoke in the house.'

'So you moved the sitting room into the garden.'

'Er… yeah. Kind of. I'm really sorry. I bring the sofa inside every evening and I won't let it get wet. And I'm not dropping any ash on it.'

Part of me was angry with Graeme, but I was mostly amused and impressed by his resourcefulness, and slightly jealous that I hadn't thought of it first. I don't smoke, but watching TV outside on a nice warm evening did sound amazing.

'Fine,' I said. 'Just make sure it all looks normal when we get back.'

'I will. I promise. You're not going to tell Rachel are you?'

'Of course I'm not going to tell Rachel. She will go fucking mental.'

'You got through to Graeme? How is he?' asked Rachel nervously, when I returned to the pool table.

'Yeah, it sounds like he's doing really well. The house and cats are absolutely fine.'

'Phew. That's great to hear. Maybe I underestimated him.'

'Yeah, I think you did.'

The six–hour bus journey was tough going and we arrived in Puno just after 3am to discover the temperature outside had dropped considerably. The ticket office was closed and there were no buses until morning, so we joined the dozens of other people huddled together on the bus station floor. Sleep was impossible, so we sat and read our books and did regular circuits of the bus station to try and keep warm.

At about 6.30am there was a mad scramble as the ticket office opened. I managed to get a spot in line and successfully bought two tickets for the first bus of the day to Bolivia's capital La Paz, which departed half an hour later. The ticket seller assured me that the bus was 'directo' and that we would definitely not have to change.

'Hello,' said a familiar voice behind me a few minutes later.

I turned to find Portuguese David Blaine standing there with a slightly demented expression on his face.

'Hello. Good to see you again, Portu…' I started, before realising his name wasn't actually Portuguese David Blaine and I didn't even know his real name. 'What is your name?'

'Vasco, but people call me…'

'David Blaine?' I interrupted.

'No! People call me Vaz.'

'Oh, right, sorry.'

'What is your name?'

'George. Nice to meet you properly, Vaz,' I said, shaking his hand.

'What about your girlfriend? What is her name?' he said, looking over to the far corner of the building where he had already clocked Rachel sitting.

'Rachel,' I said. 'And she's not my girlfriend.'

His eyes lit up.

'Oh. Really?'

'She's my wife.'

'Oh, ok. Congratulations.'

It turned out Vaz was also booked onto the 7am bus. I'm sure it was a complete coincidence. I doubt that he had been secretly following us (Rachel) since we finished our Colca Canyon tour.

Anyway, he seemed a nice guy, and it was good to have some company for the bus journey to La Paz.

# FIFTEEN

Despite our sleepless night, Rachel and I were excited about visiting Bolivia, and we were even looking forward to the prospect of a scenic bus journey which would definitely be direct, and we would not have to change.

The bus ride was our most magnificent yet, hugging the shores of the majestic Lake Titicaca – the largest lake in South America. We hoped to have time to visit the lake properly on our way back into Peru.

Halfway through the journey, we reached the Bolivian border and were all asked to get off the bus. We didn't have a clue where we were going or what we were required to do, so just followed along behind everyone else. As it was Peruvian Independence Day, the place was particularly hectic, and it felt like we would be there for some time.

The Peruvian immigration was straightforward enough, and we got all the correct stamps in our passports, with only a brief snigger at my passport photo from the officials, and then joined a longer queue on the Bolivian side. After a long wait, and a longer laugh at my passport photo, we passed through this one too without any problems.

A man whom we recognised as being the co–driver from our bus then stopped our group and said something in Spanish which didn't go down too well with the other passengers. A group of Peruvian and Bolivian ladies – all dressed in long skirts and dresses, with multiple shawls and brightly coloured scarves – started yelling angrily at the young man and one shoved him in the chest.

'What did he say?' I asked Vaz, who was still lurking near us.

'He said that we have to change buses because our bus will not be crossing the border.'

'Ok,' I said. 'Why are the ladies so cross with him?'

'Because they were told the bus was direct and we definitely wouldn't have to change. Nobody told us and now we have to go back to the other bus to collect all our luggage.'

'But we've already got our bags,' I said, gesturing to our rucksacks on our backs.

'Aren't those just your day sacks? What about your proper bags?'

'No, this is all we have.'

'Wow. You travel light. I've got to go back for my bag. Save me a seat.'

We were able to walk past all the ladies who were still abusing the poor co–driver and be the first onto the empty bus on the Bolivian side. Only it wasn't a bus. It was a really shitty little minibus about half the size of the previous one.

We took our places near the back and it was another hour before Portuguese, I mean Vaz, and the rest of the passengers returned with their luggage. They had to queue again at Bolivian immigration to show the stamp that proved they had already queued at immigration to get the stamp.

We did try to save a seat for Vaz, but one of the Bolivian ladies gave me a piece of her mind after I tried to suggest that the seat was taken. I didn't dare push it any further.

All of the seats on the bus soon filled up, yet more and more people continued to file on. I was just about to offer to give up my seat to someone more deserving, when a lady just squashed herself next to us on the two–person seat anyway. We sat there with our rucksacks on our fronts as more people continued to pile onto the bus. They kept on coming. Soon others had joined us on our seat, perched on our laps, and the aisle was stacked several people deep. Each passenger who boarded the bus issued a fresh rant at the driver who sat patiently, shrugging his shoulders every time he received a new barrage of abuse.

The bus eventually departed, but then had to stop after a couple of hundred metres because some passengers had shouted to alert the driver that several bags had fallen off the roof. There was nowhere to store everyone's luggage, so it was just tied haphazardly to the top of the minibus.

Despite being full, this bus was a 'colectivo', which meant it also stopped to pick up more passengers along the way. Each time it slowed to a stop, another tirade of insults was shouted at the poor driver. Rachel and I sat there smiling about the whole situation. We had initially been smug to get our seats. Little did we realise that we would be sharing these seats with many other people. Still, it made for a very entertaining bus journey. And at least we still had our bags with us. The bus made regular stops to pick up fallen luggage, and, judging by the extreme anger expressed by some passengers when we eventually reached La Paz, some bags never made it.

Arriving in La Paz was an unforgettable experience. From the shores of Lake Titicaca, we passed through the vast expanse of the altiplano. Most of this land lies fallow all year round. The lack of transport infrastructure, a struggling economy, and the heavy risk of both droughts and floods, mean that it is not practical to farm large sections of the altiplano. As we approached the suburbs of El Alto – La Paz's adjacent city – the area became more and more urban along the roadside, but it still didn't have the impact we had been anticipating on reaching Bolivia's capital city.

And then we turned a corner and La Paz was revealed below us in all its glory. The city sits in a huge canyon formed by the Choqueyapu River, with streets and buildings flanking the valley's sides. Its buildings and architecture won't win any beauty awards, but La Paz's setting is unrivalled.

We reached the city's main bus terminal shortly after midday and got a taxi with Vasco to a hostel. We thought we had lost him in the melee at the bus station, but he was sticking closely to us (Rachel). The first few hostels were all full but then we found one that did have one room available.

'We could share?' suggested Vaz.

'That's very kind,' I said. 'You take this room. We'll try at the hostel next door.'

'Sure?'

'Sure.'

We booked a room at neighbouring El Solario and opened the door to our room to be hit by an overpowering stench.

'What is that smell?' said Rachel, covering her mouth and nose with her hand.

'I don't know. It smells like petrol.'

'We can't sleep here.'

'Maybe if we open the windows it will go away.'

I tried the windows, but the safety catch would only allow them to open about an inch.

'We really can't stay here,' she said. 'We will die.'

The man at reception assured me the smell was floor polish. Unless they polish their floors with diesel, I think it's very unlikely. Rachel and I had slept in some pretty questionable places in the past, and didn't consider ourselves fussy (apart from our planned romantic first wedding anniversary with the beds visible to those eating in the restaurant), but on this occasion, we thought there was a good chance that if we went to sleep at El Solario, we may never have woken up again. He reluctantly gave us a refund and we got a room at nearby Happy Days Hostel instead.

La Paz famously claims to leave tourists breathless. Partly because of its setting, but mostly because of its lack of oxygen. At 3,500m, La Paz is the highest capital city in the world.

It was a city like no other we had ever visited before. Just stepping outside the hostel door, you could feel its buzz and energy, as mopeds and taxis screeched up and down the street, seemingly on whichever side of the road they fancied.

We wandered the cobbled streets for a couple of hours, and from what we could gather, La Paz was one giant market. Every inch of space was taken up with a street seller peddling their wares. And it wasn't even a recognised market day.

Vasco joined us for dinner at a Lebanese restaurant (when in Bolivia…) called Yasseps. The food was delicious, but the staff were unwelcoming and Vasco still slightly creepy. When he heard that we had had to check out of our hotel because of the fumes, he was disappointed we had still chosen not to share with him.

Vasco had plans to head off the next day on a mountain bike ride down the *'world's most dangerous road'*. The notorious Yungas Road descends 56km from La Paz to Coroico and has become a popular destination for thrill–seeking mountain bikers in recent decades. Vaz wanted us both (Rachel) to come along with him. Rachel had said from the outset that she would never do it.

'You go ahead, George, and do it without me, if you want,' she had said, in a way that made it very clear she didn't want me to do it. I was secretly relieved that I had an excuse not to go. We said our goodbyes to Vasco and wished him safe travels.

# SIXTEEN

The altitude was noticeable as we wheezed our way around La Paz the following morning, admiring the variety of things for sale. We wanted to buy some presents for friends and family back home, but travelling so light, we had no room to carry anything at all. Having travelled successfully for three weeks with one small rucksack each, we felt like we had proven to ourselves that we could get by without too much stuff. There was no reason why we had to continue to do so.

So rather than sensibly buying a small additional rucksack to accommodate a few presents, we bought a stupidly big PVC zipped bag about a metre square, in red check pattern. These bags are popular all over South America to store everything from laundry to shopping. We figured if we were going to break our self–inflicted hand luggage allowance, we might as well break it in style.

Up until now, Rachel and I had been forced to be restrained when it came to purchases, as we simply had no room to carry anything extra. With our vast new bag to fill, we went a little crazy in the markets of La Paz. I'm blaming the altitude.

It is a fact that almost everything for sale in the Andes is either made from alpaca, or features a picture of an alpaca on it. We bought alpaca hats, alpaca scarves and alpaca gloves – all made from alpaca wool, and adorned with knitted pictures of alpacas too. We also bought a couple of ridiculous woollen ponchos that we had no need for and would most likely never wear, simply because we had room for them.

We stopped regularly at cafes to ease the effect of the altitude, and ate various snacks from street sellers. I pride myself on having a decent natural sense of direction, but lost in the rabbit warren of La Paz's streets, I didn't have a clue where we were. I'm blaming the altitude.

We stumbled upon a cinema that was only showing one film. It was, predictably, about Che Guevara. Despite being dead for 30 years, Che Guevara was still the biggest celebrity in Bolivia. The few items of clothing that didn't feature an alpaca, featured pictures of Che instead.

By the time we found out where we were, we had wandered several miles out of the city centre, so we got a taxi back to our hostel and collapsed into a deep post–shopping slumber. I blame the altitude.


The following morning, I woke early and walked up to the markets on the higher streets above our hostel. I usually hate shopping, and back in England I will do anything to avoid it. But I couldn't get enough of the markets in La Paz.

Every corner I turned, there was a new sight to behold, and the smile on my face grew wider and wider. Almost every stall was run by a Bolivian lady, wearing her long flowing dress, shawls, petticoats and the trademark bowler hat.

These bowler hats were introduced to Bolivia by mistake. A shipment of hats, produced in England, was sent over to the British rail–workers who were stationed in the region in the mid–1800s. The hats were far too small for the men to wear, but rather than get rid of them, they were offered to Bolivian women who were led to believe these hats were all the rage for women in

Europe and North America. They have been a prominent part of Bolivian heritage ever since.

These women in their bowler hats at the market were sat amongst their wares, with heaps of oranges, grapefruit, or chilies stacked up around them. I wanted to know how they created the display in the mornings. The lady presumably had to take her place at the stall, while the goods were then piled around her. She would then be unable to move for the rest of the day.

I stumbled upon the notorious Mercado de las Brujas – Witches' Market – where the definition of weird purchases is rewritten. Here you can buy an array of bizarre things, such as potions, voodoo dolls, statues, dried frogs, herbal 'stimulants' and dried llama foetuses. The llama foetuses are said to ward off evil spirits, and are often built into the foundations of new houses in Bolivia to ensure a happy household.

By the time I got back to the hostel, Rachel was up and showered and ready to start the day. I told her all about the markets. She had not wanted to come with me earlier, fearing the altitude of the higher streets would be too much, and choosing a lie–in instead.

'That sounds amazing,' she said. 'Let's go and see it.'

'But I've just got back from there.'

'Well it sounds really good. I'd really like to see the markets.'

'But I told you this morning that I was going to look at them and asked if you wanted to come and you said you didn't.'

'I didn't want to go earlier.'

'Then why do you want to go now?'

'Because you said it was really good. And I've had a nice lie–in.'

'Actually, it wasn't that great. In fact, I've just remembered how rubbish it was.'

'Too late for that. Let's go!'


We had a nice breakfast at a nearby cafe and then wandered back up to the markets again. Thankfully, Rachel was impressed, and I enjoyed it equally the second time around. Our PVC laundry bag was filling up nicely, and we added plenty more alpaca tat to take home with us.

'What about one of the dried llama foetuses?' I suggested.

'What about them?'

'Maybe we should buy one to take home?'

'How about…. no?'

'But they are supposed to bring good luck.'

'I don't care. We are not taking a dried llama foetus home. However much luck it might bring.'

'We've still got room in our bag.'

'George, forget it. If you buy a dried llama foetus, you are going on the rest of the trip on your own.'

'I won't be on my own. I'll have my dried llama foetus to keep me company.'

'Well, I hope you and your dried llama foetus have a long and happy life together.'

'Thanks. We will.'


We had a cheap and cheerful lunch consisting of the Bolivian specialty of fried meat, fried egg and fried rice, at a little restaurant called Pot Pourri. All that walking at high altitude – and possibly the wine they served with lunch – had made Rachel sleepy. She went back to the hostel for a nap while I continued shopping. I had a giant bag to fill.

A charango is a stringed instrument, popular in the Andes. They were traditionally made using the shell of an armadillo, but are now more commonly made from wood. Charangoes were for sale all over La Paz., with entire streets devoted to them.

Back in England, I had been playing in a band for many years. So, for some strange reason, I decided to buy two charangoes – one for me and one for my guitar playing friend Mark. Mark had never shown any interest in South American musical instruments. But now that I was in La Paz, it was essential I bought two charangoes. We had a bag to fill.

I spent almost four hours that afternoon searching the shops and learning everything there was to know about an instrument I didn't even know existed before we arrived in South America. It was extremely unlikely I would ever learn to play a charango, but at the time it felt incredibly important. The charangoes all looked identical, but each had very subtle differences in the colour of the wood, and the pattern of the grain, which made the decision–making process so much harder.

I eventually settled on two charangoes, and bought a couple of horrendous looking padded cases for them too. Mark would be delighted.

I don't think Mark's charango ever made it out of the case for more than a couple of seconds, and neither has mine. I still have it though, just in case I decide to become a charango player later in life. At least they took up a decent amount of space in our new bag.

'Why on earth did you buy two charangoes?' laughed Rachel, when I returned to the hostel.

'Just be grateful I didn't buy any dried llama foetuses.'

'That's true.'


Later that evening, we had some over–priced and extremely disappointing cocktails at Sol Y Luna where Rachel and I had our first proper argument of the trip. It began as a slight disagreement after I tried and failed to order a bowl of olives – possibly the most middle–class argument it is possible to have – and extended into a long and heated discussion of what we would do once we returned home. More specifically, what I was going to do once we returned home. Rachel had been supportive of my decision to leave my job as a Data Information Officer, but now the realisation was setting in that I didn't have a job to go back to, it was making her understandably nervous. I tried to reassure her and tell her it would all work out ok, but we both went to bed angry. Rachel, because she was anxious about my future, and me because I didn't get my olives.

# SEVENTEEN

The concern over my career was mostly forgotten by the following morning, as were the olives, because it marked the start of one of the most highly–anticipated legs of our trip. We were going to the jungle!

We took a bus to El Alto International Airport – which, at the time, was the highest commercial airport in the world (airports at higher altitudes have since opened in China) – and checked in to our flight to Rurrenabaque – the gateway town to the Amazon rainforest.

When they announced our flight was ready to board, we followed a group of half a dozen people through some double doors and out onto the runway.

'That's not our plane, is it?' said Rachel, pointing to an aeroplane not much bigger than a minibus.

'Uh, yeah, it looks like it might be.'

'It can't be. That's not a real plane.'

'Of course it is. It's just a plane for fewer passengers.'

'I thought this place we are going to is popular with tourists?'

'It is! But that's popular by South American backpacking standards. Not popular enough to have 747s flying into the jungle every hour. Plus, I wouldn't want to be in a large plane trying to get enough height to fly over those bad boys.' I pointed at the rugged peaks of the Andes mountain range that overlooks La Paz.

'The Andes? We're not flying over those, are we?'

'Yes we are! The jungle is on the other side of them.'

'I'm really not looking forward to this. What if we crash into the mountains?'

'We won't. They've been flying planes from this airport for years. The Andes do look very close though, don't they? And very big.'

'Stop it,' she said. 'You're really not helping matters.'

The plane looked bigger from the outside than it was inside. It turned out to be smaller than most minibuses, with just 11 seats, including the pilot and co–pilot. Rachel and I sat directly behind the pilot and we could have reached out and touched him if we wanted to. We didn't want to. We didn't want to divert his attention away from the aircraft's controls until we were well over the Andes and safely landed in the jungle.

The plane took off in the vague direction of the Andes, but then started banking heavily left.

'Ah, see, I knew we wouldn't fly over those,' said Rachel. 'We are obviously going around them,'

'The Andes stretch for thousands of miles. We can't go around them. We are definitely going to have to go over them at some point.'

The plane kept banking left, and over the course of the next five minutes had completed a full 360 degrees turn and was facing back towards the mountains, this time at a significantly higher altitude.

'It's a bit like one of those spiral entrances to multi–storey car parks, isn't it?' I said.

'Er… no. I don't remember ever feeling like my life was about to end driving up one of those.'

'I have. When you are driving.'

The plane straightened up and continued on its course towards the Andes, as Rachel shot me one of her menacing looks. It was a truly incredible flight. My stomach did back flips as we crested the ridge of the mountains, the pilot pulling back heavily on the controls the entire way, and the snow–dusted crags seemed almost within touching distance.

The flight lasted about 45 minutes, and after crossing the magnificent peaks, we descended gradually down over the other side. The vegetation below us became thicker and greener, the tree canopies so densely packed together it resembled a field of genetically modified broccoli that had got way out of control.

A clearing appeared as the plane slowly approached the ground, but there was no sign of a runway or any sort of airport out of my window.

'Where are we?' said Rachel, squashing her face up to the glass.

'I assume we'll soon see Rurrenabaque and I guess there will be a runway any minute now.'

The plane got lower still, and I could see its prominent shadow on the grass below. The shadow got bigger and bigger until the plane's wheels touched gently down onto the ground. I strained my neck to see if there was a thin patch of asphalt below us that I hadn't been able to see properly before. There wasn't.

'Ok,' I said. 'Apparently the runway is made of grass.'

'I am so glad I didn't know that before we took off.'

'Well we still have to take off again when we leave,' I reminded her.

'Why do you always have to say things like that?'

'Sorry.'

Rurrenabaque Airport consisted of a rickety blue single–roomed building, just a few yards from where the plane landed. I have seen much bigger village halls. It was delightful.

Rurrenabaque is a small isolated town on the Rio Beni, a couple of hundred miles north–east of La Paz. It has increased in popularity in recent years as a starting point for excursions to the jungle and the pampas – two vastly different regions of the Amazon river basin. We were going to go on tours to visit both.

Our room at hostel El Porteño was vast and airy with an unnecessarily high ceiling and large windows. It was bigger than both the aeroplane and the airport, and the circulating air provided much needed relief from the heat.

My poor Spanish was evident when I ordered us each a toasted ham and cheese sandwich at a neighbouring cafe by pointing to the pictures of the toasted ham and cheese sandwiches on the wall, and asking for, in Spanish, what I thought was two toasted ham and cheese sandwiches. What arrived were two normal ham and cheese sandwiches, which were perfectly decent but not toasted. I think what I said must have translated as something like, *'hello, we would like two of these but definitely NOT toasted please.'*

After ten minutes in the humidity of the Amazon, the sandwiches had slowly started to resemble their photos on the menu. There is no need for ovens in Rurrenabaque. The jungle is one big toastie machine.

I was given directions to the town's Post Office, because I needed to mail a CD of photos home as a backup. When I reached the address scribbled on the back of my hand, it appeared to just be someone's house. I knocked. A lady answered.

'Dónde está the post office?' I asked.

'It's me,' she said in English. 'I am post office.'

'Oh, bueno. I would like to post this to Inglaterra por favor.'

'60 Bolivianos.'

'Gracias. Cuando does it get collected?'

From what I understood, she told me she would post it in La Paz next time she visited. I asked her when that was likely to be, and she said she wasn't sure, but it would probably be later in the month or possibly next month. I tried to backtrack on our transaction, but I had already paid her the money and secretly thought it was the greatest post office I had ever visited.

The CD of photos did make it back to our house in Northampton, but we beat it by about two months.

I was then given an address for the town's launderette, which I scribbled on the back of my other hand. Again, this proved to be someone's house. The lady – not the post office lady – took the bag of dirty clothes from us and told us it would be ready the following day. It was fascinating to see how the entrepreneurial locals had adapted to the influx of tourists to their jungle town.

In the evening, we played pool and ate pizza in the atmospheric and touristy Moskkito Bar. By touristy, I mean that there were about half a dozen other non–Bolivians in the bar. South America was anything but touristy.

# EIGHTEEN

After breakfast the following morning, we went to the meeting point at the shore of the Rio Beni for the start of our three–day jungle tour. It transpired that Rachel and I were the only people booked onto this tour, so they merged us with three people from another group as well. As we had established with our Colca Canyon tour, all the groups are largely the same anyway.

Our new group consisted of a quiet and introverted French couple named Bernard and Andrea, and a girl from Israel named Orit, who was extremely chatty and didn't stop talking for two days.

Our guide was a round and cheerful man named Jose Luis. We expected jungle guides to be dressed either entirely in khaki, camouflage or partially shredded clothing, but Jose Luis wore a baggy pair of jeans and a skin–tight green retro Reebok t–shirt. He did, however, have a machete with him at all times. He spoke no English, but was full of enthusiasm and almost as excited as we were for the start of our jungle trip.

We climbed into a long wooden boat of dubious safety. It was basically a canoe with an outboard motor held together with duct tape. But it looked like it had been floating on that river for many decades, and we hoped it would at least last for the duration of our journey.

The Rio Beni stretches over 1,000km through the Amazon basin. It was wide, calm and the colour of chicken soup. We sat peacefully for three hours as the boat headed upriver towards our camp.

The riverbank was dotted with all sorts of exotic looking birds, perched on branches watching us pass. Each time we saw a new species, Rachel and I would point and let out an audible sign of excitement, despite the fact we had no clue what each bird was. On hearing our eagerness, our guide, Jose Luis, would look in the direction we were pointing and say, 'bird.' We would then say 'bird' and he would smile which made us smile. We never did find out what type of birds they were. But Jose Luis confirmed each time that they were indeed birds.

Compared to our countless journeys on buses, colectivos, taxis, milk floats, and aeroplanes, this river trip was the most relaxing transportation of our time in South America so far. There were no sheer drops to contend with, no deadly overtaking manoeuvres, no bumpy pot–hole ridden roads, no immigration control, no laughing at passport photos, no fear of nose–diving into the Andes mountains and no people selling boiled sweets or chipas. At regular intervals we would pass small isolated villages or houses on the riverbank, accessible only by river, and each time a group of children would run down to the waterside and smile and wave to us as we passed. We would smile and wave back. The journey to our jungle camp was worth the fee alone.

Jose Luis branched off the Rio Beni and followed one of its tributaries – the Rio Tuichi – further into the jungle. We eventually pulled up alongside a small clearing on the riverbank, Jose Luis tied up the boat, and we disembarked. We were deep in the Amazon rainforest by this point, and had not passed any form of civilisation for well over an hour.

It was a 15–minute walk from the banks of the Rio Tuichi to our camp, following Jose Luis along a well–trodden path through the trees. Our camp was a collection of half a dozen small wooden huts on stilts in a clearing. We had assumed we would be sharing a tent or at least a dormitory with others on the tour, so it was a pleasant surprise to be given our own little cabin. The single–roomed hut was just big enough for a double bed with a basic mattress and a mosquito net hanging over it. It was far more luxurious than either Rachel or I had envisaged.

The heat and humidity had been a bit of a shock since flying in from La Paz. Our clothes, damp and sweaty, clung tightly to our bodies. But it wasn't as bad as either of us feared. Despite the temperature being in the mid–30s, it was the middle of winter, and we knew that the jungle could get a whole lot hotter.

Jose Luis had laid out some cheese and bread and salad which we ate while we chatted to our camp mates. Rachel and I used our poor Spanish to include Jose Luis in the conversation as much as possible, and Andrea (from France), who was fluent in English and Spanish (and French, obviously), translated the bits of his answers that we didn't understand. Which was most of it.

Jose Luis did, however, speak the international language of football and reeled off a list of Manchester United players. United were his favourite team. He then showed me a newspaper that a fellow guide had dropped off earlier in the day containing the previous weekend's scores. It turns out you can check football results in the jungle.

The afternoon was spent taking a leisurely three–hour walk through the rainforest with Jose Luis as our guide. I expected our jungle tour to be mostly looking at exotic jungle animals like monkeys, snakes and jaguars, with Jose Luis having to fight off surprise crocodile attacks every few minutes with his machete. But we mostly just looked at trees.

The trees were surprisingly fascinating though. We learned – through Andrea's translation – all about which types of trees were poisonous, which were edible, which you could drink water from, and which had certain medicinal uses. Neither Rachel nor I retained any of this information, so we would just as likely accidentally poison ourselves as cure athlete's foot if forced to fend for ourselves in the jungle.

The group's favourite tree by far was the walking tree. It probably has a proper name, but in the jungle, it is just known as a walking tree. Because it walks. The tree does not have a single trunk. Instead, it has about a dozen 'legs' providing its stability. The fight for sunlight in the rainforest is key, with all plant species battling with one another to get as much sun as possible. The walking tree will never be as high as the others, so can't compete in that department. Its leaves are not as big as some other plants, so it can't contend there either. However, the walking tree more than makes up for these inadequacies with its ability to move its position on the jungle floor to find a better spot to maximise its daylight exposure. Over time, it grows new roots in the direction of the light, with some claiming these trees can move up to 20 metres per year.

More recent studies by party–poopers have suggested that this is a jungle myth, and although walking trees grow new roots and old ones die, they don't actually move anywhere. I choose to ignore these studies, because I believe in walking trees. I was marvelling at one of them on our jungle tour, I turned to say something to Rachel, and by the time I turned back again it had gone. Stick that in your study.

A friendly Danish couple named Anna and Rob joined our group during dinner after they missed the morning departure and had to wait for an evening boat.

We went on another walk after dark. It is possible it was the same walk, but it looked very different in the darkness. The thick tree canopy blocked out the moonlight and we shuffled along slowly, guided by the faint beams of our head torches.

Every so often one of the group would shriek then whisper 'lobo' – 'spider'. We would then point it out to Jose Luis and ask him if it was an 'amigo'.

'Si. Amigo,' he would usually respond, to reassure us that that particular spider was a friend to us and was not dangerous. Some of these spiders were the size of tarantulas, because, it turns out, they were tarantulas. The Amazonian tarantulas were the least of our worries, however, and according to Jose Luis they were amigos.

Occasionally, we would ask Jose Luis about a spider and he would tell us in his very serious voice, 'lobo no amigo. Muy peligroso' – 'spider is no friend – it is very dangerous'.

Jose Luis found one such spider resting on a huge leaf. Andrea informed us (after translating Jose Luis's words) that it was a Brazilian wandering spider – perhaps the most dangerous spider on earth. Its bite can kill a human in 25 minutes. If the bite isn't fatal, its venom can cause its male victims to have four–hour erections. So, possibly it's an amigo too.

Whenever Jose Luis pointed out a muy peligroso lobo, we would back slowly away from the spider, usually resulting in us getting tangled in another web behind us, and then whirling around frenziedly to try to escape. Every cracking twig, hooting of an owl, or rustle of a leaf gave cause for concern that there was perhaps some other muy peligroso animals going to jump out on us at any moment.

It was genuinely terrifying. But it became so ridiculously scary and farcical that it almost felt like we were actors in some low–budget horror movie and not taking part in real life. Our laughter – instigated largely by Orit the Israeli – was contagious and we giggled our way around the forest, crashing comically into spiderwebs at every turn. Even Jose Luis was enjoying his tour and when we arrived back to camp we all had a group hug as though we had survived some near–death experience.

# NINETEEN

The following morning, after a breakfast of bread and honey, we went on another long walk to look at more trees. Jose Luis sure liked his trees. The lobos weren't so abundant during the day, and despite there being very little in the way of jungle animals, it was extremely pleasurable to just spend time in the middle of nowhere doing very little.

We did see several snakes, a group of howler monkeys – doing their howling in the treetops above us – a small rodent–like creature, several species of ant, and a variety of different animals with wings that Jose Luis identified as '*birds*'.

We came across one huge tree wrapped in thick vines that we were able to climb. Jose Luis cut one of these vines free with his machete and we were able to take it in turns to swing Tarzan–style between the trees.

Rachel and I loved the simplicity of our time in the jungle. South America had been more than we hoped for. We had seen and experienced some amazing things, with our senses being constantly stimulated – perhaps overly so – and always moving from one place to the next. It was sometimes impossible to take it all in when there was so much going on. In the jungle, everything became so much more straightforward. Our days consisted mostly of taking leisurely walks, looking at trees, and always ending up back where we started. We were loving every minute of jungle life.

We headed back to camp for lunch, and Bernard, Andrea and Orit got a boat back to Rurrenabaque, having only booked a two–

day tour. The Danish couple and Rachel and I were joined by some replacements – a young British couple named Dave and Wendy who were travelling around South America with their nine–year–old daughter Aleah for a year.

After lunch, we expected to go on another walk to look at trees, but we were surprised (and slightly disappointed) to discover that Jose Luis had an afternoon of handicrafts planned for us at the camp. Like everything in the jungle, it turned out to be far more enjoyable than we expected.

We were given a bowl of little nuts called coquito nuts. They resembled tiny coconuts, shrunken and dried to the size of a hollow grape. We sanded these nuts down using a variety of three different grades of sandpaper – depending on what stage of the process we were at. Rachel then threaded several of these nuts onto a piece of string to make a necklace.

I decided to keep sanding mine down until I had made a ring. I was going to give it to Rachel as a present that she would almost certainly never wear. It took me two hours of delicate sanding to get the hollow coquito nut down to the size of a ring. It was smooth and black and beautifully shiny. It was almost perfect. *It just needs perhaps one last polish*, I thought, as I rubbed the sandpaper gently over it for the final time. The delicate ring cracked all the way through.

'OH FUCKING BOLLOCKS!' I shouted.

Jose Luis looked up from the other end of the table with an expression that suggested he didn't know the meaning of what I had said, but he knew from my tone that I most certainly was not happy.

'I broke the ring,' I said, holding up my afternoon's work – a worthless cracked shitty piece of nut.

'Oh fur–king bol–locks,' said Jose Luis, before erupting into laughter that echoed through the trees around us. 'Oh fur–king bol–locks'.

'Fucking bollocks indeed,' I laughed. 'Oh well. Rachel, I made this for you.'

'Thank you. I love it,' she said.

'It's broken,' I said.

'Yeah, I know. I kind of heard you. It's still very sweet. Thank you.'


In the early evening, we walked down to the Rio Tuichi and swam in the shallow water as the sun began to set. We walked back to camp where over dinner we had a chance to chat to Dave, Wendy and Aleah. They were a lovely family and it was inspiring to see what incredible life experiences Aleah was gaining at such an early age from her travels with her mum and dad.

We did another night walk, this time along the river bank. Without trees for Jose Luis to talk about, his focus turned to looking for animals. There were a surprising number of animals hanging out down by the river at night. We saw frogs of all colours and shapes (mostly frog–shaped), birds, a small caiman, spiders (both amigos and no amigos), insects and what Jose Luis described as 'lazy birds', which seemed to be a variety of non–flying bird.


We chatted to Jose Luis around the campfire later that night – with our limited Spanish and his limited English – about his background and how he ended up as a jungle guide. He told us how he grew up in one of the communities along the Rio Beni that we had passed on our boat ride up the river. The occasional journey down the river to Rurrenabaque was as far as his world extended as a child. But he knew the jungle better than anyone. It was his playground. It was his back garden.

As a child, tourists to the area were extremely rare. But as their numbers increased in the '90s, he started assisting with organised tours, providing some much–needed local knowledge. It wasn't long before he was assigned his own groups, and he had been a lead guide ever since.

During our time in the jungle, Rachel and I had worked our way through our entire Spanish repertoire that we had learned during our 12 weeks of language lessons with Pillar. We asked Jose Luis many times if we could have the bill, we asked him repeatedly where the nearest toilet was, we asked him if he had any brothers or sisters, we ordered many paellas with a large glass of sangria, and we made enquiries about what time the next train to Madrid departed.

Jose Luis was always very good–natured and seemed to enjoy listening to us speak in Spanish, even if our conversation was a bit on the irrelevant side. Little did he realise that we hadn't yet used our secret weapon on him – the phrase book. As we sat around the fire that night, we passed around my *Penguin Spanish Phrase Book* (for anyone unfamiliar, Penguin is the publisher, not a particular dialect of Spanish spoken by penguins). We all took it in turns to read random Spanish sentences from the book to Jose Luis. 90% of the scenarios in the book would never be needed by a tourist anywhere, and when spoken in the middle of the Bolivian jungle by a group of non–Spanish–speaking gringos, it made for some top–quality campfire entertainment.

*Can you fix my heels? These stains won't come out. I want to hire a large car. Can the heating be turned down? Would you like to go to the cinema? I have broken my dentures.*

To begin with, Jose Luis looked a little bemused by the whole situation, but by the time we had all taken our turn, he was crying with laughter and pleading for us to go around the circle again.

*Where is the nearest tennis court? Can I hire skiing equipment? We want to take a coach tour round the sights. Is there a jazz club here? My nose keeps bleeding. What time is the floorshow?*

Rachel and I had grown incredibly fond of Jose Luis. The more time we spent with him, the more we liked him. He was understandably proud of his jungle and relished the enthusiasm our group showed for it.

After our final jungle breakfast the following morning, we did another three–hour walk looking at more trees; Jose Luis gave us a recap of some of his favourites. We then returned to camp for lunch, before saying our goodbyes and getting a boat back to Rurrenabaque. Jose Luis wasn't coming back with us, as he had another group arriving later that day. We had only been with him three days, but it was surprisingly emotional saying goodbye to Jose Luis and his jungle camp.

The boat stopped on the way back to give us the chance to look at a group of macaws (or, to use the correct collective noun, a pandemonium of parrots) in a tree on the riverbank. We took a couple of photos, but we weren't close enough to see them properly. We smiled at the young guy driving the boat and gave him a thumbs–up, which we meant as a polite way of saying *'hey, thanks for stopping, it was good to see the macaws. Now… vamos!'* He took it to mean, *'wow, these macaws are the best thing I have ever seen. Let's hang out here a while longer.'*

We feigned interest for a few more minutes, expecting him to start up the engine at any moment, but he didn't. The other passengers on the boat had all lost interest a long time ago and were deep in conversation with each other and not paying the macaws the slightest bit of interest. Rachel and I stopped looking at them too, and hoped our lack of interest would spur him into action. But still we sat there.

I then momentarily thought he was waiting all this time for us to get off the boat, and that we had actually been moored up near Rurrenabaque all this time. I pointed to me and the rest of the group, and then to the shore, trying to ask him if we should disembark. He then said something to me in Spanish and I mistakenly said *'sí'* before realising he must have said, *'would you like to hang out here for fucking ages longer?'* because he said *'bueno'* and then he lit a cigarette and we hung out there for fucking ages longer. We were watching that bloody pandemonium of parrots off in the distance for almost an hour.

We eventually arrived back in Rurre late afternoon (we could call it Rurre now, rather than Rurrenabaque, as it was our second visit), and checked back into Hostel El Porteño.

In the evening we ate pizza and drank cocktails at the Moskkito Bar, accompanied by the sound of blaring pop music, and reminisced about our time in the jungle. It hadn't been anything like what we had expected. We imagined we would be hacking our way through dense undergrowth with machetes and dodging wild animals, but in reality, we just followed Jose Luis around lots of paths through what often felt more like a normal woodland than a jungle. But we had had the best time. It had been so much more fun than we predicted, and it was a shock to be back in the hustle and bustle of Rurrenabaque, which three days earlier had felt like the sleepiest town in the world.

As we sat and sipped our margaritas, a toad the size of a football hopped into the bar and sat in the middle of the floor. A few locals wandered in and out and didn't seem to think it out of the ordinary in the slightest. It really was the biggest toad that we had ever seen. Possibly the biggest toad that had ever lived. It sat there staring at us suspiciously, before the barman eventually ushered it outside with a broom. It was ironic that we saw our most impressive wild animal in a cocktail bar in Rurre, rather than on our three-day jungle tour.

We played pool for half an hour, but it didn't do anything to ease the post-jungle blues, so we walked back to our hostel and had an early night.

# TWENTY

I woke early the following day and explored the streets of Rurrenabaque while Rachel slept. The town is set out in a grid system, only a few blocks long and a few blocks wide. Most of the shops, restaurants and hotels are concentrated in one small area of the town, with the surrounding streets made up of predominantly single storey wooden houses. I was walking down one of these residential streets when I saw a strange vehicle coming towards me in the middle of the road. It was the size of a car, but gliding silently. There was a large sign attached to the roof emblazoned with what looked like the word *CAKE*. I was convinced I was hallucinating. But as it got closer, I realised it was real. The contraption was a four–wheeled bicycle – or quadracycle – driven by a man with a white beard and a panama hat. The sign did indeed say *CAKE* and the front of his quadracycle had been converted into a makeshift table–top, covered with half a dozen mouth–watering cakes.

He came to a stop in front of me.

'Buenos dias,' I said.

'English?' he asked.

'Yes, was my accent that bad?'

'No. I thought I'd save us the hassle of speaking to each other in bad Spanish.'

'Thanks. Are you American?'

'Floridian,' he said.

'Cool. How did a Floridian end up selling cake on a bicycle in the Bolivian jungle?'

'I saw a gap in the market,' he said.

We chatted for a while about life in Bolivia. Each day, the Rurrenabaque Cake Man baked half a dozen cakes and then cycled around the streets of Rurre, selling slices to both tourists and locals. He didn't feel the need to expand his range, or branch out into other products. He didn't even need a shop name or fancy branding. The simple hand–painted sign of *CAKE* was all that he required. I was very impressed, and slightly envious of his lifestyle.

I bought a slice of coffee and walnut cake and a slice of lemon drizzle and paid my money. As he gave me my change, he thrust a leaflet into my hand.

*THE DA VINCI CODE IS RIDICULOUS*, it said.

I went to take the leaflet from him, but he held on tightly to the other end of it.

'The Da Vinci Code is ridiculous,' he said, staring at me intently.

'Yeah, it's just a fictional novel,' I said.

'It doesn't reflect the true values of Christianity,' he said, finally releasing his grip on the piece of paper.

'Ok, thanks. I look forward to reading it. Your leaflet, I mean. Not the Da Vinci code. I won't be reading that. It's ridiculous.'

I laughed. He didn't. Instead, he handed me another leaflet.

This one had the headline, *HAVE YOU BEEN IMPLANTED WITH A GOVERNMENT MICROCHIP?*

'Err…'

'Well?' he said. 'Have you?'

'Er… no. I don't think so.'

'How do you know? The government are trying to control us.'

'Which government?'

'The American government.'

'But I'm British.'

'And the British government.'

'Ok, thanks for the warning.'

'You might already have been chipped,' he said.

'I'll go and get checked out.'

I stuffed his other leaflet into my pocket, took my cake, and headed briskly back towards the hostel. He cycled slowly behind me.

'The path of true Christianity shall be found only by those who seek…' he said.

*But what does cake have to do with all of this?* I thought.

When I got back to the hostel I was slightly reluctant to eat the cake in case it had been drugged. But I was so hungry and it looked so good.

'So, why did this guy pick Rurrenabaque to come and spread all his conspiracy theories?' said Rachel, after I told her about my encounter.

'I don't know. Maybe he knew he would have a captive audience, especially with the lure of the cake.'

'It is damn good cake.'


We had completed one jungle tour, but had another three–day trip still to come. Next up was the pampas, exploring the animal rich wetlands of the Bolivian Amazon.

We had been warned about the mosquitos in the pampas, so went shopping for some Amazonian strength repellent. Rachel bought a new long–sleeved shirt especially for the trip, and I bought a new sun hat as I had lost mine somewhere in the jungle amongst the lobos.

As we waited at our designated meeting spot, it became apparent that we were again the only two to have booked spots with our tour operator. We were teamed up with four Israelis from another group – three male and a female – who were all very friendly, very hairy (except the female), and very loud.

We had a bumpy and uncomfortable three–hour jeep ride – stopping briefly for lunch – until we reached a small tributary called the Rio Yacuma. From there we travelled by boat a further three hours up river, following a network of smaller channels that interlaced through the pampas.

It suddenly became clear where all the animals we had been expecting to see in the jungle were. They were all hanging out in the pampas. Everywhere we looked there was wildlife. Crocodiles, caiman, turtles, herons, storks and sloths occupied every tree, bush and patch of ground we passed along the riverbank. It was almost like there was not enough land to house all the animals.

We reached our camp by early evening. It consisted of a couple of large wooden dormitory style bedrooms, built a few metres from the top of the river bank. We had dinner and chatted to our Israeli companions. Well, they chatted, and we sat there and listened.

After dinner, Melvin, our young and hyperactive guide, took us out in the boat on a night tour. Melvin certainly looked the part as a jungle guide, with his camouflage combat trousers and a black string vest. He complemented this look with a pristine pink cotton shirt which he wore with the buttons undone to show off his string vest. It was quite the look.

Our expectations were set fairly low for the night tour, and we didn't imagine we would see much wildlife from the boat in the dark. But we were wrong. Every sweep of torchlight that we shone across the water revealed several sets of alligator and caiman eyes. They burned red and menacingly and we didn't want to keep the torch light on them too long for fear of angering them.

Melvin switched the motor off and let the boat glide slowly parallel to the shore. Mid–conversation, he rolled up the sleeves of his pink shirt, leaned over the side of the boat and plunged his arms into the oily blackness of the river. There was a frantic splashing and Melvin sat back down on his seat, holding a small caiman in his hands, one hand supporting the middle of the animal, the other holding its jaw shut.

Moments earlier it had been a threatening pair of red piercing eyes in the water. Now it was a defenceless animal in the firm grip of a human.

'You want to touch?' said Melvin.

*Not really,* I thought. *I want you to put it back. It looks terrified.*

*But how often would I get the chance to stroke a caiman?*

I reached out and touched it and it felt exactly like I expected it to. Sort of caimany.

'Bueno. Now put it back, por favor,' I said.


It was an incredible feeling to be floating through the pampas with a dazzling sky above us, and nothing but the sound of nature around us. Actually, that's not true. The sky was indeed mesmerising, without any light pollution for hundreds of miles, but we heard no evidence of nature whatsoever as our fellow group members talked incessantly throughout the boat trip, at a volume that would have been audible from every one of those incredible stars above.

We returned to camp and Rachel and I sat on the small decking at the front of our hut to play cards. While on the river, we had noticed a few mosquitoes, but the movement of our boat had kept their numbers to a minimum. Now that we were back at camp, on the damp and muddy banks of the river, word had spread amongst the mosquito population that some tasty gringos had arrived. And it was feeding time.

I have always been particularly prone to insect bites, so after noticing their presence, I put on a long–sleeved t–shirt over my t–shirt and tucked my socks into my trousers. Rachel dealt the cards.

'Ow, get off, you bastard,' I said swiping one away as it sucked on my exposed hand. Another bit me on my other hand, so I retrieved an extra pair of socks from my rucksack and wore them as gloves, tucked over my t–shirt. My face was now the only exposed part of my body and I made regular swipes at that to keep the buggers away, much to the amusement of Rachel, who mosquitoes seemed to show no interest in.

Before coming to South America, we had received all of the necessary malaria, dengue fever, yellow fever and Saturday night fever vaccinations, but that didn't make the mosquitoes any less of a pain in the arse. Quite literally.

'Ahh, you little shit!' I shouted, squashing one on my bum cheek.

'What's the matter? How did it hurt you by just landing on you?' said Rachel.

'It bit me!'

'No it didn't. You're wearing clothes.'

'Well it bloody well did bite me! Ouch, there was another one,' I said, flapping wildly at a patch on my back that I couldn't quite reach.

I watched another one land on my trousers, just above my knee. I swear it looked up at me and with its eyes said, *'watch this, motherfucker',* before it plunged its snout, or whatever the hell a mosquito bites with, through the thick fabric of my trousers and into my leg.

'WATCH THIS, MOTHERFUCKER!' I said, as I brought my hand down on top of it with far more force than was necessary, splattering its blood–filled body all over my trousers, and causing considerably more pain to my leg than the bite itself.

'George, you are being a bit dramatic. They can't bite through clothing, surely? You're being paranoid.'

'These Amazonian mosquitos can bite through anything. Believe me. I doubt you would be safe in a suit of armour.' I lifted my shirt to reveal a series of bright red bite marks which I proudly showed to Rachel.

'Alright, I believe you.'

'Why don't they ever bite you?'

'I don't know.'

'I obviously taste way better than you,' I said.

'It's because you are just sweatier and smellier than me.'

'Thanks. You're the one that married me.'

'I only married you because I knew you'd make an amazing mosquito deterrent for me in times like this.'

'Well this sweaty smelly mosquito deterrent is going to bed now to take refuge under the mosquito net, so you'll be their only option out here.'

'Mosquito net? Pah! They will chew through that in no time. There will be nothing left of you by morning. Good night, my love.'

# TWENTY-ONE

Far from being nothing left of me, by morning I had inflated to twice my usual size. Every inch of me was swollen, itchy and sore. The mosquitoes had somehow found their way through the net, or chewed through it like Rachel had warned, and feasted on me all night long. I covered myself in cream and tried to block out the discomfort as much as possible.

Anaconda hunting isn't high up on the 'things to do' list of most people's holidays. But when you are in the Amazon, for some reason it seems like a normal thing to do.

Most of the tour operators offered '*anaconda hunting*' as part of their Pampas tour package. In fact, it seemed to be their main selling point, with photos of tourists draped with giant anacondas plastered all over the ticket offices. None of the groups were able to guarantee we would find an anaconda, but all said that there was a good chance of seeing one.

When choosing our pampas tour, as they all offered what appeared to be the same package, and me being of a frugal nature, I opted for the one that was $3 cheaper than the others.

We walked down to meet Melvin at the riverside early the following morning to set off on our anaconda hunt. We looked around at the rest of the group and noticed that they were all wearing long wellies and waterproof trousers. Rachel and I were standing there in our sandals.

'Hola,' I said to Melvin. 'Where do we get our boots from?'

'Que?'

'Our boots. Wellington boots. Cuando do we get ours from?'

'You not have any?'

'No.'

'We not have boots for you.'

'What about these guys?' I said, pointing to the Israelis.

'They booked with other company. That company give boots for anaconda hunt.'

'But when we booked it, all the tour groups said that all footwear for the anaconda hunt was provided.'

'Not us. We cheaper. People in this group bring own boots.'

Rachel shot me an evil look.

'George, how much did you save by booking the cheaper tour?' she asked me.

'Er… $3.'

'You skimped on $3 for them not to provide wellies?'

'All the tours looked identical. If I'd known they didn't provide wellies I would of course have booked the more expensive tour.'

'Well that's good to know. Anyway, there is no way on earth that I am walking through a snake filled swamp in my sandals.'

'I suppose that's a fair enough demand,' I said. 'Melvin, do you have ANYTHING else we could wear? Por favor! We only have our sandals.'

'Sandals is ok,' he said. 'Anacondas not bite.'

I looked at Rachel.

'See, it's ok. Anacondas don't bite,' I said. 'It will be fine for us to wear sandals.'

I looked at Melvin, shrugged my shoulders and rolled my eyes to suggest that I knew my wife was being irrational, and why couldn't she just lighten up and wade through a swamp and hunt for anacondas in her sandals. Secretly, I wanted to run home and cry.

'Do you have anything we could borrow?' I asked again. 'I will pay the extra $3.'

'Wait here,' said Melvin. 'I look.'

In the meantime, Rachel and I put on our socks that we had brought with us, in anticipation of the knee–high waders Melvin was going to find for us.

'We have this,' he said, holding up a pair of retro white Puma trainers. The sole was flapping around on one of them, completely detached from the shoe, leaving a gaping hole in the toe.

'Gracias. Is that all you have?' I asked.

'Si. No more.'

Rachel and I looked at each other.

'It's better than nothing, I guess,' I said. 'You wear the shoes.'

'What? And you'll just wear your sandals?'

'It doesn't look like I have much choice.'

'What about this huge hole?' said Rachel to Melvin. 'Won't animals get through that? Muy peligroso animals!'

'No, no, no,' he said. 'Anacondas are very, very big. They not fit through hole. They wrap around your leg.'

He clocked the look of sheer terror on Rachel's face.

'It's ok. I get tape. Fix hole,' he said.


With Rachel's trainers sellotaped up, and me standing in my socks and sandals, we climbed aboard the boat and were ready to go. I was prepared to break the first rule of fashion (no socks with sandals) for the sake of an extra layer of protection, even if it was only a thin layer of cotton.

After a short boat journey, Melvin tied up the boat and we began the walk towards the swamps. As our group assembled by a cluster of trees on the edge of a vast area of marshland, Melvin began what we assumed would be an extensive safety briefing of what we should and shouldn't do during the hunt.

'Ok. We walk in water. If you stand on snake, you shout *MELVIN* and then stand still. Vamos!'

That was it.

'But... but...' I tried to ask, curious to know whether there was anything else in the swamp that was likely to hurt us. We had established from chatting to the Israelis on the walk that anacondas do have teeth and they can bite, but they are not venomous.

'But they still have teeth?' Rachel had asked.

'Oh yeah. Very sharp teeth,' one of them had said. 'But it's not the teeth you need to worry about. They will have crushed you to death before you die from blood loss.'

The group all laughed amongst themselves and Rachel looked as though she might pass out.

'I'm sure they are exaggerating,' I said, trying to block the images from my mind about the anacondas I had seen in films.

The murky water came midway up our shins as we waded out through the swamp. Other than the flies, there was no sign of animal life, and it seemed implausible that we would find an anaconda in this never–ending marshland.

In the distance, we could see another two tour groups, each of similar size to ours, walking along in two separate picket lines in

146

different areas. We could also see that they were all part of the fancy $3 more expensive groups, with their matching thigh–length waders glistening in the sun. The smug bastards.

Our group set off in similar fashion, shuffling slowly, no more than a couple of feet away from each other. It made sense to drag our feet gently through the water, rather than taking big steps. If I was an anaconda, minding my own business at the bottom of a bog, I think I would be less likely to crush someone to death if their foot casually brushed into me, rather than having my head aggressively trodden on.

I turned and noticed that Rachel was no longer next to me. She was following directly behind, copying my footsteps precisely, to use me as a human shield against any muy peligroso animals. I pointed out that she had left an anaconda sized hole in our group's picket line, and she reluctantly resumed her position.

'How are your trainers?' I asked.

'Oh, wonderful. My feet feel totally dry and protected.'

'Really?'

'What do you think?' she said, shooting me another of those classic glares that reminded me of the $3 I had saved by taking the cheaper tour. 'The sellotape fell off after about ten seconds. And how are your socks and sandals?'

'Absolutely wonderful. I really feel like I am at one with nature. All these losers wearing wellies are not fully embracing the experience.'

We looked around longingly at the rest of the group, all wearing substantial footwear.

'Yeah, they all look so jealous of us, with their comfy protected feet,' she smiled for the first time since we began the hunt.

We were searching for anacondas in the Bolivian jungle. Despite our less than ideal circumstances, it was impossible not to be slightly excited about the whole ludicrous situation.

The hunt was scheduled to last for three hours, and we had been warned there was a possibility that even after three hours, none of the groups would find anything. Melvin told us the other two groups had been hunting for nearly two hours already and had not yet found so much as a tadpole.

We had been walking for less than 20 minutes, when Rachel shrieked to the right of me.

'What is it?' I asked.

'I touched something big. And it moved.'

'Really?' I said, looking down at the motionless surface of the water in front of her.

'Yes, really. It was big and solid and moved when my foot touched it.'

'Are you sure it wasn't just a log? Or a rock?'

'Do logs or rocks move?'

'No... it's just... well...'

'You think I'm making it up?'

'Of course I don't think you're making it up. Maybe just being a little overly–jumpy.'

'Something definitely moved.'

'We should tell Melvin then.'

'But what if it is a log or a rock?' she said.

'I thought you said it moved.'

'It did.'

'Right, then we should tell Melvin. MELVIN!' I shouted. 'Rachel thinks she's found something.'

'Stay still,' he said. 'I come.'

'It's probably just noth… OH MY GOD!… it moved again. It's definitely alive.'

'Stay still,' Melvin said again, wading quickly towards us.

'It was somewhere down there,' said Rachel, pointing to her feet.

Melvin casually rolled up the sleeves of his pink shirt and dipped his bare arms into the brown water.

'Ah, she got one!' he said. 'Big one.'

There was a brief thrashing and we caught a glimpse of the yellow patterned skin breaking the surface of the water as the snake tried to escape Melvin's grip.

He slowly pulled both hands from the water to reveal an enormous anaconda. It was at least twelve feet long, and more than eight inches wide. It was stunning and graceful, yet at the same time powerful and petrifying. I couldn't take my eyes off it.

There were gasps from the rest of the group as they all huddled around to get a closer look. Even Melvin, who presumably did this daily, looked childishly excited by Rachel's find.

Melvin shouted out across the marshland to the other two tour groups that we had found one, and they all turned and began converging upon us.

'Here, you found it, you hold it,' said Melvin, untangling the snake from his arms and draping it around Rachel's shoulders before she had a chance to protest. Rachel stood frozen with fear as it coiled itself around her arm.

By now, the other two groups had reached ours, and so about 25 people were assembled watching Rachel with her trophy. A barrage of questions fired in her direction in a variety of accents. *How did she find it? Did it try to eat her? Was she scared when she found it?* Rachel stood there too nervous to even speak in case it caused the anaconda to divert its attention to her neck instead.

I could see that the anaconda had begun to wrap itself even tighter around Rachel's arm and there was a definite feeling of panic radiating from Rachel's stricken eyes.

'Is it squeezing you tightly?' I said.

She gave a hurried nod.

'Melvin, I think it's trying to crush her,' I said, as Melvin had become distracted by one of the flirtatious girls from the other group.

'Oh, lo siento. Sorry,' he said, and it took him some considerable effort to unwrap the incredible snake from Rachel's arm.

There was no need for the anaconda hunt to continue. We were unlikely to find another, and certainly not one as big. We spent another five minutes having the snake passed around the group, then Melvin released it back into the water and we watched it gracefully slither back under the surface. All three tour groups began the slog back towards their various camps, full of wonder about our morning's excursion.

'That was incredible,' I said to Rachel. 'Look at all these people here and you were the only one to find an anaconda.'

'It must be the lucky Puma trainers,' she said. 'I've become quite attached to them. I might ask Melvin if I can keep them.'

'See, it wasn't so bad after all. And think of that $3 we saved! We were only in there 20 minutes. It would've hardly been worth paying extra.'

She scowled at me to let me know that I was far from being let off the hook.

# TWENTY-TWO

With the anaconda tour far shorter than anticipated, we had a few hours free before lunch. Melvin suggested we should have a swim in the river. The Israelis all jumped about excitedly. I laughed at Melvin, assuming that he was joking, what with all the caiman we had seen, the anacondas, and the fact that we were going piranha fishing in the same stretch of river later that afternoon. Melvin didn't appear to be joking, though.

'What about the caiman?' I said.

'They not hurt you. They scared.'

'What about the very hungry ones?'

'Hmmm, maybe,' laughed Melvin. 'Swimmers no get bit by caiman here.' He paused. 'Well, not for long time.'

'What about piranhas?' I said.

'Piranhas don't eat you. Only in James Bond. They very small.'

'But if there are lots of them might they attack a person?'

'No. Only if you bleeding. Or if you in tight space.'

'What do you reckon?' I said to Rachel. 'Do you want to swim?'

'You've got to be kidding. I did the anaconda hunting in those stupid trainers, but there is no chance you will get me to swim in that river with piranhas and caiman. You can if you want. I'll come and watch.'

We all clambered into a boat and Melvin drove us a few hundred metres up the river where it was slightly wider, and the piranhas would presumably feel a little less confined, and therefore less munchy.

'Here good place to swim,' he said.

I caught a glimpse of something large breaking the surface of the water just next to the boat.

'Was that a caiman?' I asked.

'No. Pink dolphin,' said Melvin.

I looked again, and a flash of pink emerged from the water. And then another. There were at least three of them. We had heard stories about the legendary Amazon pink river dolphins, but weren't sure they actually existed and certainly didn't think we would get to see them. They were at least six–foot–long with a pointed snout – basically they were dolphins, but pink – and both beautiful and surreal.

'Dolphins mean it safe to swim,' said Melvin. 'Pink dolphin eat piranha.'

The Israelis didn't need any more persuading and had already ripped off their t–shirts and jumped over the side of the boat.

'Come on!' shouted Daniel, the most talkative of the group. 'It's amazing. When are you going to get another chance to swim with pink dolphins in the Amazon?'

I looked at Rachel who wore an expression that said it was an experience she was more than happy to live without. Daniel did have a point. This was a once in a lifetime opportunity.

'Our passports and our money are under the mattress in the bunkhouse,' I said to Rachel as I took off my t–shirt.

'That's not funny.'

'Sorry. I'm only joking. Maybe we should have bought a dried llama foetus after all. To ward off the piranhas and caiman.'

'That's not funny either.'

I climbed over the edge of the boat and swam quickly over to join the rest of the group. Their noisiness would surely be a deterrent to any predator. The water was warm and earthy, and the fear of what lay beneath the surface certainly made it a memorable experience. The occasional glimpse of pink in the water around us enabled me to tick the '*swimming with dolphins*' thing off my bucket list, even if a brown, piranha and caiman infested river in the Amazon is not the usual dream scenario.

'It's not piranha that hurt you,' said Melvin, once we were all safely back in the boat.

'What do you mean? I thought you said the caiman wouldn't bother us?'

'No. Not caiman.'

'Then what?'

'Candiru.'

'What is candiru?'

'Candiru a small fish.'

'What does it do?'

'It swim up inside your penis and get stuck. Then eat your penis from inside.'

'WHAT THE FUCK, MELVIN? ARE YOU SERIOUS?'

The Israelis all started laughing hysterically.

'Yeah, we were warned about those too,' said Daniel. 'But don't worry, they have to swim up a stream of urine to get into your penis, so they can only get up there if you take a piss.'

'But I did take a piss!' I shouted. 'That's the only reason I went swimming. I didn't think I could hold it until we got back to camp.'

They all laughed even harder.

'Oh. You should have held it, mate,' said Daniel.

'Why didn't anyone warn me?'

Melvin found this hilarious too, as did Rachel, but I failed to see the funny side.

'Why are you all laughing? How do you know about this fish, Melvin?'

'Ray Mears,' he said.

'You've met Ray Mears? Has he been on one of your pampas tours?'

'No, I see candiru on Ray Mears. On TV.'

'RAY MEARS GOT HIS PENIS EATEN OFF FROM THE INSIDE BY A SMALL FISH ON TV?'

'No!' laughed Melvin. 'We watch Ray Mears TV show. He talk about candiru. He very funny.'

'I don't think it's supposed to be funny,' I said.

'He very funny.'

After lunch we went piranha fishing in the very same waters we had been swimming in. Melvin set up our fishing lines – which consisted of a hook attached to a piece of wire with some sardine flesh on the end – that we dangled into the water.

It wasn't long before we started getting bites. For such a small fish, piranhas are disproportionally strong. We lifted them into the boat where they thrashed angrily around, still attached to the line.

The piranha is a deceptively beautiful fish from a distance. Its skin is a bright silver and orange that shimmers like a hologram. And then you look at its face and it's the scariest motherfucker you have ever seen. Intense orange eyes that can see inside your soul and a mouth so fearsome you don't want to look at it for too long.

The teeth look like they have been drawn on by a child trying to design the ugliest monster they could imagine.

'I can't believe you swam with those this morning,' said Rachel.

'If we had done the piranha fishing before then I definitely wouldn't have.'

Needless to say, once we had reeled in the piranha, none of us were too keen on removing the hooks from their mouths.

'It just like normal fish,' said Melvin.

'Er, no it's not, Melvin,' said Daniel. 'Normal fish don't have massive big fangs.'

We left the hook removal to Melvin.

Between us we caught half a bucket full of piranhas, which Melvin would be barbequing for our dinner. Lucky us.

# TWENTY-THREE

We were heading back to camp when someone spotted some squirrel monkeys in a bush on the riverbank. Melvin steered the boat towards them so we could get a closer look. He switched off the engine, but we were still drifting at a considerable speed towards the muddy bank. Most of us saw this coming so braced ourselves for impact. Rachel, who had been distracted by the monkeys, was not prepared, and as the boat hit the riverbank, she lost her balance and fell backwards off her seat and somehow slid arse first into the bucket of piranhas.

I watched it all happen from the next wooden bench. The look on Rachel's face is something that I will remember forever. She flailed around hysterically for a few seconds with her arms and legs in the air like an upturned turtle, as I clambered over the bench to try and help her. I reached out an arm and pulled her quickly to her feet, careful not to spill the contents of the bucket on the floor of the boat in the process.

'Holy shit! Are you ok?' I asked, trying so hard not to laugh.

'I don't know,' said Rachel, still clearly shaken, as she checked her bottom for any sign of teeth marks. 'I think so. Why the hell did he just crash the boat?'

'I don't think he did it on purpose.'

Melvin and the Israelis were all too engrossed in the monkeys and hadn't noticed Rachel's little incident with the piranhas.

'That's the scariest thing that has ever happened to me,' she said.

'Worse than the Mandango Trail?'

'Much worse!'

'It was incredible. I can't believe you just sat in a bucket of piranhas.'

'It's not as if I chose to sit there!' she snapped.

'I know, but it was genuinely one of the funniest things I have ever seen.'

'Funny? Thanks a lot. There was nothing funny about that at all. Why are you such an idiot?'

'Sorry, but you just sat in a bucket full of piranhas.'

'AND? Which part of that is funny?'

'The part where we have a bucket of some of the most notoriously dangerous animals in the world, and you somehow sat in it.'

I sensed that as the realisation was setting in that she hadn't been harmed, Rachel too was beginning to see the funny side.

'But they could have attacked me! I could have been killed or had some severe injury.'

'Well, obviously it would not have been as funny if that happened.'

'Not AS funny? But still funny?'

'Well, no, not if you'd died or been seriously injured of course.'

'OK?' asked Melvin, sensing our little domestic dispute from the other end of the boat.

'Yes, we're fine thanks. Rachel just sat in the bucket of piranhas.'

'Haha, that very funny!' said Melvin.

'See!' I said. 'I told you it was funny.'

She gave a little smile.

'Look, I'm really glad they didn't eat you,' I said, putting my arm around her. 'Let's go and see these monkeys.'

A group of six or seven squirrel monkeys, each the size of a small cat, lurked tentatively in the bushes, their distinctive black and yellow fur clearly visible through the fauna. Melvin reached into a carrier bag under his seat and pulled out a bunch of bananas, and cut each one in half. This clearly wasn't a chance encounter, but a scheduled part of his tour. He handed us a couple of banana segments each, and then held out one of his own pieces at arm's length towards the monkeys.

Within seconds, one of the more confident monkeys emerged from its cover, climbed onto the edge of our boat and began confidently nibbling on Melvin's banana (grow up!). Melvin encouraged us all to do the same. Hold out our own, I mean, not nibble on Melvin's banana too.

Half a dozen other monkeys emerged from the undergrowth. They were all soon clambering onto the edge of the boat and feasting off the banana segments that we held in our hands. We all squealed with childish glee.

But then a feeling of guilt overcame me.

'Is this right?' I said quietly to Rachel. 'Should we be doing this?'

'You mean feeding the monkeys?'

'Yeah.'

'I know. It does feel a bit wrong,' she said.

'It feels very wrong.'

All of the jungle and pampas tour groups claimed to be proudly supporting eco-tourism, but feeding wild animals by hand didn't seem to fit in with this ethos. It was difficult for us to criticise Melvin; he was only doing it because it was popular with the tourists. And why wouldn't it be? Although we knew it probably wasn't environmentally or ecologically correct, we couldn't escape the excitement that there were monkeys on our boat in the middle of the Amazon rainforest and that they were eating bananas from our hands.

'Isn't it just the Amazonian equivalent of feeding the ducks at the park back in England?' said Rachel. 'I bet the locals have been feeding these monkeys bananas for hundreds of years.'

'Yeah, that's probably true I suppose. I think it's more serious than that, though. Isn't it supposed to be a possible danger for the monkeys? If they get more confident around humans then they might be more susceptible to getting hunted by other predators, or even other humans. Or they might become more aggressive towards humans if they expect to be fed.'

'That makes sense. But why doesn't it cause those same problems with ducks?'

'It does! There are some seriously angry ducks at the park. Just you wait, when we get home to Northampton, it will be completely taken over by ducks.'

Once back at camp, Melvin barbecued the piranha for us to sample for dinner. There was very little meat on them. They were mostly bone, teeth and evilness.

Later that evening while Rachel and I were playing cards in one of the single beds in the dormitory, under the limited protection of our mosquito net, we heard the sound of cheering close to our hut. We stuck our heads outside to see what was going on and saw another tour group from the neighbouring hut gathered at the top of the river bank.

One of their guides was at the front of the group, grinning away as he held on tightly to a rope. The assembled crowd were egging him on with whatever it was he was doing. We followed our gaze along the rope to a huge chunk of raw meat – the skinned carcass of some dead animal. And there, at the water's edge, its eyes just breaking the surface, was a giant caiman. It lurked just a metre from the meat and only four or five metres from the tourists. The guide gave the rope a flick so that the meat moved ever so slightly. The motionless caiman kept its eyes transfixed on the bait before launching an attack. With an almighty surge, it powered its huge body – all four metres of it – towards the carcass, jaws stretched wide. The guide, who had obviously done this before, pulled the meat away just in time as the caiman's huge jaws clamped shut onto thin air. The bait now lay another metre further up the bank from the caiman. The crowd went absolutely mental.

'What the hell is he doing?' said Rachel.

'Trying to lure a huge dangerous animal up the riverbank into a tourist camp, by the look of things.'

'And we thought feeding the monkeys bananas overstepped the boundary of eco–tourism. This is another level.'

Neither of us wanted to be involved with this spectacle any longer so went back into our cabin and closed the door, propping a chair against it, just in case.

We lay in bed listening as the whooping and cheering got louder and louder. We half expected it to turn to shrieks as the guide or one of the tourists was gobbled up, but by the sound of things the caiman eventually got tired of the antics too and retreated to the river. Until next time, when it might venture further up the riverbank into camp in search of food. Or revenge.

# TWENTY-FOUR

Melvin woke us at 5.30am the following morning for our sunrise river cruise. Despite the early start, the Israelis were in full voice and shouted incessantly to each other like the world's most irritating alarm clock. We arrived at the designated spot to watch the sunrise, but a thick mist lingered above the river and we could only just make out the other end of the small boat we were in. Melvin did his best to describe how the sunrise would have looked had we been able to see. This was not too difficult to imagine, having seen a sunrise before.

We returned to camp for breakfast, packed our bags, and then got back on the boat that would take us all the way down the river back to the port. The early start had taken its toll on the rest of our group and they thankfully dozed for most of the way back. We stopped to watch a group of capybaras, rolling in the mud very close to the riverbank (there doesn't seem to be a collective noun for the capybara. Let's go with a 'calamity'). Resembling guinea pigs the size of large dogs, capybaras are perhaps the strangest looking animals I have ever seen. They reminded me of the *Rodents of Unusual Size* in the film *The Princess Bride*. They definitely do exist. We tried not to look at the calamity of capybaras too enthusiastically in case the guy driving the boat lit a cigarette and made us watch them for fucking ages longer. After a quick lunch at the port, we were collected by a jeep to begin the long and bumpy drive back to Rurre. We checked back into El Porteño for the third time, and after a few compulsory post–tour cocktails in the Moskkito Bar, we had an early night.

I went out in search of breakfast the following morning and found myself lured, seemingly against my will, to the adjacent street where I met the CAKE man again. He had cast some sort of spell over me and knew I would return.

'Have you thought about what I told you?' he said.

'Er... yeah,'

'And? What do you think?'

'About which bit?'

'All of it. The governmental microchipping, the Da Vinci Code... everything.'

'Well, yes, you make some great points,' I said.

'I speak the truth. That's why you came back.'

'I came back because you make even better cake.'

'The cake lasts but a moment. The issues I address last forever,' he said, placing another leaflet into my hand after I paid for another two slices of cake.

*IS YOUR PET A GOVERNMENT SPY?* the headline said.

I stuffed it into my pocket.

'Make sure you read it,' he said.

'I will. Thanks for the cake.'


After back–to–back jungle and pampas trips, it was enjoyable to spend a lazy day around Rurrenabaque, reading, writing our journals and emailing home from the town's local internet café with dialup internet so slow it would have almost been quicker to hand deliver our messages back to the UK.

Rachel wasn't feeling too well. I did momentarily wonder if she had been drugged by the cake man, and became concerned that we were both soon going to drift off into a deep sleep and wake up holed up in some remote jungle cabin, being quoted passages from the Da Vinci Code until we relented to the Cake Man's conspiracy theories. However, I felt absolutely fine.

We went to a café called Tacura for lunch, but Rachel couldn't face eating anything. I ordered one chicken burrito with my best Spanish, and even held up one finger to illustrate that we only wanted one. The lady brought two burritos and placed one in front of Rachel. I did the noble thing and ate both, because that's the kind of thoughtful guy I am.

Having had an afternoon nap, Rachel was happy to come and sit in the Moskkito Bar in the evening, which seemed to be hosting a '*gringo freaks of the Amazon*' themed night, because we spoke to an eclectic bunch of travellers. We met Kurt, an American who was driving across Bolivia on a quad bike, for no other reason than he thought it would be "rad". We met Steve, an English guy who was so stoned that when I asked him how long he had been in Rurrenabaque, he showed genuine surprise and concern that he was even in Bolivia. He thought he was still in Argentina. We met another English guy called Tom who didn't stop talking all evening about a band he was in back home called *The Flying Tokyo Flagship Band*. They were on the verge of greatness and everyone in the world would soon know their name. He was so enthusiastic and passionate about his band that I believed every word he said. So much so, that I wrote *The Flying Tokyo Flagship Band* on my hand so that I could remember that moment. I recently googled *The Flying Tokyo Flagship Band* to find out how things turned out. Google returned zero results. I am sure they are still on the verge of greatness.

Dave, Wendy and their daughter Aleah, whom we had met on our jungle tour, were also in the Moskkito Bar. We played pool and drank cocktails until past midnight, comparing stories from our different pampas trips. They had been unsuccessful with their anaconda hunting, and were very envious of Rachel's find. They were not so envious of our footwear selection.

Rachel claimed to be feeling a little better as she danced clumsily around the pool table. I suggested we should perhaps quit while we were ahead and go back to the hostel.

'Ok, after this song finisheseses,' she slurred, as a familiar bassline pounded through the speakers.

'*TOMMY USED TO WORK ON THE DOCKS…*' she screamed, punching the air not even remotely in time to the music.

'Rachel, you haven't had anything to eat today. I think we should get you to bed.'

'I'm fine. Really. I feel sooooo much better. *SHE SAYS, WE'VE GOTTA HOLD ON TO WHAT WE'VE GOT…*'

It was no use trying to compete with Bon Jovi. I was never going to win. I downed the rest of my margarita and went to the bar to get another round in, raising both arms in the air on the way to join in the chorus.

'*WOAH… WE'RE HALFWAY THERE…*'


The following morning, Rachel was feeling a whole different kind of sick to the previous day as she was hit with the mother of all hangovers. She insisted that her illness had worsened, but I reminded her of the multiple cocktails she had consumed, which she had insisted at the time were medicinal.

We went for breakfast at Tacura where we had eaten lunch the day before. Rachel couldn't face the thought of any food, so I ordered one plate of eggs using my best Spanish and held up one finger to show I only wanted one. The lady brought two plates of eggs and placed one in front of Rachel. I did the noble thing and ate both, because that's the kind of thoughtful guy I am.

It was time to bid farewell to Rurrenabaque, a town we had grown very fond of during our few days there. A town that had embraced the relatively recent influx of tourists to its remote location in the middle of the Amazon jungle with style. Whether that was by charging tourists to take their mail to the post office whenever they next happened to be going to La Paz, or laundering clothes while doing their own daily wash, or giving diners two of everything even if they only ordered one, to conducting unforgettable tours into one of the world's most incredible wildernesses, to selling slices of cake and preaching extreme Christianity from a quadracycle. It was a town full of character and characters.

Taking off on the grass runway from Rurrenabaque airport was nowhere near as scary as we anticipated. Rachel's pounding headache provided her with ample distraction to stop her mind from worrying about such trivialities as crashing to certain death in the mountains.

We were back in La Paz by lunchtime and greeted by bright blue sky and cold crisp air. Having grown used to the humidity of the jungle, the thin air of La Paz was a shock to the system and didn't help Rachel's hangover, I mean, illness. I bought two vegetable pitas from a street seller, but Rachel couldn't face hers, so I did the noble thing.

We checked back into Happy Days hostel – half expecting Portuguese David Blaine to be there waiting for us – and Rachel went for an afternoon nap to try and recuperate.

Our ridiculously big shopping bag still had some space in it, so I went out in search of tat. I returned to the hostel later with two alpaca fur cushions.

'What the hell are those?' said Rachel.

'Alpaca fur cushions.'

'They are revolting,' she laughed. 'Who did you buy those for?'

'The cats.'

'The cats? You bought presents for our cats?'

'Yes. We've bought presents for nearly everyone else. And there was some space left in the bag.'

'Are you sure those cushions aren't actually made OF cat? They look remarkably similar.'

'No, of course they are not made of cat!' I said, suddenly questioning my purchase. 'The lady who sold me them said they were genuine alpaca fur.'

'Oh well, in that case they must be.'

Our cats – Father Dougal and Batfink – hissed at the cushions when they first saw them and never ventured anywhere near them again.

# TWENTY-FIVE

Our dinner of coke and popcorn the night before had worked its wonders on Rachel and she was feeling considerably better by morning. Which was a relief, because we had a full day of Bolivian public transport to contend with. After a taxi journey from our hostel to the bus station, we boarded a bus to Oruro where we got a train to Uyuni for the start of our tour of the world–famous salt flats – the Salar de Uyuni.

The train journey from Oruro to Uyuni was magnificent. The views across the dry and inhospitable altiplano were superb, but it was the speed, or lack of, that was the train's biggest appeal. It moved at little more than walking pace the entire way. It felt like it was in the process of either slowing down at a station, or about to hook–up onto a faster engine for the entire journey. A journey that lasted almost nine hours. Still, the train was state–of–the–art, by South American standards, and even had a small television showing films.

As we chugged along at a snail's pace, Rachel flicked through the photos on my camera of our trip so far.

'These are really good,' she said.

'Thanks. They are ok. I'm still getting to grips with how the camera works.'

'You should seriously think about doing photography as a career.'

'Yeah right.'

'Honestly, you should. You've talked about it in the past.'

I had been interested in photography for many years. I bought my first film SLR before going to university and spent all of my free time there in the darkroom, developing my own photos. I then took a module in digital photography, just as the medium was taking off. Our tutor bought the class some state–of–the–art digital cameras that boasted an industry–leading 1 megapixel.

Just before flying to South America, I bought my first digital SLR. It was silver and shiny, and I was worried it would attract a lot of attention on our travels, so I covered every part of it in black tape, to make it look a little less bling, and a little more like an old film SLR.

Rachel had obviously been thinking about my future, but I had become so immersed in our holiday that I had not had time to think about what would happen when we got back home. I didn't have a job to go back to, which was both exciting and terrifying.

I knew that I didn't need a job that would earn me lots of money. I didn't need a job that would require me to travel the world. I didn't need a company car or private healthcare. I just needed something that would stimulate me, allow me a little creative input, and stop me from wishing away the days between weekends.

While working as a Data Information Officer, I had photographed the wedding of some friends of mine and enjoyed the experience enormously. I had toyed with the idea of pursuing it as a career, but knew I had a very long way to go before I could possibly start charging people for my services. I was prepared to learn, though, and put in the hard work until I was good enough.

'You could contact some local photographers when we get home and try and get some work experience,' said Rachel.

'Aren't I a bit old for work experience?'

'Of course not.'

'But I would have to work for free. That's not going to help pay the bills.'

'I'm starting my new job when we get home, so you won't have to work full time.'

'I know, but…'

'But what? You were right,' she said. 'We'll survive. Everything is going to work out ok.'


We arrived in the town of Uyuni at 10.00 pm. It was minus 20°C. Uyuni is the most popular gateway town for the Salar de Uyuni, so accommodation was in plentiful supply. We found a cheap room at Residencial Sucre – which surely translates as '*the sugar house*', and sounds a lot more like a brothel than a hostel. I did wonder at the time why they asked me if I wanted the room for a night or just an hour.


I woke with a jolt early the next morning, bursting for the toilet. I had woken several times in the night needing to go, but the air on my face had been so cold I couldn't bring myself to get out of bed. There was no holding it in any longer. I dashed from the room wearing only a pair of boxer shorts, grabbing a towel so that I could shower at the same time. During the same trip, I mean, not at the same time as going to the toilet. The bathroom was about ten metres from our room, but accessed via the outside and the cold hit me the second I opened our bedroom door. My chest compressed instantly, and combined with the altitude, it was a real effort to force in a lungful of air. I set foot on the tarmac and my bare foot instantly stuck to the layer of frost that had formed on the ground. I prised it away, springing from toe to toe until I had covered the distance to the bathroom.

The water in the shower was only marginally above freezing so my shower was over very quickly. Without any clothes to change into, I was forced to dance back to our bedroom in just my small towel. I burst through the door and startled Rachel who, until my entrance, had been fast asleep.

'What's wrong?' she said, clocking the look of pain on my face.

I tried to speak but my body had contracted so much I couldn't form any words.

'F–f–f–f–f….' I stammered.

'Are you ok? What happened?'

'F–f–f–f…'

'George, you're scaring me. What is it?'

'F–f–f–f…ucking f–f–f–f–freezing.'

'Why the hell would you go outside dressed like that?'

'B–b–b–b–bursting for a w–w–w–wee.'

It was another half an hour and the application of every item of clothing that I owned – including the thermal long johns with the hole in the crotch – before I was able to stop my teeth chattering and begin to feel the blood flowing once again to my extremities.


Spanning over 4,000 square miles, and sitting at 3,656 meters above sea level, the Salar de Uyuni is the world's largest salt flat. It was formed thousands of years ago after the evaporation of several prehistoric lakes. After a breakfast of Ritz Crackers (other snack crackers are available), we set off to book our Salar de Uyuni tour.

There were variations of trip durations on offer, ranging from one to four days, and there was an option of either returning to Uyuni or ending the tour at the Chilean border. After looking at the map, I suggested it would be potentially easier for us to do a three–day tour and get back to Peru via Chile, rather than retracing our steps through Bolivia on the world's slowest train.

All of the three–day tours looked identical, but after experiencing the wrath of Rachel when I had saved us $3 on our welly–free pampas trip, I decided to splash out and not book us onto the cheapest tour. I booked the second cheapest instead. It cost $3 more.

We settled on a tour group called Salar Paula, paid our money, and were told to be back in a couple of hours for departure. In the meantime, we left our bags at the office and went to explore the nearby Cementerio de Trenes – the train graveyard.

Uyuni was once an important transport hub in Bolivia, but for decades the rusty carcasses of many trains have rested on the edge of the salt flat, a couple of miles outside Uyuni. Rachel and I were the only people there, and it was a slightly haunting experience to see these huge and once so powerful contraptions gradually eroded away by the salt and the rain.

The Cementerio de Trenes is now basically an adult's adventure playground, and we spent half an hour climbing the rusty ladders, walking along the train roofs and jumping from carriage to carriage like we were Indiana Jones, making the most of the experience knowing we were unlikely to ever be back there again.

An hour later, after meeting up with the rest of our tour group, we set off on our three–day tour. Our first stop was the Cementerio de Trenes, where we spent an hour climbing the rusty ladders, walking along the train roofs and jumping from carriage to carriage like we were Indiana Jones, making the most of the experience knowing we were unlikely to ever be back there again.

# TWENTY-SIX

There were six of us in our tour group: a British guy named Jos who was in South America partly on holiday and partly to research an academic paper he was writing on something I didn't understand. Jos was travelling with his Italian girlfriend Fran. We were also joined by an Italian couple who were recently married and touring South America for their honeymoon. Our tour guide, a tiny man named Valerio, didn't speak any English, but he was very cheerful and eager. The seven of us squashed into the back of a Toyota Landcruiser with our bags strapped to the roof, including our bulging bag containing ponchos, charangoes, and the alpaca cushions for our cats, and set off across the Salar de Uyuni.

The wheels of the Landcruiser crunched on the crisp salt crust as Valerio drove us out onto the Salar. It wasn't long before the town of Uyuni was a speck on the horizon behind us, and the immense salt flats stretched endlessly to the horizon in every direction. The bright blue cloudless sky contrasted perfectly with the blinding white of the salt. We had all been told to wear sunglasses throughout the tour because of the risk of snow blindness, or salt blindness. It was a surreal and otherworldly experience, and with no reference points to go by, it was impossible to gauge any perspective of how far away things were.

A small building appeared on the horizon, and despite Valerio driving at a fair speed, it took a considerable amount of time for us to reach it. The building was the Hotel de Sal Luna Salada – the salt hotel. We were given a tour of the hotel, which is built entirely from blocks of salt. The beds are made from salt, the chairs are made from salt, the tables are made from salt, the duvets are made from salt. Actually, cotton probably. I don't know. Definitely not salt.

'Hotel de Sal Luna Salada?' whispered Rachel. 'Does that translate as the hotel made of salt, moon and salad?'

'Ha, I think salad is 'ensalada'. Although I would love to see a hotel made entirely of salad. There's definitely a gap in the market for that.'

'Will our accommodation tonight be a bit like this place? I love it.'

'Er... no. I think tonight's accommodation will be a little more, well, rustic.'

'What do you mean by rustic?'

'Well, shit, I guess.'

'I bet for $3 more we would have been staying at the salt hotel, rather than just looking at it.'

I didn't bother responding to her and just rolled my eyes.


After a quick picnic lunch outside the hotel, prepared by Valerio, we drove for another hour to the Isla De Pescado – the island of the fish. Valerio told us, via a translation from Jos, that it got its name because from a distance the island resembles a fish. It doesn't.

As we got closer to the island, we realised Isla De Pescado would be more appropriately named Isla De Cactus. It is a bizarre prominent rocky outcrop in the middle of an enormous expanse of bright white nothingness, where hundreds of giant cacti thrive. It is a setting that would look improbable even in a cartoon.

We had an hour to walk the network of rocky paths that criss–cross the island. The centrepiece is Cactu Gigante, which, based on the assumption that these plants grow 1cm per year, is 1203 years old (there was a signpost with this information on it. I didn't measure it). The views from the top of the island were phenomenal, and took our appreciation of the Salar de Uyuni to a whole new level.

What I remember most about Isla De Pescado, though, is that it is where I left my beloved purple fleece that Rachel had affectionately named 'The Big Aubergine'. By mid–afternoon, the sun was blazing down on us and I removed The Big Aubergine as we walked amongst the cacti. It is there, visible, in many of the photos that we took. But it wasn't with me later in the day when the temperature plummeted well below freezing. The temperature range in the Salar is one of the more extremes on earth. It can reach up to 20°C during the day in August and drop to minus 20°C the same night. It was a really stupid place for me to lose The Big Aubergine – the only jumper I had brought with me to South America.

Back in the truck, Valerio left the salt and headed onto the dry and dusty land that borders the Salar. The terrain became hillier as patches of vegetation became visible on the slightly more fertile land.

We arrived in the village of San Juan by early evening where we would be staying the night. We were greeted by about a dozen young children who were obviously used to the influx of tour groups to their small village, but still excited by our presence… and presents. Rachel and I had brought a few little things with us to South America to give to children – pencils, stickers, balloons –

which they were very grateful for. We all had a game of football on a gravel pitch as the sun set, before being called in for dinner.

Our accommodation was a bunkhouse, where a lovely Bolivian lady cooked us a stew that looked revolting and tasted worse. But we were cold and hungry, it was hot and plentiful, and she was delightful, so we wolfed it all down.

Rachel and I were both suffering dodgy stomachs in the morning. I don't want to imply it was the lady's stew, but it was definitely the lady's stew. The entire group were all feeling ropey, but we piled into the Landcruiser and carried on regardless.

From San Juan, Valerio drove us up through rocky crags to Laguna Hedionda – the stinking lake – which more than lived up to its name. Despite the saline water and sulphurous aroma, hundreds of pink and white flamingos have made the lake their home.

We continued upwards and into the Siloli Desert. The bright white salt of the previous day had given way to sand and stone, as we drove to several more lagunas, each with water a different colour to the last.

We passed many impressive rock formations. The most famous and photographed of all is the Arbol de Piedra – the stone tree. This cleverly named rock looks like a tree, but is made of stone. Standing at seven metres high, the wind and sand have eroded the lower part over centuries, forming a trunk that makes the whole thing look precariously balanced.

Valerio was very respectful of this natural monument and, despite being the only tour group there, he wouldn't allow us to get too close to it, for fear that too much tourist activity would speed up the erosion process.

Each time we stopped, Valerio seemed keen for us not to linger too long and ushered us back into the Landcruiser almost as soon as we had set foot on the ground. The previous day he had seemed so chilled and relaxed that it was strange to see him now so agitated and concerned about the time. Jos asked him what the rush was, and Valerio looked very animated and pointed off towards the horizon and then mimed something that looked like a steering wheel, all while explaining to Jos in frantic Spanish about why he was rushing.

'He says that he is rushing so that we get the best accommodation tonight,' said Jos.

'What does he mean? I thought the accommodation is all pre–booked,' I said.

'Last night's accommodation was reserved for us, but tonight there are many different places we could stay, and Valerio says it's first come first served for the best places.'

'How bad can it be?' I asked.

Jos translated this to Valerio and his response didn't need translating. Valerio's face told us that those in the slower groups would be sleeping somewhere really shit.

'Right, let's get going,' said Rachel climbing quickly into the backseat of the Landcruiser.

'Vamos!' we all said in unison.

Valerio laughed, turned the ignition, and then floored it.

After another hour at full–speed, we stopped for lunch at some other peculiar rocks and ate pasta and meatballs that our host the previous night had prepared for us.

'Do you think we should eat this after how we all felt this morning after last night's meal?' asked Jos.

I surveyed the desolate landscape.

'I don't think there is a lot of choice.'

All the while during the meal, Valerio had his eyes fixed on the horizon behind us. There aren't roads, as such, across the Salar, but well–marked tracks that the different tour groups tend to stick to.

After about five minutes, Valerio's eyes widened. We turned to see a tiny cloud of dust in the distance. It was another tour group.

'Vamos!' he shouted.

We stuffed our faces full of as many meatballs as we could. Valerio threw all the bowls into a large plastic box and we were back on the move before we even had a chance to swallow.

I patted Rachel excitedly on the knee.

'Valerio is awesome,' I said. 'We wouldn't have got this level of service on the $3 cheaper tour!'


Valerio didn't ease off the accelerator for the next few hours. All six members of our group had booked our three–day excursion to see the wonders of the Salar. Now it was all about getting to our accommodation as soon as possible, and it added a new sense of drama and excitement to our journey.

Having slept badly the previous night, most of us began to doze in the back of the Landcruiser. We were woken after an hour by Valerio who was shouting at us excitedly.

'Mira! Mira!' he said, pointing erratically up the road ahead. 'Look! Look!'

We all sat up, bleary eyed, and stared into the distance, where a flock of about half a dozen birds were congregating on the track.

'Muy raro,' said Valerio excitedly.

'Those birds are very rare,' translated Jos.

'MUY raro,' Valerio emphasised.

'They are VERY rare,' said Jos.

'Thanks Jos, we got that,' I said.

We watched them intently as we got closer, Valerio not taking his foot off the accelerator. The birds looked a little like guinea fowl; short and fat and happier on the ground than in the air. We continued to get nearer to them, and still Valerio showed no signs of stopping. He was presumably just going to drive around them instead.

'MUY MUY raro,' said Valerio.

'Very, very rare,' said Jos.

'Yes, Jos, we know!' we all shouted.

As we got within a few metres of them, it was clear that if Valerio was going to avoid the birds, he was going to have to take evasive action, so we gripped the seats in front of us to brace ourselves for the dramatic swerve.

Only Valerio didn't swerve. He just ploughed on straight through them. I looked behind to see the limp bodies of three of the birds bouncing down the track in a cloud of feathers.

I looked at Rachel whose eyes were wider than I thought physically possible, and her hand was clamped tightly over her face to prevent herself screaming. A faint little gasp was still audible from her mouth. The Italian couple, who rarely said anything, muttered something to each other and looked completely dumbfounded. Jos, who was sat in the passenger seat next to Valerio, just stared at him with a look of disbelief. Only Fran, Jos's fiery Italian girlfriend, knew how to vocalise what we were all feeling. She unbuckled her seatbelt and leaned into the gap between the driver and passenger seats and began a long and angry rant at Valerio in both Italian and English. Valerio didn't understand what she was saying, but definitely got the gist of it. We all joined in and vocalised our disgust, and then Jos added some token Spanish vitriol for good measure.

Valerio looked as shocked and surprised as the rest of us, but his shock and surprise was about what he could have possibly done wrong.

Fran continued to berate him for several minutes.

'Ellos son solo pájaros,' whimpered Valerio.

'What did he say?' yelled Fran.

'He said they were only birds,' said Jos.

'Only birds!' she shouted. 'So that makes it ok to mindlessly run them over? And they weren't just any old birds, were they? They were rare birds.'

'MUY raro birds,' I added. 'MUY MUY raro birds.'

'Stop it, George,' said Rachel.

It was a strange situation. My initial anger towards Valerio turned to surprise and then soon to sympathy. It was just a clash of cultures and beliefs. Valerio hadn't sped up or deliberately tried to run them over. They just happened to be in his way, and, to him, they were only birds – albeit very very rare birds – and they weren't worth slowing down or swerving for.

'That was unbelievable,' whispered Rachel, when she had finally recovered from the shock.

'Imagine what would have happened in the $3 cheaper tours,' I said. 'They would be running over alpacas, climbing all over the stone tree and chopping down cacti left, right and centre.'

'Please stop talking.'

'Sorry. At least we are still on track for the best accommodation.'

'That's true,' smiled Rachel.

Valerio was subdued for the rest of the afternoon. He knew he had upset us and we all felt a little guilty for being so critical of his differing set of values. We stopped again late afternoon at the incredible Laguna Colorada – the Red Lagoon. This lake is famous for its blood–red water, coloured by a cocktail of sediment and algae. Vast numbers of Andean flamingo, and the world's largest population of the smaller James's flamingo, feed off this algae giving them their garish pink colour. We sat in silence and watched the birds strut their stuff across the laguna.

Valerio's encounter with the rare birds had been almost forgotten by the time we pulled up outside the night's accommodation and realised we were the first tour group to arrive. We gave Valerio a big pat on the back to show him he had redeemed himself, and he smiled for the first time in hours.

The luxury accommodation that we had bagged was a large breezeblock–built room with about a dozen single beds. It was basic but functional.

We spent the evening playing cards with the rest of our group, plus a few stragglers from another tour group who shared our dormitory. Several other groups pulled up at various intervals later in the day. The other tour guides and Valerio would have a slanging match with each other across the dusty parking area, and the irate tour group leader would wave his arms around erratically after realising all the decent accommodation was taken, before wheel–spinning away to find somewhere else to stay. We sat there smugly eating our spaghetti.

As soon as the sun went down the temperature plummeted. Valerio told us that we would need to wear everything we owned, and he provided plenty of blankets to help keep us warm. These blankets were a welcome sight, as I took a moment to think about The Big Aubergine, all alone amongst the cacti on the Isla De Pescado. Individual beds seemed to be a big waste of body heat, so Rachel and I shared a single bed. As did Jos and Fran. With each other, I mean, not the four of us. The newly married Italian couple decided that sharing a bed in a public room was not acceptable, so remained in their separate beds. And to think that Italians are known as being one of the most passionate nationalities in the world.

Rachel and I have very different body temperatures. I sleep in no more than a pair of boxer shorts all year round. The summer duvet is plenty warm enough for me in the winter, and I would leave the window open a little all year if I was allowed. Rachel, on the other hand, favours pyjamas, thick winter duvet, socks, several blankets piled onto her side of the bed, with her thick dressing gown also draped over the top for extra warmth. The arrangement works fine at home in a double bed, with her side piled to within a few feet of the ceiling and mine several feet below.

Sharing a single bed in the sub–zero Bolivian Andes proved more problematic. After putting on everything we owned, including our ponchos, alpaca hats and gloves, Rachel then took all the blankets from my neighbouring single bed, plus a handful of others from a crate Valerio had brought in case we needed them, and piled them onto the bed. We even used the alpaca/cat fur cushions.

The weight of the bedding alone made it difficult to breathe, and I did think we would more likely die from suffocation than hypothermia. We could feel the chilly air brushing gently on our faces, but the rest of our bodies were delightfully cosy. We drifted off to sleep with mixed emotions: delight that Valerio proved his worth as the fastest driver on the Salar, but sadness and guilt for the casualties along the way.

# TWENTY-SEVEN

At 2am I woke with a start. My clothes were damp and sticky (no, not like that!). My forehead was beaded with sweat and my head was pulsating under my woolly hat. After the initial relief wore off that I hadn't wet myself or 'wet' myself, I then thought I had developed some serious fever in the night. Rachel stirred slightly as I slipped out from under the duvet. As the cool air swept over me, I felt instant relief. I had been slowly cooking to death throughout the night. I removed my hat, gloves, poncho, t–shirts, long johns and socks, and climbed back under the weight of the blankets in just my boxer shorts and slept like a baby until morning.

We were woken by a sprightly Valerio at 5am for our sunrise excursion. It took me a while to wake Rachel. She seemed to have slipped into some sort of oven–roast coma.

'How could you sleep with all those clothes on?' I asked.

'I think that's the best night's sleep I've ever had,' she said. 'I have never felt so toasty. I'm going to start sleeping with my hat, gloves, poncho and clothes on when we get home, too.'

'Nice to see the honeymoon period of our marriage is well and truly over,' I said.


The Sol de Mañana (morning sun) is a geothermal field in the south west of Bolivia, where we headed to watch the sunrise. The area covers several square kilometres and is dotted with boiling mud pools and fumaroles that spouted steam and gases from the volcanic activity below. The sky was clouded over and, yet again, we didn't see the sunrise. But it was still a magical experience, and I don't think it is possible to get up for the sunrise and regret it, even if the sun is hidden. You feel like you are winning the day before it has even started.

It was a further 30–minute drive for a dip in some hot springs before breakfast. The hot springs we had visited in Baños and in Chivay during our Colca Canyon tour were both basically over–heated, overcrowded public swimming pools. Nothing about them felt natural, apart from the dirty brown colour. The hot springs that we visited on the final morning of our Salar de Uyuni tour were far more memorable.

It was a natural spring, miles from anywhere at about 5,000m above sea level, that had been shaped and excavated to allow for people to bath in it, but still maintaining its authentic feel. It wasn't even 8am and the thin air was still bitterly cold, which made the thermal waters of the hot springs even more welcoming. We were the first group to arrive and had the entire pool to ourselves for a while, before it slowly filled up with more gringos.

It was a fun atmosphere as tourists of many different nationalities compared stories of the Salar's magic while we bathed. It was also the first time any of us would have had a wash in three days, but we tried not to think about that too much. It was all fun and games until a big ginger Welshman, wearing absolutely nothing to hide his big ginger bollocks, ran and dive–bombed into the pool right next to us, and suddenly all we could think about was how none of us had washed in three days.

We visited one final lagoon – Laguna Verde – where I was disappointed not to see any green flamingos, before Valerio dropped Rachel and me at the Chilean border. We said goodbye to the rest of the group who were about to begin their 400km journey back to Uyuni, before going their separate ways. Rachel and I were heading up through Chile, back into Peru and then onto Cusco for the final leg of our trip.

We had another farcical border crossing, walking backwards and forwards getting various exit and entry stamps, having my passport photo laughed at multiple times by both Bolivian and Chilean officials, before boarding a bus to the pretty town of San Pedro de Atacama.

We had only intended to visit Ecuador, Peru and Bolivia on our trip, and felt a little dirty (we were) as we roamed the streets of San Pedro de Atacama while we waited for our bus to the city of Calama. It felt like we were being unfaithful to our other countries, and without wishing any disrespect to Chile, we wanted to get back into Peru as soon as possible.

On arriving in Calama, where we would get our connection to Arica on the Peruvian border, we discovered that there were no spaces on any buses to Arica that day. I tried in my broken Spanish to explain to the woman in the ticket office that there must surely be a way. In South America, there was always a way.

'No more seats,' she said.

'We don't mind standing,'

'No standing. Not possible.'

'Can we sit on the dashboard?'

'Que?' she said

'Is there a milk truck we can catch instead?'

The lady just stared at me.

'You know. A truck that delivers the milk. Trucko de leche, maybe? We could ride on the back. Help sell the chickens. The pollos.'

She continued to stare at me.

'George, let's leave it,' said Rachel. 'I don't think it's quite the same here.'

We bought tickets for a bus that left late the following night, giving us 36 hours in a city we hadn't planned to stop in.

Before La Paz, killing time without anywhere to stay had not been a problem. We just wandered aimlessly with our meagre possessions on our backs. Since La Paz, and our senseless shopping benders, I now had a stupidly big bag, full to the brim with ridiculous souvenirs to haul with me everywhere we went. Buying that additional bag no longer felt like such a clever idea.

Chile was a world away from the parts of Peru, Bolivia and Ecuador we had travelled through. The previous day we had woken in a small village consisting of a handful of basic structures, where the children were delighted to receive some pencils and had been enraptured by a balloon. Calama, by comparison, was a bustling metropolis. A city that would not have looked out of place in the United States. The cars were bigger and better than anything we had seen in South America, the houses smarter, people walked the streets in suits, we saw more shirts and ties in the space of ten minutes than we had combined since arriving in Quito all those weeks ago. It was difficult to take it all in. La Paz had felt crazy and chaotic, but in a very different way. Being suddenly dumped back into a developed city brought with it a whole new type of anxiety. Car horns sounded, we could hear several police and ambulance sirens in the distance, and bright illuminated signs to high street stores we recognised flashed all around us. Standing there with our backpacks and our giant red checked PVC bag, in a city not unlike those we knew back home, we felt very much like we didn't belong.

As we were walking the streets, looking for somewhere to stay, we turned to see a small dog following us. It was a brown and scraggy–looking mongrel, with big sorry eyes pleading for us to love it. Or, more likely, feed it.

We had seen hundreds of other stray dogs during our time in South America. But they had all looked and acted like strays, and either been very skittish and nervous of us, or yappy and prone to nipping. This one looked different.

'George, look at the cutesy wootsey lickle doggy woggy,' said Rachel in an affected baby voice.

'It's very sweet but don't encourage it. It's just a stray.'

'How can such a cutesy wootsey lickle doggy woggy not belong to someone? Can we keep it?'

'Er… what do you think?'

'Yes?'

'Of course we can't keep it. We are backpacking in South America.'

'We've only got a week left. And we can ship it home. Pleeeease.'

'No! Firstly, we don't know for sure that it doesn't belong to someone, and secondly, I doubt it's even possible to ship a stray dog from Chile to the UK. And if it is, then it would probably have to stay in quarantine for months and months. It looks fairly happy here in Calamari or whatever the name of this place is.'

'Calama. Even I know that. Look at him! I think he likes us.'

'That's because you keep looking at it and talking to it in a really silly voice. Don't make eye contact.'

'I can't help it.'

We walked several more blocks, changing direction at random, trying to lose the dog, but it stayed closely behind us, not taking its eyes off Rachel. I did wonder if it was perhaps the reincarnation of Portuguese David Blaine.

We approached a large shopping mall and decided to go in, assuming the dog would not want to follow us, and would latch on to someone else instead. Not literally. It didn't seem in the least bit vicious. The automated doors slid open and we stoically continued onwards, fearing eye contact would only encourage it.

Rachel was the first to look back after we were deep inside the mall.

'Oh look, the lickle cutesy wootsey doggy woggy is still here. He's followed us. He wants to come shopping too.'

'That lickle cutesy wootsey doggy woggy is not coming shopping with us! We are not even going shopping.'

'Then why are we inside a shopping centre?'

'To try and get rid of the dog!'

We continued walking and the dog kept following. I was trying my best to ignore it, Rachel wasn't trying very hard at all. A security guard patrolling the mall approached us at speed from the other side of the plaza. He shouted something at us, pointing angrily at the dog, which might possibly have been him saying *welcome to our mall! I hope you and your cutesy wootsey lickle doggy woggy have a pleasant visit*,' but I think was perhaps something a little less friendly.

'No mi perro,' I said, pointing to the dog and shrugging my shoulders. 'It's not my dog.'

'No?' he said.

'No.'

He interpreted this as me giving him permission to kick the dog. It was only a very gentle nudge with his foot, but he then swung his foot back for a harder go. Rachel and I both shouted 'NO' at the same time and the security guard stopped mid swing.

'We will take him outside,' I said, pointing to the door.

'Si. Bueno.'

We ushered the dog to follow us, and it duly obliged, thinking we were finally welcoming it into our family. It scampered along, its eyes now lit up with the prospect of being loved for perhaps the first time in its life.

After a few failed attempts, we eventually got it to wait on the other side of the door, as we re-entered the mall. Looking back, we could see its excited face, tongue hanging out, and a look of expectation that we would only be gone for a moment and would surely return to it very soon to love it for the rest of its life.

We never returned.


Surrounded by all of the opulence in the Calama shopping mall, we realised we didn't want any of it. Overpriced designer clothes and jewellery felt at odds with what we had experienced of South America so far. We would have preferred a lady sat on a pile of oranges, or a stall selling dried llama foetuses any day. Or even a preacher on a quadracycle selling cake.

We walked straight through the mall without entering a single shop, and exited at the far end so that we would not be detected by our dog. Look at me, all these years later, and I'm still referring to it as 'our dog'. I don't think either of us have ever fully recovered. It's probably still sitting by that shopping mall in Calama waiting for us to return.

We checked into a nearby hostel, bought a couple of oversized beers, a big piece of cheese, and a box of crackers, and sat in our room, reluctant to be a part of the developed world outside.

# TWENTY-EIGHT

By morning, this reluctance had turned to mild excitement. I sat and watched two back–to–back Premier League football matches on a TV in our bedroom, and then we went and ate lunch at a fancy Chinese restaurant (when in Chile…). We walked through the mall again, from the opposite end to where we left the dog, this time perusing a few of the shops and feeling a little more at home. Without our rucksacks, we no longer felt like vagabonds. Rachel and I both bought a pair of jeans each, as it was the first time in South America that we had seen clothing that matched fashions from this millennium.

To then complete our immersion back into big city life, we spent the afternoon watching TWO films at the cinema, back to back. A little after 8 pm, we retrieved our bags from the hostel, and headed to the bus station where we boarded a night bus to Arica close to the Peruvian border in northern Chile.

So as not to get too used to the modern world, and to ease ourselves back into the traveller lifestyle, we bought a couple of dubious looking 'Doggies' hot dogs from a little trader at the bus station.

'I wonder what ever happened to that cutesy wootsey lickle doggy woggy?' I said to Rachel, as I took a bite of my hot dog.

'You're sick. I can't eat this now. You have it.'

'Thanks,' I said. 'Oldest trick in the book.'


We had taken several night buses in South America, and had accumulated a total of about ten minutes sleep combined. Our night bus across Chile was the best of the lot. The seats were comfortable, we didn't have anyone sitting on our laps, and we slept solidly for most of the journey. It was almost as enjoyable as a milk truck.

We arrived in Arica, well rested, at 6am. We had been warned the border crossing back into Peru could be a little complicated when negotiating it by foot, and extremely time–consuming by bus. We had been advised to pay for a taxi instead, so handed our passports and a wad of dollars to a driver named Isaac and trusted him to work his magic.

The crossing was seamless and worth every cent. We didn't even have to get out of the taxi. Isaac did all the talking, presented our documents and then drove us to the bus station in the town of Tacna on the Peruvian side of the border. He didn't even laugh at my passport photo, so we tipped him generously.


I don't include Chile on the list of countries I have visited. I don't have a list, but if I did, Chile would not be on it. We were there for less than 48 hours, and a good chunk of that time was spent on buses. The rest was spent in a shopping mall, cinema and walking 'our dog'. We will definitely go back one day, so that I can officially add Chile to my list. If I had one.


Despite the comfort and luxury of our overnight bus trip, and the ease of our taxi journey across the border, we almost missed the sense of adventure and chaos we had felt on boarding every other bit of public transport in South America. Sitting on dashboards next to windscreens with bullet holes in, standing in milk trucks, having other passengers sitting on our laps, and suitcases falling off the roof, was part of what made travelling in South America so much fun.

This nostalgia for proper South American travel lasted only minutes. The connecting bus we caught from Tacna to Puno across Peru was one of the worst we have ever experienced. It was 12 hours on rough, winding roads. The bus had a blow out – thankfully on one of the few stretches of straight road, rather than one of the many precipitous mountain passes – which took a while to fix. We were then stopped by police who searched the entire bus, passengers, and all of our luggage. Then to top it all off, the lady sitting directly in front of us, picked nits from her son's hair for the entire journey. The one redeeming feature of the experience was a delicious lomo saltado (beef stir-fry) that we ate during one of the few rest stops along the way.

The buses we took during our time in South America varied in their state of crapness. But all – except the bus we got from Calama to Arica in Chile – were immeasurably crap. Our buses frequently broke down. In the UK, if this happens, the bus driver phones for assistance and the passengers sit and wait for a replacement to arrive. In South America, the bus driver and his co–driver disappear beneath the bus armed with some wire, duct tape and a wooden stick and will almost always have the bus up and running again within minutes. All buses in South America are essentially held together with wire and duct tape.

White crosses dotted the roadside wherever we went, signifying where fatalities had occurred following a crash or a vehicle disappearing over the edge of the cliff. Catholicism is the dominant religion in South America, and our drivers would often do the sign of the cross each time we passed one of these white crosses. But they were everywhere, so our drivers spent most of the time with one hand on the wheel and the other praying to God to keep them safe, ironically as they were driving one handed around a blind bend with a precipitous drop to one side. I'm sure God would be looking down from above in despair saying, 'Gracias, amigos, I appreciate all the love, but keep both hands on the wheel, por favor.'

We arrived in Puno late in the evening, after a long and tedious day's travelling and found a hostel near to the station. Just before bed, I decided to check my email at the hostel's lone computer. There was a message from my mum. The subject was *SAD NEWS*.

It had been over a week since we had checked our email. We had no phone signal in Bolivia or Chile and had been completely uncontactable. *Had my mum been trying to get in touch with me all this time? What was this sad news that she was about to impart?*

'Everything ok?' asked Rachel.

'I don't know. I'm a bit nervous about opening this email. It says *SAD NEWS*.'

'Hopefully it's nothing serious. You'd better open it.'

I clicked the email and it took an age for the dialup internet to load the text. It was short and to the point.

*Hi Dord,*

*Sad news. The next series of ER will apparently be the last. I thought you would want to know. I hope you are having a wonderful time in the Salar de Uyuni. Looking forward to hearing all about it.*

*Love, Mum xx*

'What is it?' said Rachel, as I shook my head in disbelief.

'Un–be–lievable. Her '*sad*' news is that *ER* is ending.'

'*ER* the TV show?'

'Yes.'

'Oh, that is sad news. I like that show.'

'I know, so do I. But I thought someone had died or something!'

'Ha, well at least they haven't.'

I replied to the email, politely asking Mum never to title an email '*SAD NEWS*' again unless she had some genuinely sad news to report.

We only had time for a very quick stroll around Puno the following morning before catching an early bus to Cusco. Leaving the shores of Lake Titicaca, the bus traversed the altiplano with sweeping vistas all the way to Cusco. A lunch of perfectly ripe avocados squashed into a freshly baked roll made for a surprisingly enjoyable journey.

Leaving our Salar de Uyuni tour at the Chilean border was intended as a shortcut, but it had taken us three days to get across Chile and Peru to Cusco. I was finding it increasingly hard to justify to Rachel that I had made the right decision, and when we bumped into someone we recognised from the hot springs on our Salar tour (not the ginger–bollocked Welshman), and found that they had been back in Cusco for over 24 hours, my reasoning didn't seem so concrete.

'Maybe they just flew back from the Salar,' I said.

'I don't think that's even possible,' said Rachel.

'Well, if we had managed to get on one of those earlier buses in Calamari we would have been here 36 hours earlier.'

'I suppose. And it was Calama, not calamari.'

'But, if we had got the earlier bus, we would never have met our dog.'

'Oh god, please stop mentioning our dog. I'm trying not to think about it.'

# TWENTY-NINE

Cusco is one of the most popular tourist destinations in the whole of South America. The city is an eclectic mix of colonial Spanish architecture, built on and around its Inca ruins. Cusco sits at the head of what is known as The Sacred Valley of the Incas, with the famous Inca citadel of Machu Picchu at the far end. Machu Picchu is Peru's most popular tourist attraction; the ancient Inca ruins are recognisable the world over. We had left this highlight to the end of our trip.

It was 3 pm when we arrived in Cusco. We got a taxi from the bus station to the weirdly named Hostal Royal Frankenstein, decked out with kitsch wallpaper, palm trees and murals of Frankenstein's monster. It's what the Incas would have wanted. The hostel was the most energetic and backpacker-friendly we had stayed in; the air filled with excited chatter from people about to start the Inca Trail or those just back from Machu Picchu. Hostal Royal Frankenstein even provided complimentary hair straighteners, much to Rachel's delight.

Machu Picchu sits high above the small town of Aguas Calientes, about 50 miles northwest of Cusco. Aguas Calientes is inaccessible by road and can only be reached by train (and then a bus ride or walk up the mountain to Machu Picchu). Or it can act as the finishing point of an organised multi–day hike following the Inca Trail. Inca Trail expeditions range from two to five days, with varying routes and distances. Rachel and I had hoped to end our time in South America by hiking the Inca Trail. But midway through our trip, we realised that for us to do the expedition, we would have to sacrifice one of our other trips because of time constraints. We decided that they were all too important to us and we would instead visit Machu Picchu by train, and save hiking the Inca Trail for another time.

With only a few days left before our flight back to the UK from Lima, it was essential that we bought our train tickets to Aguas Calientes to make sure we got to visit what promised to be one of the most memorable places of our time in South America. As soon as we had dumped our bags in the hostel, we set off to the ticket office to book our seats.

The ticket office had already closed for the day.

'Don't worry,' I said to Rachel, 'I'll make sure I'm here first thing tomorrow morning to get us tickets.'

In the meantime, we booked ourselves onto a day's Sacred Valley tour for the following morning. The Sacred Valley – or the Urubamba Valley – includes lots of archaeological Inca sites that are impressive, but nowhere near as impressive as Machu Picchu.

The streets of Cusco were more touristy than anything we had seen in South America. But not in a bad way. It is a stunning city with beautiful cobbled streets and winding narrow passageways, and the mass of tourists and shops selling alpaca everything gave the city a real buzz. We had been made to feel extremely welcome almost everywhere we went in South America, but there was no doubt we always stood out as gringos. In Cusco, we blended in with the hundreds of other backpackers who roamed the streets, and it was nice to feel strangely invisible.

Despite the frequent upset stomachs, we had eaten well in South America, and mostly enjoyed the food. We often didn't have much choice of where or what to eat, as the towns and villages we had been staying in were so small. In Cusco, every other building was a restaurant, each with an amiable waiter or waitress standing outside, trying their hardest to entice tourists off the street. With so many places to choose from, it was overwhelming trying to make our decision.

'Where do you want to eat?' I asked Rachel.

'I don't mind. They all look good.'

'This place looks popular,' I said, looking at a brightly coloured building with tables crammed full of people both inside and out, all looking like they were having the time of their lives. A smiling waiter approached.

'English?' he said.

'Si,' we said.

'Hungry?' he said.

'Si,' I said. 'Hungrymundo.'

'Hungry in Spanish is hambriento,' he laughed.

'That's what I said!'

'Come with me.'

We followed him towards the bustling restaurant. *This is going to be so great*, we thought. We caught glimpses of the plates of food people were tucking into and it all looked incredible. We skirted in-between a couple of tables, but instead of going through the front door, the waiter went through a side door that led up some stairs adjacent to the restaurant.

'Wait, I thought we were eating down there.'

'It's full down there. We have more tables up here,' he said.

202

'Ok, but it's the same restaurant is it?'

'Same food, yes,' he said.

Upstairs there was a large room full of tables laid out for dinner. All were empty apart from one other couple sat at the far end of the room. They looked far from happy, and compared to the atmosphere down on street level, it was like walking into a funeral parlour. We sat down and ordered a couple of beers.

'Is this the same restaurant?' Rachel asked me after the waiter had left the room.

'No, I think we've been scammed. Oh well, he said the food is exactly the same.'

The food wasn't the same. I don't know what it was, but it was one of the worst meals we had ever eaten. To make matters worse, our table by the window looked down directly onto the restaurant below, as the joyful people tucked into their plates of glorious food.

Our waiter was annoyingly delightful throughout, and it made it very difficult to resent him for luring us into this shithole. It was good to support a struggling business, even if the chef was incompetent. Or so we kept telling ourselves.

'Maybe one day everyone will be flocking upstairs, and the tables below will be deserted,' I said. 'And we'll be able to tell people we knew this place before it was famous.'

'And before the food was edible?' said Rachel.

I left the hostel early the following morning and went to try again to buy train tickets to the small town of Aguas Calientes for our Machu Picchu trip. I was there before opening time, but the queue already stretched around the block. I reluctantly joined the end. As the minutes ticked by, and the queue only moved ever so slightly, it became clear that I wasn't going to reach the front of the queue before our Sacred Valley tour departed. I returned to the hostel to break the news to Rachel.

'So, does that mean we won't get to see Machu Picchu at all?' she said.

'We still have one more chance tomorrow to get tickets.'

'And if we can't get tickets tomorrow?'

'Then I don't think we will be able to visit Machu Picchu this time.'

'I really hope we can. I've been looking forward to it since we booked our flights to South America.'

'Me too. But it's been there for hundreds of years and will be there for hundreds more. I will go to the ticket office even earlier tomorrow and will try my hardest to get tickets for a train later tomorrow.'

The Sacred Valley tour was brilliant, and we knew it would at least be part compensation if we didn't get to see the main attraction. During the day we visited the impressive archaeological sites of Pisac, Ollantaytambo and Chinchero.

This was the first organised day tour we had been on during our time in South America. All the other tours had been multi–day trips, and they seemed to attract similar types of people to Rachel and me – albeit from many different countries. All were relatively young, fit and healthy, and prepared to rough it a little. The Sacred Valley tour attracted a completely different demographic. There were a few other backpackers on our bus, but most of the group were much older, larger and less mobile tourists, visiting Cusco as part of an organised tour of Peru. At each stop on the Sacred Valley tour, Rachel and I would explore the ruins far and wide, climbing to the highest accessible points, seeing as much of the sites as we could within our allocated time. The majority of the group would disembark at each stop and then not explore much further than the gift shop. Some decided not to even get off the bus. They were all a really lovely bunch, though, and their enthusiasm and eagerness to hear all about our trip – where we had been and what we had seen – made us feel like genuine explorers.

'You swam with piranhas?'

'You hiked the Mandango Trail?'

'You hunted for anacondas in a swamp?' said one of them, his jaw almost touching the floor.

'Yes,' said Rachel. 'And George did it wearing a pair of sandals.'

'I did wear a pair of socks with the sandals, much to my shame,' I said, before noticing he was sporting a socks and sandals combo. 'Not that there is ANYTHING wrong with that.'


We returned to Cusco at 7 pm and spent some time chatting to other backpackers at Hostel Royal Frankenstein. There was more talk about Machu Picchu and how it had been the best thing they had seen in their lives. There we were, days away from flying back to England, and we still didn't have any train tickets.

For dinner, we ignored all the enthusiastic waiters in the street, and headed straight for a restaurant called Chez Maggie which was extremely popular. While not at all Peruvian, the nachos and fajitas were probably the best thing we had eaten in weeks.

I woke before dawn the next day and walked to the ticket office long before it opened. There were two other Brits and an American already there. They were trying to buy train tickets for the following day. I was hoping for tickets for the same day. I didn't hold out much hope.

The queue slowly built up behind me and when the ticket office eventually opened, those in front of me successfully bought their tickets and offered me a '*good luck*' as they passed.

'Dos boletos for today, por favor,' I said to the man in the ticket office.

He looked at his computer screen and shook his head, sucking air through his teeth, which is the international noise for '*I don't think so, sonny Jim. That's a big ask.*'

'Por favoooooooor' I said, unsure whether that works the same way as '*Pleeeeeeeease.*'

His eyes scanned the screen as he scrolled down with his mouse. 'No… no… no... no… ah… si! Tengo dos boletos para el Vistadome.'

'No entiendo,' I said. 'I don't understand.'

'I have two tickets available today. But it's for the Vistadome from Ollantaytambo to Aguas Calientes. They are the last two tickets.'

'Fantástico! Qué es the Vistadome?'

'It's a train with glass ceiling. It's more expensive. And your seats – they not together.'

'I'll take them! Muchas gracias, señor! Muchas muchas gracias.'

By the look of surprise on the man's face, I don't think he had ever seen someone so excited to buy train tickets. I skipped back to the hostel (yes, genuinely), where Rachel had just woken up.

'How did you get on?' she asked hopefully.

I put on an Oscar–winning performance of dejection.

'No luck,' I said. 'There were no tickets available for the train today.'

'Oh well. Well done for trying. You were right, Machu Picchu will still be there next time.'

'Yeah, there were no tickets for the train…. But I managed to get the last two tickets…. for the VISTADOME!'

'The Vistadome? What's that?'

'It's basically a train. But with a glass ceiling.'

'Wait? So we are going to Machu Picchu?'

'We sure are!' I said, waving the tickets. 'We get the train to Aguas Calientes this afternoon, and we go to Machu Picchu tomorrow.'

'Oh my god, that's amazing!' she said, throwing her arms around me.

I didn't think it was possible for someone to be more excited about train tickets than me, but Rachel had managed it.

'There is one problem, though. We are sitting at opposite ends of the carriage,' I said.

'Even better!' she said. 'Only joking. Thank you. You did brilliantly.'

# THIRTY

We bought our Machu Picchu entry tickets from an agency in Cusco to save on queueing on the day, and then caught a bus to Urumbamba and a colectivo to Ollantaytambo. We had a look around the market, ate a fruit salad each (both of us were so ecstatic about the train that we decided to live dangerously), and boarded the Vistadome to Aguas Calientes.

The Vistadome was indeed fantástico. Not so much because of the somewhat exaggerated glass ceiling (it just had a small extra row of windows on the edge of the roof), but it was a truly spectacular train journey, with wonderful scenery to either side and above. And we were on our way to Machu Picchu, baby!

Aguas Calientes is an odd little town. It has the feeling of being hastily assembled to cope with a sudden influx of tourists. Which is exactly what it was. Once a tiny rural farming settlement, it became an important transportation hub after the rediscovery and excavation of Machu Picchu by American historian Hiram Bingham in 1911.

We found a room in a hostel that had been so hastily built that it had opened for business long before it was finished. And once functioning as a hostel, it appeared they decided not to bother finishing it. Our room was on the second floor, and the staircase continued upwards after our bedroom. But there was no third floor, and the steps disappeared suddenly over the side of the building.

Aguas Calientes – meaning 'hot waters' – is named after the town's hot springs, so we took an obligatory trip to the slightly smelly communal baths at the top of the town. It was just before closing time and there were only a couple of other people there. We sat in silence, looking at the steep sides of the densely vegetated valley, knowing that somewhere up above us, sat Machu Picchu. We couldn't stop grinning.

We had an early start in the morning, so after a quick beer and a menu turistico at one of the many restaurants on the main street, we returned to our half–built hostel, ensuring that we stopped when we got to the second floor.

There are buses available to transport tourists from Aguas Calientes up the steep winding road to the entrance of Machu Picchu. We had been told by a couple of different people, and our guide book, that these buses didn't operate early enough to get to the site in time for sunrise. If we wanted to see the sunrise, our only option was to walk up the mountain.

We woke at 4am and stuffed our few belongings into our rucksack. We had left most of our things – including our ridiculously big bag of presents – at the hostel in Cusco until our return. We had with us a change of underwear, our waterproofs, a camera, and that was about all.

Between us we had one lousy headtorch that was so weak it barely illuminated the ground in front of us. We started slowly up the road, following the switchbacks as they weaved up the hillside. We could see a couple of torch beams on the road below us, but the night was quiet and still.

When we were about halfway up, after 40 minutes of walking, we heard the rumble of an engine below us. We turned to see the sweeping headlights of a vehicle coming up the mountain. The noise grew louder and as it turned the next corner and steamed past us, we realised it was a bus.

'What?' said Rachel. 'I thought buses don't go up the mountain this early?'

'Maybe that was just a bus for the staff or something?'

We carried on walking. A few minutes later, another bus passed us. This one was definitely not a staff bus, judging by the faces of the teenagers with their noses squashed against the back windscreen pointing and laughing at us. One little shit with a FC Barcelona baseball cap even raised his middle finger at us. Over the next half an hour, several more buses passed us.

We eventually reached the entrance gate, puffing and sweating, to be greeted by a throng of tourists from the coaches forming a chaotic queue in the dark at the entry booth.

'So we got up especially early, walked for an hour and a half up a mountain, and we still have to queue behind this lot?' said Rachel, looking distinctly pissed off.

'It's ok, follow me,' I said, spotting a separate entrance gate for people with pre–booked tickets that was about to open. There was no queue.

As we walked past the crowd of people waiting to buy their tickets, I caught sight of the FC Barcelona baseball cap kid, looking at me disbelievingly. I raised my middle finger at him and smiled, then we flashed our pre–booked tickets at the entrance booth clerk, and we were two of the day's first visitors through the gates into Machu Picchu.

# THIRTY-ONE

The famous view of Machu Picchu is from the Caretaker's Hut, a short walk up some steep steps to the left. Those finishing the Inca Trail tend to get their first glimpse of the site from the Sungate, an hour's hike further on. After already walking up the mountain before sunrise, the Caretaker's Hut was more than adequate for us.

As we walked slowly up to the viewpoint, still in partial darkness, we forced ourselves not to look back over our shoulders at Machu Picchu behind us. We wanted to see it for the first time from above. There were two others at the Caretaker's Hut when we arrived, and we greeted them with a whispered 'hola'. It felt too early and serene to be talking at normal volume to one another.

'Ready?' I said to Rachel, holding her hand.

'Ready!' she said, her face bursting with excitement.

We slowly turned around to look down over the ancient Inca ruins. Only they weren't there. All we could see was a thick blanket of cloud sitting snugly on top of them in the half–light.

'Oh,' I said.

'Oh,' said Rachel.

'Apparently it usually clears around sunrise,' said one of the other tourists in an American accent. Presumably because he was American, rather than someone fond of doing accents at 6.30am.

Rising above the clouds, we could see the magnificent peak of Huayna Picchu, overlooking Machu Picchu from the other end of the site. A group of llamas wandered about by the viewing area. I think they were more likely there scavenging for food from tourists, rather than to watch the sunrise, but I might be wrong.

Right on cue at 7am, we caught our first glimpse of the sun hitting the top of Huayna Picchu, as it rose over the mountains behind us. Several other tourists had arrived at the Caretaker's Hut by this point, but they were all hushed and respectful, not wanting to ruin the moment.

The famous ruins still sat in partial cloud, but as predicted, as the air warmed up, the clouds slowly dissipated, revealing Machu Picchu in all its glory. There was a collective gasp from everyone around us.

Despite the hundreds of times I had seen this view on postcards, posters, guidebooks and travel programs, I wasn't prepared for its beauty. Straddled elegantly on the dip between two mountains, surrounded by thick green forest on all sides below, it fully deserves its place as one of the 'new' seven wonders of the world.

Machu Picchu was built in the mid–15th–century, but looks a lot older. It is widely believed to have been a royal estate, but the Incas didn't have a written language so there are no records to verify this. There is no doubt, however, that the Incas had a fine eye for a good location. Sitting at 2,430m, Machu Picchu is not as high up as it seems. It is confusingly 1,000 meters lower than Cusco. However, because of its prominence and sheer magnificence, it feels like you are standing on top of the world.

Huayna Picchu, the peak that sits above Machu Picchu, can also be climbed for views of the site from the other end. Due to the dangerous and occasionally precipitous nature of the trail, numbers are restricted to a few hundred per day. Walkers had to check in at a hut and register their details before setting off, and check out on the way back, to ensure all those who began the trip returned home.

After sitting for a while with the llamas, marveling at the view from the Caretaker's Hut, Rachel and I set off to the other end of the site to climb Huayna Picchu, before all of the day's tickets had been allocated.

The first part of the climb takes about half an hour as it ascends steeply, but the path is adequately wide and there are not too many ominous drops. Ten minutes from the top, things get a little trickier. First up there is a stone staircase that extends sharply up the side of an enormous Inca wall. There is no handrail, and a terrifying drop to one side. My legs turned to jelly on seeing it.

'Oh. My. God,' said Rachel when she locked eyes on it. 'We're not going up there, are we?'

'It looks like the only way up,' I said.

'I can't do that. Remember what I was like on the Mandango Trail?'

'You got through that in the end.'

'I had to shuffle along on my arse.'

'So did I. But this is different.'

'Yes, it's worse!'

'That's because it's almost impossible to climb stairs on your arse. Look, you've searched for anacondas in a swamp since then. And sat in a bucket of piranhas. It won't be nearly as scary as that. It's just a normal staircase.'

'Normal staircases don't result in instant death if you stumble.'

'You won't stumble.'

'I might.'

She didn't.

Rachel took a deep breath, and we made it slowly up the stairs, where we then had to crawl through a small tunnel in the rocks, before hauling ourselves up a metal ladder bolted to the rock.

There were several spectacular vantage points over the ruins of Machu Picchu below. We stopped at each one to rest and take in the view. The final section – now roped off to the public – is a set of 600–year–old individual stone steps jutting out of the wall up to another lookout, with a precipitous drop below each one.

'Just the Stairs of Death to go,' I said, instantly regretting my choice of words.

'The what?'

'Just these last steps to go, I said.'

'Did you just call them the Stairs of Death?'

'No!'

'Yes, you did. Why would you call them the Stairs of Death?'

'I... I... did I call them that? I don't think I did.'

'Yes you did.'

'Well, that's what they are known as.'

'Who by?'

'Everyone. The Stairs of Death are legendary. I mean, look at them!'

At this point, a group of four hikers came up the trail behind us, blocking our route back down.

'Are you going up?' one of them asked.

I looked at Rachel. 'Are we?'

'I guess so,' she said, setting foot on the first stone and tentatively stepping up to the next. 'You'd better catch me if I fall.'

Our rucksacks, which only contained the bare essentials, suddenly felt like they were full of rocks, as the apprehension of being put off balance set in. With a group of people now assembled behind us, we were forced to act bravely and push on.

We eventually reached the top and sat down to admire the sweeping views of Machu Picchu behind us. 'Well done,' I said, putting my arm around Rachel. 'We made it up the Stairs of Death.'

'STOP calling them that! We still have to go down them.'

By now, there was not a cloud in the sky, and the sun illuminated Machu Picchu far below us.

Huayna Picchu is also a prominent archaeological site, consisting of a collection of terraces and temples. It is believed to have been the home of the city's high priest, who resided there with a group of local virgins. As you do.

The Incas are regarded as having been an incredibly advanced and forward–thinking civilisation. But as we sat looking down onto Machu Picchu, I started to wonder if they have perhaps been given too much credit. Yes, their locations were breathtakingly beautiful, and their stonework incredible, but most of their structures now lie in ruins. Perhaps the Incas were actually just a bit shit at building.

Look at the pyramids in Egypt. Built about 2560 BC. That's 4,000 years before Machu Picchu. And many of them are still standing. Britain's Stonehenge is believed to have been assembled at about the same time. It is still standing. The Pantheon in Rome was built at the beginning of the first millennium. 1500 years before the Incas. It is still immaculate. I have been to pubs that were entertaining rowdy drinkers for 500 years before the Incas even existed, and they still look as solid (and grubby) as the day they were built.

Because most Inca sites lie in ruins, they all look significantly older than they are. As I sat on top of Huayna Picchu ruminating about this theory, I began to express my cynicism about the Inca civilisation to Rachel.

'Should you be slagging off the Incas, when we are sitting on top of one of their ancient sites?' she said.

'What do you mean?'

'Well, firstly we've got to climb down these 600–year–old steps that you have just claimed 'weren't built to last'. Secondly, weren't the Incas big believers in curses and human sacrifice?'

'Er… yeah. And?'

'Well, if I was an Inca god, then you've set yourself up as a bit of an obvious target for sacrifice now. Here you are, sitting on top of a mountain, the Stairs of Death still to navigate on the way down, and you have said that the entire Inca civilisation was 'a bit shit at building'.'

'Well… I just…'

'It's too late now. The damage is done.'

Needless to say, the descent of Huayna Picchu was a little nervy, and I never said a bad word about the Incas ever again. And it's not like I will express my opinions about them in a book.

After successfully making it back down to Machu Picchu, we spent a leisurely few hours exploring the extensive site, with its countless different rooms and terraces. I was vocally admiring the Inca stonework at every opportunity, and trying to ignore the fact that a lot of the site had been rebuilt from the crumbled remains since its discovery.

We walked back up to the now crowded Caretaker's Hut for more views of Machu Picchu in full sun, and then sat and ate our sandwiches and posed for photos with the llamas.

'What time is our train?' Rachel asked.

'4.30 pm, I think.'

'What time is it now?'

'12ish, I guess,' I said, pulling my phone from my pocket. 'Oh shit! It's 3.20 pm! How did that happen? It was only sunrise recently.'

Time had somehow been sucked away from us as we had explored Machu Picchu. Maybe it was the Inca curses? And now we were all the way up at the Caretaker's Hut on the top of a mountain, with a train to catch from Aguas Calientes at the very bottom in a little over an hour.

We hastily stuffed our water bottles and food wrappers into our rucksacks.

'Is there a later train?' asked Rachel.

'No, this was all they had. If we miss this train then we will be stuck in Aguas Calientes for another day or two, which means we will miss our flight to Lima tomorrow and then miss our flight back to England.'

We began descending the steps from the Caretaker's Hut at a ridiculous speed, accidentally photobombing many tourists' holiday snaps along the way.

Outside the entrance gate our hearts sank. There was a queue of over a hundred people waiting for the bus back down the mountain.

'We're not going to get there in time,' said Rachel.

'We can still make it!' I said.

'No, we can't! Look at that queue! We will have to wait for at least four buses until it's our turn.'

'We don't need the bus. We can run.'

'What? You can't be serious? Remember how tough it was this morning?'

'That was uphill. Now we've got gravity on our side.'

'George, I really don't think that's a wise idea. I don't think we will make it in time. We might as well accept the fact that we are going to miss our flight tomorrow and look at booking an alternative instead.'

'We've got to at least try. Vamos!'

Rachel sighed heavily, tightened her rucksack straps, and set off after me down the road. We followed the switchbacks down half of the mountain, but each time I glanced at my phone, the chances of us making the train seemed less likely. The sun was beating down on us and it was tough going.

'Wait, what's this?' said Rachel as we rounded one of the many corners.

'What's what?'

'This path.'

'It looks like it cuts off the corner,' I said. 'That's handy.'

'Do you think they have them on the other corners too?'

I looked across the road to the switchback we had just traversed and noticed a small gap through the trees that would have been impossible to see in the early morning darkness.

'Er… yeah, it looks like they do. That makes things a little easier.'

'You mean we've been running around all these stupid switchbacks when we could have just gone straight down the mountain following the steps?'

'Yes. We could have done that when we climbed up the mountain this morning too.'

We made good progress down the second half of the mountain, thanks to the revolutionary discovery of the path, and arrived back in Aguas Calientes sweatier than either of us had ever been before, which was not ideal preparation for a two–hour train journey.

With five minutes to spare until our train, I even had time to buy a Peruvian national football shirt from a market trader outside the station. It was a gift for my friend Damo, who claims his grandma invented banoffee pie. We still had a football shirt sized gap in our present bag to fill back at Hostel Royal Frankenstein.

'See, I told you we would make it,' I said, giving Rachel a hug.

'Don't get too close. I stink.'

'Me too. At least we haven't got to sit near each other on the train.'

We felt a strange unexpected rush of adrenaline. We had been fortunate enough to have seen one of the world's most extraordinary sights at sunrise, and then climbed a notoriously tricky peak involving ladders, tunnels and rock ledges. But that was nothing to the feeling of elation we experienced from sitting on a train we felt certain we would miss an hour earlier. We couldn't stop smiling at each other across the crowded carriage. The faces of those sitting next to our reeking bodies were not so enthusiastic.

After our failed attempt to get the hostel in Arequipa to hold a room for us when we visited Colca Canyon, only for them to launder our clothes instead, we were delighted to arrive back at Hostel Royal Frankenstein and discover a room reserved for us as promised, and our bags still there and clothes as dirty as when we left them. I could pretend that my Spanish had improved by this point, and that my instructions had been flawless, but the truth is the owner was German and spoke fluent English.

# THIRTY-TWO

Guinea pig, or 'cuy', as it is known, is a popular delicacy in the Andes. I had managed to avoid eating it until now, but as it was our last night in South America, I thought I should give it a try. Rachel ordered the chicken Kiev.

'Chicken Kiev. That's a nice traditional Peruvian dish to have on our last night in South America,' I said.

'Is it Peruvian?'

'No of course it's not. I was being sarcastic. It's called chicken Kiev.'

'And?'

'Kiev is in the Ukraine. So it probably originated there, I guess.'

'Or maybe the city of Kiev was named after a really popular chicken dish from Peru?'

'Er... yeah, maybe.'

I had seen cuy served to a customer in another restaurant. It was a whole guinea pig, skinned and roasted, but still with its head and legs attached. I assumed this was some freakish restaurant in rural Peru, and that here in tourist–friendly Cusco I would be served a beautifully presented fillet of guinea pig, bearing no resemblance to its former rodenty incarnation. Instead, I got the horror show too.

My plate arrived with a whole guinea pig, legs, head and all, lying on its back in the middle of my plate. But what was more disconcerting was its expression. It had its mouth wide open, baring its teeth, with its claws out ready to attack. It certainly didn't make me warm to it.

'Well, that looks, ermm, delicious,' said Rachel, taking a bite of her breaded chicken Kiev.

'Thanks,' I said. 'I can't wait to get started.'

'Great, then start.'

'Fine. I will.'

I picked up my knife and fork and began prodding it. I'm not sure why. It was definitely dead.

'No, no,' said a voice to my left. I turned to see one of the waiters standing beside me mimicking eating something with his hands.

'Oh, so I eat it like a corn on the cob? Like mazorca de maiz?' I said, delighted that I knew a phrase in Spanish.

'Si, si! Mazorca de maiz!'

'Bueno!' I said. 'This meal just gets better and better.'

He then continued to stand there while I picked up the cuy, trying to work out how to hold it without its spikey claws getting in the way. I looked up to the waiter and he stood there still grinning at me and gave me a thumbs up.

I took a bite. It was much crunchier than I anticipated. Once I was through the crispy skin, it didn't taste as bad as I was expecting. It tasted, predictably, a bit like chicken. Obviously nowhere near as good as a chicken Kiev, but good nonetheless.

'Mmmm,' I said to the waiter, reciprocating the thumbs up at the same time. He grinned even more.

I swallowed the mouthful and he continued to stare at me, clearly waiting for more. I rotated the guinea pig in my hands and went for another bite. This time one of its claws poked me in the eye and I let out a squeal. The waiter laughed and moved on to find his next gringo to torment.

It was a bit disconcerting having something look at me, baring its teeth as I ate. And no, I don't mean the waiter. I made a decent effort on the cuy. It certainly wasn't the most enjoyable meal I have ever had, but it wasn't the worst. As we sat with our beers overlooking one of Cusco's main squares, we reflected on what an incredible honeymoon it had been.

Our time in Peru, Bolivia and Ecuador had come to an end. The following morning we caught a flight to Lima where we got our connecting flight back to the UK. South America had been more than we could have imagined. We had never before witnessed nature in such wild and extreme forms - powerful snakes, deadly spiders, terrifying yet strangely beautiful piranhas, pink river dolphins, salt flats, trees that walked (if you believed hard enough), majestic mountains, mighty rivers, curious monkeys, rodents of unusual size, hot springs, geysers, toads the size of footballs, awe-inspiring condors and countless other 'birds'. Travelling for six weeks in the shadows of volcanoes was a humbling experience. It made us feel small and insignificant, but it also made us feel incredibly alive and appreciative of the world around us.

South America had taken us further out of our comfort zones than we ever thought possible. We had experienced things and seen places we believed were only for hardened adventurers. We had both conquered fears, and overcome many challenges, and the continent had undoubtedly made us both stronger and braver than we were before. There was nothing I would have changed. Except maybe next time I would stick to the Peruvian classic, chicken Kiev.

We arrived back home to Northampton late the following night and were relieved to find the house still standing, the cats still alive, and the furniture mostly where we left it.

'Graeme has done good,' said Rachel.

'Never in doubt,' I said.

A couple of days after returning home, Rachel started her new career as a teacher. Over the following months, I began regularly assisting two local photographers. I shadowed them at weddings and corporate shoots, gaining valuable experience and developing my skills.

At the same time, I signed up with a few recruitment agencies and worked a series of jobs that made my role as a Data Information Officer seem exhilarating. But I didn't care. I was no longer trapped, because I was actively taking steps to change my future.

Travelling in South America had opened my eyes to how passionate people can be about life. From the market stallholders, to the tour guides, to the bus drivers, to the street cashiers and jungle cake sellers, and the many other travellers we met during our journey, they were all so full of enthusiasm for everything they did. They were passionate about where they lived, passionate about their job – whatever it entailed – and passionate about their existence on this earth. I hoped some of this had rubbed off on me and would stay with me forever.

The photographers I had been assisting started passing paid jobs my way whenever they were double–booked. I put together a portfolio, built a basic website, did a leaflet drop around Northampton and began actively promoting myself as a photographer. I had been telling people for a while that I was a photographer, and slowly but surely, the bookings started to come in, and I started to believe it myself.

Rachel and I managed to save some money between us, and we travelled again during the school holidays the following summer. This time to Australia. And this time, I had a new passport with a brand–new photo.

When we returned to the UK from Australia the following year, I told the recruitment agencies that I was no longer looking for work. I was setting off on my own to forge a career as a photographer. A few days after making this momentous decision – and almost a year to the day after returning from South America – I had some time to kill before my next photography booking. I found myself standing at Land's End wearing nothing but a pair of boxer shorts.

But that is another story.

# ACKNOWLEDGEMENTS

Firstly, a huge thank you to all of our kind and generous friends and family who contributed to our honeymoon fund at our wedding. Without you all, this trip would not have been possible.

Thanks to Rachel for sharing this adventure in South America with me.

Thanks to Robin Hommel for your proofreading help. Big thanks to Becky Beer for your wonderful editing advice and for being such a pilkunnussija.

And lastly, thanks as always to YOU for reading my book (unless you've just skipped all the way to the end to read the acknowledgements, which is absolutely fine, but a little weird). It means an awful lot to me that you have chosen to spend your time reading about an adventure of mine. Thanks again, and if you keep reading, I'll keep writing.

If you enjoyed reading *Travels with Rachel*, I would be extremely grateful if you would consider posting a short review on Amazon. Reviews are SO important for authors, so any way in which you can help spread the word is hugely appreciated. Thank you.

Photos to accompany this book will be added to my Facebook page shortly, so please LIKE that to keep up-to-date. Photos for all my other books are already on there.

www.facebook.com/georgemahood

I have a useless website that I don't update at all, but there is a mailing list sign up page if you would like to join and be one of the first to hear of my new books. Signed paperback copies of all my books are available from my website's 'shop'.

www.georgemahood.com

I am on Twitter for general ramblings: @georgemahood

And Instagram too @georgemahood

Or you can drop me an email with any comments, feedback or criticism. It's always great to hear from readers.

george@georgemahood.com

I have written several other books! They are all available at very reasonable prices on Amazon. Please take a look…

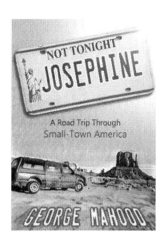

## NOT TONIGHT, JOSEPHINE:

### A Road Trip Through Small-Town America

Two Brits, George and Mark, set off from New York City to explore the back roads of America. In this calamity-ridden travel tale, George sets out in true clichéd fashion to discover the real America.

Throw in plenty of run-ins with the police, rapidly dwindling finances and Josephine – the worst car in the world – and you have all the ingredients for a classic American road trip. Will George and Mark make it all the way to California?

And then there is Rachel, George's girlfriend, left back in England. Would travelling to the United States without her turn out to be the stupidest decision he had ever made?

## FREE COUNTRY:

### A Penniless Adventure the Length of Britain

The plan is simple. George and Ben have three weeks to cycle 1000 miles from the bottom of England to the top of Scotland. There is just one small problem... they have no bikes, no clothes, no food and no money. Setting off in just a pair of Union Jack boxer shorts, they attempt to rely on the generosity of the British public for everything from food to accommodation, clothes to shoes, and bikes to beer.

During the most hilarious adventure, George and Ben encounter some of Great Britain's most eccentric and extraordinary characters and find themselves in the most ridiculous situations. Free Country is guaranteed to make you laugh (you may even shed a tear). It will restore your faith in humanity and leave you with a big smile on your face and a warm feeling inside.

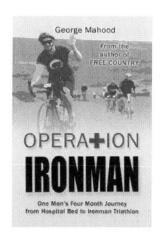

## OPERATION IRONMAN:

### One Man's Four Month Journey from Hospital Bed to Ironman Triathlon

Operation Ironman follows George Mahood's inspiring and entertaining journey from a hospital bed to an Ironman triathlon. After major surgery to remove a spinal cord tumour, George set himself the ultimate challenge –

a 2.4 mile swim,a 112 mile bike ride,

and a 26.2 mile run,

all to be completed within 16 hours.

He couldn't swim more than a length of front crawl, he had never ridden a proper road bike, he had not run further than 10k in 18 months... and he had never worn Lycra.

He had four months to prepare. Could he do it?

**EVERY DAY IS A HOLIDAY**

George Mahood had a nice, easy, comfortable life. He had a job, a house, a wife and kids. But something was missing. He felt like he was missing out on a lot of what the world had to offer.

He then discovered that it was Bubble Wrap Appreciation Day. The day after that was National Curmudgeon Day, and the day after that was Inane Answering Machine Message Day. In fact, the calendar is FULL of these quirky, weird and wonderful events. He realised that somebody somewhere had created these holidays, believing that they were important enough to warrant their own official day. Surely he should therefore be more appreciative of their existence? So he decided to try and celebrate them all. He hoped that at the end of the challenge he would be transformed into a happier, more intelligent and more content person.

Follow George on his hilarious, life changing adventure as he tries to balance his normal life with a wealth of new experiences, people, facts and ridiculous situations. It's a rip-roaring, life-affirming, roller-coaster of a ride, where every day is a holiday.

# CONTENTS

# ABOUT THE AUTHOR

Yasmin Alibhai-Brown came to the UK from Uganda in 1972 just before Asians were expelled by Idi Amin. After completing her MPhil at Oxford, she went on to teach immigrants and then later to work in adult education as a lecturer and head of department. In 1988 she turned to journalism, joining the *New Society* and later the *New Statesman and Society*. Since 1990 she has worked as a freelance journalist writing for the *Guardian*, the *Independent* and other papers. She is also a radio and television broadcaster. In 1995 she joined the Institute of Public Policy Research as a research fellow working on race and politics. She is married with a 19-year-old son and a 5-year-old daughter.

# ACKNOWLEDGEMENTS

This book would have not have been written without the many hours that were freely given to me by countless elders from the ethnic minority communities, their families and their carers.

I am deeply grateful to them all. I feel immensely privileged to have had access to such poignant experiences and the wisdom that only age can bring. My hope is that the younger members of these families will also gain insights from this book. Immigration brings with it many gains but it is also an arduous journey. These people survived to describe both sides of the story.

My thanks to Pardeep Gill who assisted me on this project, and to Age Concern for their commitment to this issue. And finally thanks with all my heart to my mother Jena who taught me to value old age, my husband Colin and my children Ari and Leila who, as ever, kept me buoyant.

*Yasmin Alibhai-Brown*

# INTRODUCTION

The kind of care required and received by ethnic minority elders is influenced by their history, by culture, by public attitudes towards elders in general and by changes in policies and the law. Everyone who organises or provides care for these elders needs to understand this background. What we do is determined by what we know. In this sense the term 'ethnic minorities' is used to cover all culturally distinct groups and not just people of colour.

Many people who provide care have little information about the history, values and lifestyles of the different minority groups in Britain, and without such information it is not possible to assess properly the physical and emotional needs of individual elders. Such detailed assessment is now a requirement under various new regulations and the community care legislation.

But if lack of information is a problem, having only superficial knowledge can be even more problematic. The information in a book such as this can only be basic and generalised. People are complex and unique, and may or may not conform to what we know about the communities they come from. Individual assessments should therefore never assume knowledge.

Something else to bear in mind is that minority communities do not exist in a vacuum. Politics and the media in particular influence the way people see themselves and the way they are perceived and treated in Britain.

In many ways the needs of ethnic minority elders are exactly the same as those of elders in general. They are not some species apart.

All elders want decent housing, security, companionship, an income and respect. But this does not mean that they can all be treated 'the same'. There are specific needs that are defined by the religion, the culture and the historical and contemporary experiences of ethnic minority groups, and these must be taken into account if the service they receive is to be appropriate and effective.

This book looks at the broader framework of how elders receive care and then notes the requirements and experiences of ten distinct ethnic minority groups within the general framework.

## Methodology

Some of the material has been drawn from published sources. This book is not based on a quantitative social survey, although data from such sources have been used where relevant. The aim was to use qualitative and journalistic interview techniques in order to gain in-depth insights into individual lives and perceptions. The interviews are not intended to be used to make generalisations or statistical points but to illustrate, where possible, some trends that have been mapped out by experts in this area. The 120 interviews were done over a period of three years by the author and an assistant. Some of the material was specifically for this book; the rest was for articles written previously. Many of the interviews were carried out in the relevant community languages and were then translated by the author. The names of the people interviewed have been changed.

## How this book can help

The book provides background information about various communities and also the context in which care is expected and provided. This knowledge should help the people planning the delivery of services and those working with ethnic minority elders to understand more about the lives of the elders and therefore, hopefully, provide care that is better suited to the needs of their clients.

Chapter 1 introduces the precepts of good practice when working with ethnic minority elders, and Chapter 2 outlines the general background and key issues involved. In Chapters 3 to 6 we look more specifically at the different communities. But remember, as care workers, managers and assessors, that the information is at a general level and should not be used in superficial ways. Every elder in our society is an individual who deserves to be treated with respect and real understanding.

## Key issues covered

- The care needed and received by ethnic minority elders is determined by:
  - their collective histories and memories;
  - their religion and culture;
  - society's attitudes towards elders in general;
  - cultural changes in mainstream and minority communities;
  - the way the majority population views ethnic minorities;
  - changes in the law and in the allocation of resources.
- Care workers need to be aware of all these issues and also the reasons why people came to Britain and what their early experiences were.
- Immigrants bring benefits to their new country and try to improve their own prospects. Many succeed; others fail. In the end, immigration does alter and influence values and beliefs. Elders feel this deeply.
- Continuing problems of marginalisation and discrimination mean that many ethnic minority families are caught in a trap: they cannot access appropriate services and so feel forced to rely on their limited resources, making them feel even more isolated from the mainstream community.
- Few care workers are trained to communicate with people who speak little or no English.
- Few local authorities have accurate information about ethnic minority elders in their area. Care workers may therefore have to find ways of responding to clients, sometimes without guidance from their departments.

■ Some care workers believe that service delivery should be 'colour blind' and not make special provision for ethnic minorities. This goes against the spirit of the NHS and Community Care Act 1990, which stresses the importance of taking account of each individual's religion, culture, language, etc. The 'colour blind' approach also ignores the human rights of ethnic minority elders, many of whom have worked in this country and paid their taxes.

■ It is a myth that all ethnic communities 'look after their own'. Many families cannot or will not do this any longer, and providers need to respond to this.

■ Ethnic minority elders are a minority within a minority, but this should not affect their right to appropriate care.

■ It is wrong to assume that everyone in the same community is exactly the same. Community care is supposed to be built around individuals and what they require.

# 1 Care workers, ethnic minority elders and their carers: good practice

In this book we look at various ethnic minority communities in order to gain some understanding of their lives and the issues that concern them. We also examine the historical events that brought various peoples to Britain and the broader political and social context that has influenced their lives. Our attitudes to older people and the structure of health and social services affect all elders but have particular effects on ethnic minority elders.

It is very important to stress that you should regard with caution the cultural backgrounds given in this book. You should look at them within the general historical and political context, and avoid the danger of simplifying and making superficial assumptions. As Karl Atkins, Research Fellow at the University of York, points out:

> Not only do black people have to contend with a mistaken emphasis on cultural practices in explaining their situation, they also have to deal with inappropriate generalisations. Introductory notes on black communities, present in most training material for service practitioners, often follow this pattern. One would not, for example, attempt to summarise a western approach to child rearing practices in one paragraph. Yet this is what black people are subject to.[1]

Here is what an Asian nurse said to a white elder about British family life:

> I read that you people don't like your children. You just throw them out at 16. So they throw you out when you are old. It is your culture.

How does something like this seem to white Britons? What would be the reaction if training material were published with such simplistic 'cultural explanations'? How would they be rebutted?

As care managers and workers in the field, you must have much more information in order to respond sensitively and appropriately to the needs of ethnic minority clients. You need to understand why people are in Britain, how racism has affected their lives, how they have confronted barriers, how their expectations have been met or thwarted and, lastly, the issue of ageing in a land where the norms are so different from the country they left, perhaps decades ago.

There are also the issues concerning resources and care delivery. These are of course mainly the responsibility of policy makers and politicians. As a care worker, for example, there may be little you can do about the fact that most local authorities have not yet looked at the profile of the population in their areas in order to cater for different groups needing care in the community or that tight budgets have limited the choices available, especially for ethnic minority elders. But knowing about all this helps you to understand how excluded people from ethnic minorities feel from service provision. And in a one-to-one relationship, which is what much care work is about, this knowledge gains you access to another person's world. It helps you to develop empathy, which is what this book is trying to generate.

There are many publications on policy and service delivery to ethnic minority elders. There are also many books and manuals providing practical information on the various ethnic communities. This book is concerned with improving and enhancing the one-to-one interaction between ethnic minority elders and those who are providing care and service to them.

**Martha**, a black pensioner who lives alone:

I can eat the food and all that. I don't mind it. But I think I want my home helps to talk to me and listen to my memories. But they have no time, and they don't want to listen. They don't understand anyway. How can a 20-year-old girl from Surrey understand my life?

What is needed to improve these interactions is an open-minded approach that does not judge and does not assume what an ethnic minority elder thinks or wants.

## Key issues

■ Whatever community an elder comes from, they are first and foremost individuals with varied beliefs and different degrees of how much they conform to cultural norms and lifestyles. No generalisations can or should be made about people simply on the basis of the really quite elementary information that is provided here.

■ All the groups covered in this book have had to find ways of overcoming deep prejudices against them from many in the majority population. They have had to deal, psychologically and practically, with direct and indirect discrimination throughout their lives. Again, this does not mean that every individual has had a terrible time or that we are talking about victims. Quite the contrary. When the odds are against you, you have to be stronger and more canny than those who can take their status and position for granted.

■ Elders in general are often treated with little real respect and consideration in our society. This is likely to get worse if younger people become more self-centred and ageist.

## Checklist for individual good practice

### Values and attitudes

There are many ways a care worker can make personal interaction with an ethnic minority elder more effective. Some are long-term strategies and skills that will need to evolve; others are relatively easy but important first steps. Some of these have to do with self-awareness.

DEALING WITH DIVERSITY AND PREJUDICE

Check within yourself if you feel uncomfortable with certain groups or communities, and talk this through with someone you can trust.

Remember that we all have prejudices, including people in the minority communities. Having prejudices is not something to deny or feel ashamed of. Doing nothing to change these, however, is wrong and can diminish the service you are providing.

Read more about the group, and try to talk to different people within the community. Remember that ethnic minority communities are not perfect and they too have problems that they need to sort out. You should not feel that you are wrong if you react against something that is common in a culture that is not your own. But it is up to you to find out more and then treat individuals from that community as equals. And this works both ways. As we shall see, many ethnic minority people feel that the British are cruel to their children and their old people. This is a grossly unfair stereotype, and it would be unacceptable for, say, a black care worker to base her care on these beliefs and say to a white elder: 'You should be happy that I am coming to look after you. You people don't care about the old. You like dogs more.'

CULTURE

It is important to remember that diets and lifestyles do not depend only on original cultures. They are influenced both by changes in culture as people settle in their new countries and by socio-economic factors. There is no perfect or 'normal' diet or lifestyle. All of us have evolved the way we live through historical and other influences. Most diets in the world are balanced in their original countries. Even religious restrictions that were once looked on as peculiar by the host community are now taken on as healthy alternatives. The rise in the number of vegetarians and also in the number of white people who fast are just two examples.

It is also important to remember that not all cultures believe in making light of problems, of not revealing their emotions publicly, of joking about painful and tragic events.

Care workers often have to negotiate the tricky area of family involvement. You are seen as catering not to an individual but to the family. Where there are tensions between the client and the family, it is best to discuss this with colleagues and others before taking a position.

Norms vary between groups. For example, the relationships between men and women are distinct in different cultures, although these too are changing as they are influenced by western culture. Women in many communities are in control of the home, and increasingly so as they get older. But they are expected to be the main homemakers.

Fathers, brothers and sons may behave in ways that can seem, or are, authoritarian. It is not necessary for a care worker to be in awe of difference. It is right to engage in discussions about differences, but it is not right to dismiss values because they don't conform to mainstream ideas. Asian women are often pitied by 'outsiders' for their deprived and controlled lives, but most Asian women are proud to be Asian and don't wish to be 'rescued'. Nevertheless, if there are real problems of cruelty and oppression within a minority family, it is important to take action just as you would with a white family. Culture is not an excuse for inhuman behaviour.

COMMUNICATION PROBLEMS

Communication problems can be improved greatly if small but important things are remembered. It is very important to learn the right names – however difficult and confusing – and the correct forms of address and pronunciation. This is something that gives an individual his or her identity and dignity. People often have their records mixed up and even miss appointments because of official ignorance about their names. However, never ask to look at passports or Social Security documents in order to check a name. This will cause fear and resentment.

Visits should be built around religious days, prayers and festivals. Again, checking first is very important. The effect of knowing without assuming can be very positive. Saying something like: 'Mr Ahmed, are you going to mosque on Friday?' makes Mr Ahmed feel you are trying to understand his world.

It is important to learn the formalities that are important in different groups. Most ethnic minority elders expect to be treated with respect. Humour or informality by a care worker, however well intentioned, will create barriers. The following remarks were witnessed in hospitals; they are all from white nurses speaking to male Asian elders:

Come on, Mr Singh. Why so po-faced today? No curry on the menu?

[*to a devout Muslim*] Mr Mohamed [*wrong name used*], time to go home. Get dressed; you'll soon be home. Watching the match tonight? Don't forget to get in the beer. Can I come?

There, there; just take off those pyjamas. Don't be shy. Nothing I haven't seen before, you know.

All three nurses meant well. But they only succeeded in embarrassing and alienating their patients.

Body language, physical contact and eye contact are different in different cultures. Not making eye contact is often a mark of respect, not of shiftiness or shyness. Touching between the sexes is also generally not acceptable. Sometimes basic gestures of 'yes' and 'no' are also completely different. It is important to learn and be sensitive to these subtle distinctions.

### Language barriers

Language barriers might be more difficult to resolve without an interpreter, but at the end of the day it is only by recognition of a common humanity that effective communication can take place.

There are useful books on English as a second language that you can buy and use to improve the way you talk to elders who are not proficient in English. Remember that people who do not speak English are not stupid. The British often speak only English but many ethnic minority elders speak two or three languages and dialects. The list below gives some simple ideas on ways you can improve communication in English:

- You can use pictures to 'talk' to people.
- Don't use questions when requesting actions. Tell people directly. So, instead of: 'Would you like to have your tablets, please?' say: 'Here, have your tablet, please, Mrs Patel.'
- Use gestures and (appropriate) body language.
- Speak slowly but not too loudly.
- Don't use jargon; use simple words and listen to the person so you can pick up on and use the words they know.
- Use full words rather than contractions (eg 'I have' not 'I've').
- If necessary, repeat (without showing irritation), using simpler and perhaps longer explanations.
- Allow more time, and also remember how difficult and stressful this can be for a client.
- Try to imagine being in a similar situation, in which you under-stood little or nothing of the language.

If you are using an interpreter, make sure that you have explained the context and made it very clear that censoring or re-interpreting conversations are not part of what is expected. (You can tell the interpreter that, at the end, they may talk about anxieties or issues that were not discussed.)

## Creating a secure environment

Most of the time, elders feel more secure when they know their environment and what to expect in terms of their diet etc. Respect for conventions in personal care is also essential. Washing after using the toilet is an example: for many bed-ridden patients from an ethnic minority it is traumatic if they are only wiped and not washed after they use the bedpan.

Deeply held beliefs must be treated with respect. One Hindu woman who had been widowed young was asked by her care worker why she had never remarried. The relationship between them suffered a real setback because the care worker had not known that traditional Hindu women do not remarry if they are widowed. Also important is the need for elders to have their experiences, memories and stories validated, valued and talked about. This is something care workers must learn to do in a sensitive way.

## Principles of good care practice for all elders

- Acknowledging individual beliefs and identity.
- Working in an anti-discriminatory way.
- Supporting individual rights and choices.
- Communicating effectively.
- Providing and gathering important information.
- Maintaining the confidence of those being cared for, including respecting their views and rights and confidentiality.
- Developing empathy.

These are, in fact, the requirements for candidates working towards the National Vocational Qualification (NVQ) or Scottish Vocational Qualification (SVQ) Levels 2 and 3 in Health and Social Care. Unit O, the value base unit, which is about the promotion of equality for all individuals, is a mandatory part of these qualifications.[2]

Informed choice is the right of all individuals but is something that ethnic minority elders are often denied because they are not given the information they need in a way they can understand.

For ethnic minority elders these general principles matter a great deal. The following interactions, based on real experiences, illustrate either how well the principles were followed or how they were ignored.

Now, Mrs Ahmed, it says here on the form that you are Muslim. I think I know what you are not allowed to eat. But will you let us

> know exactly what you can eat and if you want your family to bring in your meals?

Here the care worker is actually checking on the religious and cultural beliefs of the person, instead of assuming anything. But she has also informed herself enough so that she is not starting from a position of total ignorance.

> Now come on, Trevor, there's a good chap. Let's get these pyjamas off; we'll clean you up and then you can watch *Desmond.*

Most Afro-Caribbean elders would not expect to be addressed in this casual way or be talked down to like children. Although it is without malice and intended to be friendly, such an approach may cause needless irritation and loss of dignity.

> So was it very different when you all first came over, Mr Singh? The weather must have been a shock. And what did you do for food? It's great now – we can all have a curry any time we want – but what did you eat in those early days?

Here the care worker is genuinely empathetic and interested. She is giving Mr Singh the opportunity to talk about his life, something that is so important to elders, and she is making him feel proud of his culture and his contribution. And it is done in a natural and unforced way.

> I don't know how to buy such stuff. Just give me list for Sainsbury's and I'll go shopping for you. We are very short staffed you know.

People who go into the homes of elders to help them are often expected to do some shopping. This unwillingness to try to accommodate the specific needs of ethnic minority elders is partly to do with lack of time, but good care workers would try harder if their managers emphasised the importance of it.

This lady is also from Viet Nam. I brought her today so she can help us talk and you can tell her what you need.

This is an excellent example of what a good care worker can do to break down language barriers. Even if interpreters are hard to find, many of us know people who can help out.

## Personal awareness

Below is a basic checklist of the kinds of questions that care workers can ask themselves to make sure that prejudice and generalisations are not interfering with good practice.

- What do you think a family is? What is your view of the ideal family? Who should be in charge? Who has responsibilities, and to whom? (Such questions will clarify your own view and then you can analyse your responses to unfamiliar situations.)
- If you believe passionately that men and women should share in the housework, you should be aware that this view will influence how you interact with women in some ethnic communities who still play the 'traditional' role in the home.
- If you think that people who immigrate should assimilate, how will you respond – even unconsciously – to ethnic minority elders who don't speak English or who want to use their own herbal medicines?
- Similarly, you need to examine your own beliefs and views about other areas, such as:
  - illness and pain;
  - attitudes to death;
  - involvement and interference by members of the family and by professionals;
  - individual rights and family obligations;
  - immigration;
  - food and diet;
  - religion;
  - old age.

Never force your own views on ethnic minority elders – although, if you have established a rapport, you can have a discussion about any of them. Don't make derogatory remarks about other people's lifestyles. Ask for information and explanations.

# General awareness

Develop links with local groups and places of worship from the minority communities. Your department will benefit and it will make your work easier and more productive.

## *Client relationships*

Build up trust by relating to the elders and others in the family. Find out how the families work, who the provider is and what the accepted chain of respect is.

Don't perceive ethnic minority families as just victims of racism or unequal treatment. This is of course a reality, but family life is also fun, full and strong in many of these communities. Showing that you are aware of this will open many doors into family life. Say that you'd like to have a meal with them or see how they celebrate their festivals. Most ethnic minority communities will be delighted and their sense of alienation will be reduced.

Talk about the cultural preferences of clients, but don't base super-ficial judgements on the views of one person. Explore the underlying emotional life of elders. For example, when a woman says that she is happy living with the family but you can see that there are problems, you need to find a way that respects her but allows her to seek help if she needs it. Cultures are not above the law and it is not racist to question or even criticise inappropriate behaviour, as long as you do it from an informed position and you are dealing with an individual in a particular situation.

### Learning empathy

You can learn empathy by using your imagination. Imagine that you are badly injured in an accident on holiday. You are in a foreign country where you do not speak the language or understand the 'norms' or system.

- Think of your confusion and fears.
- Think about your own expectations and how you would feel if they were not met.
- Imagine how you would feel if busy people got irritated with you.
- Imagine the loneliness and the feelings of anger and desperation.

## Ethnic minority carers

There are a significant number of ethnic minority carers of elders in this country. It seems that, proportionately, being a carer is more common among the minority communities than among the white British population. The reasons for this are complex but related to the following factors:

- lack of appropriate services for ethnic minorities;
- lack of knowledge by people in ethnic minorities about what *is* available;
- deeply held beliefs that it should be the family who take care of elders and not 'strangers';
- the wishes of the elders themselves;
- low income and thus an inability to pay for services.

These carers are often isolated and rarely get the support they might need or are entitled to. And because there is so little research into this area, local authorities cannot respond in a systematic way either to the people being cared for at home or to their carers. This is why one small research project decided to look at the lives of carers from three communities in the London borough of Southwark. The report says:

Little was known about minority ethnic carers. A few community organisations had things to say about their members or users, but we knew of no attempts to seek out carers from minority communities, and no documented findings about their circumstances.[3]

A year later, in 1991, another book highlighted the same problem:

With the heightened awareness of carers and their caring roles in recent years, more information aimed specifically at them has been produced, offering signposts to such services as taking time off and help in the home. However, there has not been much written for carers of particular racial groups.[4]

So what are the experiences of and problems often faced by ethnic minority carers?

■ Getting them to accept the fact that they are doing an important job, that they are carers, not just relatives who are doing their duty.
  **Arunaben,** who looks after her infirm mother:

> We have to look after the old people, not just throw them in the dustbin. But it is very hard and nobody cares that we are doing this. I am a widow, a sister, a nothing in my family. They just think I should do this quietly. But what about me; who will look after me? I can get no pension. Really, I am telling you, I am so worried.

■ Physical problems that have to be dealt with, and which may be difficult because of certain taboos and the sheer energy and strength required.
  **Hananah,** a Muslim woman who takes care of her father-in-law:

> I have to clean his toilet. I am his daughter-in-law and we both are so shamed. In our culture men and women don't look at the bodies. So we cannot tell anybody. My husband is very sensitive so he does not do anything for his father. I think he is ashamed of him.

■ Lack of relevant information and an unawareness that it is their right to seek help. For example, almost all the people interviewed in the Southwark project did not know what was available or how to organise respite care.

**Hananah** again:

> I can't ask for the help because my husband is not unemployed. And it is a disgrace if outsiders come in to help. But we people also don't know what is there.

- Some carers may have the same language and communication problems as the elders they are caring for.
- Many carers felt worried about the physical problems of the people under their care, and what they should be doing for them. **Munira**, a woman from Pakistan who speaks hardly any English and who is looking after an elderly aunt:

> She has a heart problem. But I don't know what I can give her to eat which would not be bad for her but also tasty. I can't understand the doctors and they can't understand me.

- Poverty, inadequate housing and other problems often make the lives of both the carer and the elder unbearable. **Munira** again:

> If we had a video, maybe I can get the Indian films to pass the time for both of us. But where to get the money? My brother has no job. I am asking the mosque people next week to help. But I feel so shy to ask them.

- Some groups, such as the Afro-Caribbeans, are better able to use the services because they are aware of them and because they have few communication problems. But in the Chinese, Asian and other communities there is less awareness of what is available, how service delivery is changing, how to use the services or even how to fill in application forms or telephone for advice etc.
- Even when people have the language, getting the right information is very difficult for ethnic minority carers, particularly when there are significant structural and legal changes in the way care is provided. Remember that in a relatively short period we have had the NHS and Community Care Act 1990 (the main social services aspects implemented in April 1993) and the Carers (Recognition and Services) Act 1995, and enormous changes to the way health care is provided. Most older people, particularly

in the minority communities, have found it difficult to keep up with the changes.

■ Many people from minority communities have been made to feel that they do not have the same rights to services as white Britons. This makes them nervous, and hesitant about approaching the health or social services for help. Even when they do get help, they often feel that they must accept what they are given and be grateful, not to rock the boat.

■ The practical needs of the elders and their carers as well as the emotional needs that should be catered for and understood by care workers.

**Norma**, a 55-year-old black woman who looks after her mother:

> I took my mother to a luncheon club where this white old-age pensioner said to me that she had been mugged and that it was all so much better in the old days, in the sixties before coloureds arrived. I told her for us those were the bad old days and why was she saying that we brought all the trouble? The worker who was listening said to me 'don't mind her, she is old'; but why did she not say anything to make me feel better?

## Legislation

The Carer's (Recognition and Services) Act 1995, requiring local authorities to undertake assessments of carers' needs, has helped but many carers are not asking for assessments. This is often because they are not aware that they *can* ask for an assessment, or they think that there is no point in asking because funds are so limited. Moreover, ethnic minority carers are still thought of as wanting to 'look after their own' and they are bypassed when allocating the very limited help that is available. The myth tends to win over circumstance.

## Ethnic minority carers' needs

There are support groups for carers, and social services departments can often provide information about them. Often, however, they tend to be for all carers generally. Ethnic minority carers can be encouraged to set up their own support groups. A good place to look is day care and meeting centres for ethnic minority elders.

The information carers need is complicated and diverse. People find it hard to understand that local authorities next to each other have very different approaches to service delivery and that even straightforward situations are more complicated than they seem at first. For example, someone looking after an elder in a council flat would have to be in contact with the following:

■ social services department
■ housing department
■ GP, hospital services
■ Benefits Agency office
■ bank
■ voluntary organisations
■ local authority transport facilities
■ disability organisations

Try to imagine how difficult life can be for a person caring alone for someone who is on a very low income, unable to get out and also has to cope with all the language difficulties and problems of discrimination. It *can* be done better, and some institutions have tried to improve things. For example, the Benefits Agency has published information in a number of different languages.

Most ethnic minority elders and their carers find it very difficult to appeal against decisions or to complain about the lack of help or the kind of service they are given. This is partly because they fear that they may not be entitled to what is available, so if they make a fuss they will lose what they are getting. Silence is *not* satisfaction.

Local authorities must find out about the needs of ethnic minority elders and their carers in the areas where they live. This should include their leisure and educational needs – for example, most mobile libraries do not carry books in languages other than English unless this is requested. Working with the local communities, strategies can be developed for improving communication. Where possible, interpreters or same-group professionals should be used to help make the service fit the client.

## White care workers and ethnic minority clients

There are many excellent and committed white care workers who, daily, help to improve the lot of ethnic minority elders and also to influence and improve policies. For some the fact that they are unable to communicate fully with their clients makes them feel inadequate and unprofessional. They too would welcome help with interpreters.

**Sarah**, a nurse in west London:

I am a nurse. I believe in my profession and I really want to help these people on my ward who cannot speak English and whose sense of bewilderment is heartbreaking. But there is only so much I can do with the time and the skills I have. Interpreters are as rare as red squirrels and I feel I am failing much of the time. And you know what is so hard? That they are so grateful anyway. One old Muslim man was crying into his pillow. So I went and just held his hand, because I did not know what to do. He took his hand away because I am a woman, and then he told his son to apologise to me because I was being kind and he thought he was rude. His son told me he fought in the war. And we treat them in this way, ignoring their needs. And with all these market forces, it is getting worse for them. When I worked in London hospitals before, many of them had advocacy teams and translators; now these just don't exist.

There are many care workers like Sarah, but sadly, at the other end of the spectrum, we also have care workers who are ignorant and even resentful of the demands that ethnic minority elders make on their time and work schedules.

**Helen,** a 40-year-old home care assistant ('home help')

> Don't get me wrong, I would never say anything to them, but I feel angry that they come over here, use our systems and then expect special treatment. I mean, back in Pakistan they would be living in slums. I go in as a home help. Where are they going to get that in their country?

Besides the professional reasons why such carers should give good care to ethnic minority elders, it is a requirement in various charters, including the Patient's Charter.

## Policy issues

Those who set out and are implementing legislation passed in the last decade need to be aware of their responsibilities to elders from different communities. As a care worker, if you feel that such needs are not being met, it helps to know what the laws, policies and charters say.

The **Citizen's Charter** says that people should have more choice in the public services they receive.

The **Patient's Charter** says that patients have a right to expect certain standards in the delivery of health care:

- 'Your privacy, confidentiality, dignity and cultural beliefs will be respected at all times.'
- 'You should be given clear, understandable information in appropriate languages about services and treatments available.'
- 'There should be arrangements to ensure everyone, including people with special needs, can use the services.'

The NHS and Community Care Act 1990 says that people in need of care have the right to be assessed for services to meet their needs by a care manager. The 1990 White Paper 'Caring for People' also emphasised that ethnic minority cultural values should be recognised when planning care packages. This assessment is supposed to be based on need and a holistic approach. The package that is arranged will depend on resources but is also supposed to be reviewed and reassessed periodically.

The **Race Relations Act 1976** makes it illegal to discriminate, directly or indirectly, against ethnic minorities in the provision of services.

*Community Life*, a book published in 1990 by the Centre for Policy on Ageing, says that packages should reflect the informed choice of the customer.

These charters, legislation and policies are only saying what should be done anyway for all citizens and residents, for reasons of social justice and best practice. Yet there is evidence that even the most basic needs are not being met. For example, elders from many ethnic communities do not understand the details and instructions on medicine labels.

Even where voluntary organisations and others do try to find out what is needed, they too often depend solely on 'community leaders', who may provide them with information that could in fact be incomplete or even inaccurate. It is essential for people to double-check – with each individual – the information they have.

In some departments and organisations – even those that pride themselves on being fair – white workers often feel that too much is being done for ethnic minorities. Or there may be people who have done some in-service training on anti-racist practice and then approach ethnic minorities with a generalised set of assumptions. And there is the associated problem of not recognising that there are diverse groups within ethnic communities. What most black and Asian people feel very strongly is that they should be treated as individuals who have the same rights and are considered a part of British society. A woman interviewed for an Age Concern project in Brent said:

> We are human beings also. We have two eyes, two arms and two legs. Are our needs that drastically different that you always have to do special work on us? . . . we are the community, we are not

separate from it, living somewhere that no one can reach us. They only need to keep their eyes and ears open.'[5]

## Ethnic minority care workers

There are now many more care workers from ethnic minority communities, in both the social services and the health services. Most are found in the least well paid jobs, although some boroughs are beginning to employ people from the ethnic minorities as social workers and in more senior positions, too. Nevertheless, it cannot be assumed that, because people are themselves from a minority community, they will automatically be sensitive to the issues we have been discussing or that they see themselves as representing certain interests.

- Some, in wishing not to be seen as different personally and professionally, may take on a 'colour blind' approach or even one that is antagonistic towards cultural diversity.
- Others will feel strongly about the issues but feel too powerless or too angry to do anything about it.
- Others may have strong feelings against some minority groups and may in fact treat them with mistrust and unfairly ignore their needs.

**Mrs Ramji**, an elder who had a black home help:

> She told me she did not like us because we're Asian and that we treat black people like the servants. So I felt afraid when she came, if she was going to be angry with me.

## Responding to difficult situations

All kinds of problems can arise when care workers are looking after elders. Many of these are connected to the nature of the work, the nature of old age, pressures of the job itself, lack of resources and also the kinds of problems it is impossible for any care worker to do anything about. The way to approach the care of ethnic minority elders is:

- to understand their history and the context in which they live;
- to develop empathy for people who came here as immigrants and refugees, and who are now getting older;
- to make sure that, as far as possible, the needs of those being cared for are being addressed and met where possible;
- to understand that there are some problems that you as a care worker can do nothing about but that you should not feel angry or useless.

Remember:

- It is vital to know and understand some of the historical and cultural backgrounds of the people you are dealing with.
- But it is just as vital to treat them as individuals, always using what you know as a sounding board to check what each person believes and desires.
- As far as possible you should work in an anti-discriminatory way, giving individual consideration to people's beliefs and their identity.
- You will learn along the way. Nobody should be worried about doing or saying the right thing. As long as you are open, you will build up the skills you need.

### Institutional and wider problems

At present, in spite of good intentions and also all the statutory requirements, care for ethnic minority elders is patchy. The following is what Age Concern and the Commission for Racial Equality said in a joint briefing paper:

What understanding there is of older people from ethnic minorities tends to be clouded by stereotypes and myths. If there are to be adequate and suitable services and support to meet their needs, there is an urgent need for better understanding and comprehensive study of older people from all ethnic minority populations. Overall support and suitable provision for older people from the ethnic minorities tends to be marginalised and is fragmented.[6]

## Other factors that prevent a proper response

The increasing pressure on resources and a society that is moving away from the ideals of welfare for the vulnerable are producing unacceptable injustices. As Naina Patel says:

> Looking to this decade, . . . the NHS and Community Care Act 1990, with its market-oriented approach and unwillingness to recognize structural barriers to services to black elders, threatens to exacerbate their situation within an increasingly chaotic and shrinking welfare society . . . add to this the stereotyping, gatekeeping, organisational, individual and direct racism and one begins to appreciate how effectively these work to keep black elders 'out of the market'.[7]

We must all work hard to maintain and to improve anti-racist practice.

## Elements important for institutional good practice

- An equal-opportunity policy on employment, service delivery and harassment that is well understood by all staff.
- A database of the area served, giving a breakdown of ethnic and religious backgrounds, with age, gender and disability information as well as housing conditions.
- Needs assessments that take all these factors into account.
- Purchasing services and inspections using this information to make individual assessments.
- A working consultation process with local ethnic minority communities.
- Information and public education campaigns.
- Interpreting and translating services available.
- Complaints procedures.
- Organisations contracted to provide services such as meals-on-wheels should be expected to understand and cater for different needs.

■ Staff training so that workers can develop best practice in this kind of provision.

## Special facilities

There are controversial issues concerning special facilities for ethnic minority groups that you may need to understand. Is it fair or right for people to be separated and catered for in this way or should they just fit in with general provision for the majority population? As one activist has put it: 'It is crazy to insist that everything should be mainstreamed: old people do need some special services based on being with people who share their background and experience.'

But if mixing is inappropriate for ethnic minority elders, is it equally valid for white elders to demand the same? In the name of fairness, separate services may be an alternative, but making such a decision is not easy. Neither group should be allowed to claim territorial rights except where genuine reasons, such as fear, diet, language and customs, make the elders feel unsettled.

This book is about developing sensitivity and respect for ethnic minority elders. For too long they have been either ignored or treated as some curiosity. In the end, best practice depends on understanding that these are human beings with rights and expectations that should not be denied in a civilised society.

As Tennessee Williams wrote in his play *Sweet Bird of Youth*:

I don't ask for your pity, but just your understanding – not even that – no. Just for your recognition of me in you and the enemy, time, in us all.

# 2 Background and key issues

## Ethnic minority elders: who are they?

The term 'ethnic minorities' in Britain has largely come to mean black and Asian people. This is unfortunate and inaccurate because there are many other minority groups who don't seem to be included in the term but who also have distinct identities. How many of us, for example, would think of Jewish, Irish, Cypriot or Italian communities when we talk about minority communities? Yet, logically, we should.

There is also a problem of getting accurate data for groups such as these because national figures are not available, partly because of the way information is gathered and broken down and partly because some groups, the Jewish community in particular, are deeply suspicious of such data gathering because of their own painful history in Europe before the 1950s.

The groups we cover in this book are:

- the Black communities: Afro-Caribbean and African
- the Asian communities: Hindus, Muslims, Sikhs
- the Chinese and Vietnamese communities
- the Jewish community
- the Polish community
- the Turkish community

The reasons for choosing these minorities are that they constitute some of the largest distinct ethnic groups in Britain and also because on the whole they would be most likely to have experienced considerable discrimination or hostility during their period of settlement in this country. The only exception is the Irish community, which is not only the largest immigrant group to this country but also has suffered a history of prejudice and economic deprivation. The reason for not including them as a separate group in this book is that, in many significant ways, they share cultural characteristics with the indigenous population. But this does not mean that their experiences are not valid or that they feel that the needs of their elders are fully met.

The figures for ethnic minority communities and the white population, according to the 1991 Census, are shown in the Table below.

The total population of Great Britain was 54,889,000, 94.5 per cent of whom were white and 22.1 per cent were aged 60 or over.

The remaining 5.5 per cent were grouped as follows:

|  | All ages (rounded to 000s) | Percentage of population | Percentage of minority population over 60 years |
|---|---|---|---|
| Indian | 840,000 | 1.5 | 6.8 |
| Black Caribbean | 500,000 | 0.9 | 10.9 |
| Pakistani | 477,000 | 0.9 | 3.7 |
| Black African | 212,000 | 0.4 | 2.7 |
| Bangladeshi | 163,000 | 0.3 | 3.3 |
| Chinese | 157,000 | 0.3 | 5.7 |
| Other Black | 178,000 | 0.3 | 2.1 |
| Other Asian | 198,000 | 0.4 | 4.1 |
| Other groups | 290,000 | 0.5 | 5.0 |

Other figures put the total number of ethnic minority elders at 95,027 men and 80,483 women. These figures include Turkish, Arab and other communities not counted separately. Poles, Cypriots, eastern and central European Jews, Italians, Spaniards and Portuguese are also present in the population but not counted in these figures. There are 111,751 men and 144,717 women Irish elders.

## Other key facts and figures

- 3.22 per cent of the total ethnic minority population is elderly, compared with 16 per cent of the UK population as a whole.
- Older men outnumber older women in the ethnic minority population. In the white population older women outnumber older men.
- Black Caribbeans, Chinese and Indians have proportionately larger numbers of elders than the Bangladeshis and the Pakistanis.
- The number of elders in all minority groups is rising and is expected to increase dramatically in the next 40 years.

Except for the Irish, the largest groups of ethnic minorities have their origins in the Indian sub-continent or the Caribbean countries. There are also thousands of people from other racial, ethnic and religious communities who make up the population of Britain today. This island has, over the centuries, had all kinds of different groups coming to its shores, and it is useful to remember that the British themselves have also settled in countries around the world. Spain today has many British elders who chose to retire there.

Among the ethnic minority communities in Britain, substantial numbers of people were actually born here. Their elders came for all sorts of different reasons, part of a long flow into this country over many centuries. The important thing to remember is that all these groups have a right to be here.

The more recent migrant groups have had to struggle against many odds to find their place in society, especially those who are physically different or who have, throughout history, been victims of hatred.

## History

Most of the established population (the indigenous people) remain ignorant of the history of immigration to Britain. For example, not many people know that:

- Black and Asian people were seen in England as early as the seventeenth century.
- During colonial times, it was quite common to see Asian ayahs and lascars in the streets of London and port areas such as Liverpool.
- Three and a half million Indians volunteered to fight in World War 2 with the Allies. Thousands of Caribbeans and Africans also enlisted and fought for what they believed was a just cause.

### Early twentieth century

Polish Jews, fleeing from religious persecution, arrived in Britain in large numbers at the end of the nineteenth and beginning of the twentieth centuries. They settled in east London, Manchester and Leeds. Other Jewish refugees also arrived at around this time, mainly from Russia and Rumania. They too settled in the east end of London, Manchester and Leeds. These refugees were already bi-cultural: they were primarily Jewish, but there were language and other differences between them because they came from different countries.

### The inter-war and post-war years

As the persecution of Jewish people continued in Europe, they began to arrive in Britain in greater numbers in the 1930s and 1940s. They came from Poland, Germany and Austria. The rise of Nazism increased this flow, although until 1939 many were sent back and they ended up in concentration camps.

**David,** a Jewish elder, recalls how he felt when he found out that his grandparents were among those who were sent back and subsequently killed:

> It was like my whole world and faith collapsed. To think that this country, which I held up as a saviour of my people, had done this to my own grandparents. To be a Jew is to be always on guard after something like this. And it was not that easy for my parents here

either. There was so much hatred against us in this country. When you get old like me, you remember all that, and it hurts.

Polish Catholics also suffered at the hands of the Nazis after their country was invaded in 1939. Many of them also arrived in Britain in the 1930s and 1940s. Other groups who came over at that time included Czechs, Ukrainians, Yugoslavs, Latvians and Estonians.

Men from undivided India came to fight in Europe, and were stationed in Britain. Afro-Caribbeans also volunteered to join the Allied forces during World War 2. Many were in the Royal Air Force and were stationed in Britain.

### The 1950s and early 1960s

Italians arrived in Britain during this time. Most have settled in London, Bedford and Hertfordshire. They were recruited by the hotel and catering industry or they worked in foundries, brick-making and other heavy industries. Some took up auxiliary jobs in the National Health Service.

Portuguese and Spanish people came then, as a result of active recruitment into the hotel trade and the National Health Service. They settled in London, other areas in the south east, Liverpool and Manchester. In both communities there are large numbers of single older women who speak little English.

The hotel trade brought in Moroccans and people from the Turkish mainland. Mauritians were recruited directly and actively by the National Health Service. Many Turkish and Greek Cypriots also came to work in catering and the clothing sector. Most live in the Greater London area, particularly in the north-east part. Greek Cypriots are mainly Orthodox Christians and Turkish Cypriots are mostly Muslims.

People of Pakistani origin, mostly men, were recruited for the textile and engineering industries as part of the reconstruction process after the devastation of World War 2. People of Indian origin were, like the Pakistanis, recruited to work in the heavy industries in the post-war period. Some Bangladeshis also arrived here at that time. They started up the now widespread Indian restaurant trade.

There were special recruitment programmes in the West Indies to get personnel into sectors where there were acute labour shortages. London Transport, hotels and restaurants, and the National Health Service put out advertisements and went on recruiting drives to these countries. One of those involved in the recruitment drive was the late Enoch Powell, who subsequently changed his stance and publicly voiced his opposition to the influx of immigrants.

### The late 1960s and 1970s

Because of political upheavals in South and Central America, this period saw the arrival of refugees from Chile and other Latin American countries. There was also a flow of refugees from Czechoslovakia and other East European satellites of the Soviet Union.

Filipino workers were recruited by the employment agencies to work in the National Health Service and in the hotel and catering industries. Most of them were women and they came on the work permit system, which meant that, although they could gain the right to settle permanently, they were not allowed to send for their families to join them.

The Chinese community, mostly from Hong Kong, began to arrive at this time and, like the Bangladeshi immigrants, they concentrated on setting up and or working in restaurants.

The birth of Bangladesh after the break-up of East Pakistan in 1971 resulted in a bigger wave of migration by Bangladeshis who were worried about what the future would bring. Some of the arrivals already had family members here.

After independence, many Asians in Kenya, Tanzania and Uganda were offered the opportunity to hold on to their British passports. All three countries then began a process of Africanisation of key jobs. This coincided with strict new immigration laws that were enacted by the British government, which led to Asians from these countries and from Malawi and Zambia coming to Britain in regulated numbers. The 1968 Commonwealth Immigrants Act was responsible for making these people 'homeless' until admitted into the country that had given them passports. Then, in 1972, the military dictator Idi Amin expelled Asians en masse. These were people who had helped to build the country. Britain took in Ugandan Asians with British passports.

Vietnamese refugees came over after 1975. Many of those who risked their lives by getting on small boats and setting out to sea never made it. Some did reach Hong Kong somehow and ended up in refugee camps, from where a number came to Britain.

### The 1980s

With primary immigration all but halted, the only arrivals into Britain have been refugees such as the Iranians who came after the revolution or the Somalis who were fleeing war and starvation. Other avenues of legal entry have been strictly limited and, although there is evidence of some illegal immigrants or false refugee claimants entering Britain, the numbers are small and exaggerated by some newspapers and politicians. Most of the immigrants entering legally were families who had been waiting for years to be reunited.

Some people who came from Africa and other ex-colonies to study have also stayed on, often because they now have partners and children who are British. The Nigerians form the largest of this group.

## Where in England and Wales do ethnic minority elders live?

In general, ethnic minority communities tend to be concentrated in urban areas. More than half of them live in the south east of England. There are also large populations in the west Midlands and Greater Manchester areas. There are significant differences in the geographical distributions of these groups. For example, Chinese people outnumber other ethnic groups in Wales and Merseyside while there is a high concentration of Asians in the north west. Asians are also sub-divided into various religious and other groupings. Leicester has attracted mostly East African Asians, while in Bradford the majority of Asians are Muslims who come from a similar background and geographical area. There are vast differences in lifestyle and values between Asians, even those who share the same religion. Muslims in West Yorkshire and Muslims from East Africa have less in common than you might expect. In fact, East African Muslims and East African Hindus would have more in common with each other because they come from the same class and have a shared history.

Having a general idea of settlement pattern is not an indication of a mass identity. Knowing certain historical and geographical facts about the Scots does not mean that you can define and predict what all Scottish people do, believe and think. It is the same with ethnic minority people. They are all individuals with personal histories and preferences. And it is when you talk to such individuals that you get a picture of what life is like for ethnic minority elders.

## Issues facing ethnic minority elders

**James Harrison,** ex-war hero and retired bus driver:

I came here first to fight for this country and then back again in the sixties, when in Jamaica we were all being told how we were needed by the motherland. For all my life I worked. I have now reached the last days of my life. I am alone, my children have fled to the other side of the world, to America. My wife died, miserably, of illness and depression. I feel my life has been a complete waste. That I failed. And I will die knowing this and in a country where to be old for anyone is a sin, but for a coloured person is the biggest sin of all. My dear, you have no idea of the pain in my heart and how much I want to die. But I am a Christian and it would be wrong. Now we people are not wanted by the state and not wanted by our children.

Mr Harrison is one of the ethnic minority elders interviewed for this book. What he expresses so movingly is how many others feel about their lives. It is a sad reflection of our society that such people should feel so disenchanted. Many were once robust and optimistic individuals who came into this country from the ex-colonies and helped to inject new blood and drive into Britain at a time of tremendous post-war exhaustion. Talk to other groups, those who might have fled terror, war and other disasters, and you often get the same sense of dejection.

## Attitudes towards old age

The feelings of ethnic minority elders are shared by white British elders in our community. They too often feel undervalued, and increasingly so in a society that is becoming obsessed with youth. Many live in poverty; others are neglected and ignored. A number are the victims of young criminals and this creates fear of crime, which affects the choices they make and the way they then live.

## The welfare state

Elders are also concerned that new policies, which they do not understand, are chipping away at the services that helped them to feel secure and on which they depended. According to the Office for National Statistics, there over 9 million elders in Britain today.[1] The numbers are expected to rise steadily, but, instead of dealing with this as an important social responsibility, panic has been generated that the financial burden on those in work will multiply. Some people feel that this is to excuse the gradual erosion of state benefits that elders have learned (and earned the right) to expect. In 1989, Professor Alan Walker wrote: 'concern about the ageing of the population is being artificially amplified ... in order to legitimatise policies aimed at reducing the state's role in welfare.'[2] The media and politicians constantly present this picture of gloom and doom, and this has an effect on our elders and how we treat them.

Added to this is the general restructuring within the welfare state that has already begun to take place. When Margaret Thatcher said that there was no such thing as 'society', she was signalling a profound change of direction. In the past decade the focus of responsibility has steadily moved away from the community and the state towards the individual and the family. Many more people are now preparing to cater for their own old age through private pensions and other financial schemes.

All this is contributing to the sense of despair that many elders feel.

**William Pontin**, Mr Harrison's next door neighbour, who used to work as a postman, explains his feelings:

> Like James here, I too have worked all my life. Now we get all this news about how the old are a problem for the young and how the state cannot support us. It makes me feel like a parasite, but my taxes all those years helped to look after the old and so it's my turn now.

But, like many people who feel under threat, Mr Pontin is much less tolerant about those elders who he feels are not 'really British'.

> I don't mean James here because he worked. But all those people from Pakistan and Africa; they are just coming here to get our benefits. So there isn't enough to go around and people like me will lose what is ours by right.

### The media

For years now, the media in this country, especially the tabloid press, have given people like Mr Pontin the impression that all immigrants are 'scroungers' on this society or that they bring trouble to what was once paradise. Very few newspapers or programmes reflect the enormous contribution that immigrants have made to Britain or ever talk about their rights as British people. Many ethnic minority elders feel insulted by this kind of portrayal of their people, and for some it has become almost impossible to think of themselves as people with the same rights as indigenous folk. And as the cake available to elders in general gets smaller, ideas like those expressed by Mr Pontin acquire greater acceptance.

If, over the years, people with power and influence had made it their responsibility to educate the ordinary British public on the contribution made by black and Asian immigrants to the transport and health services, for example, perhaps we would not have this level of ignorance among the ageing white population.

This is not to say that black and Asian elders have always seen themselves as victims or that all white people have treated them unfairly. The resilience of these immigrants – their capacity to support one another and simply survive against the odds – has been one of the most impressive stories of our times. Many have also forged close relationships with individual white Britons. But these undoubtedly positive aspects of their lives should not obscure the hardships that so many encountered and continue to face.

Even Mr Harrison who feels so disappointed tells his neighbour that he thanks the Lord that he is black and that he and his friends can still sit and laugh about their time in this country. 'You should try and come along one day, William, to our club and see what good friends really are.'

### 'Scapegoating'

It is not just white elders, those who watched the country transform itself after World War 2, who so readily blame 'outsiders' for their troubles. Such views about the ethnic minorities are fairly common, even among care workers. And the attitudes are hardening at an interesting time, says Dr Mark Johnson, of Warwick University:

> It is ironic that all this discussion of the demographic time bomb and the future inability of the State to support our elders . . . in the style to which we have become accustomed, has come just at the point when many of those migrants who came to Europe during the period of post-war reconstruction, are themselves achieving retirement age.[3]

# The emotional cost of immigration

The emotional cost of immigration borne by many ethnic minority elders needs to be appreciated by everyone working with them. At the end of a long arduous journey, they still don't feel as if they belong in this country, at least partly because of the attitudes described above. Some also feel alienated because for years they treasured the idea of returning to the land where they were born and now they know it is too late. Others, when they were younger, felt able to participate in the economic life of the country – mostly at the low-income end of the employment market – but wanted to retain their cultural and religious integrity.

However, immigration the world over is a complex process and it is not possible, and perhaps not desirable, for people simply to go out to work and then withdraw into their cultural enclaves at the end of the day. Their children went to school with those in mainstream society; the family watches television; their world view is challenged and even threatened every minute of the day. The elders were not prepared for this and many did not know how to deal with the conflicts that arose. They had to cope with discrimination from the established communities as well as a dilution of their cultural beliefs – which occasionally were based on their own prejudice.

**Mr Gurdial Singh,** a retired factory worker, expresses his anguish:

I came here to work in a factory in Southall. My brother came first. After Partition there were so many problems in our villages back home. I thought I will work here for some years and then go back. I brought my wife. She got the work sewing the clothes for factories at home. It was a very difficult life.

My brother and I bought a small house. There was no heating for five years, only one paraffin heater in the living room. Then the children came and we thought they would get the best education. They got the worst education. They learnt disrespect, about dirty things like sex. I did not know my children any more. Then my daughter wanted to marry a Muslim. Imagine the shame in our community. The people in the gurdwara would not talk to us. She married anyway.

## Racism and discrimination

These changes in family life might have been more bearable if ethnic minority people had had an easier time in the outside world. But, as research has shown,[4] discrimination against the visible minorities in employment and housing has been pervasive from the time they arrived. Some individuals have done well, but for large sections of the ethnic minority community unfair practices relegated them to second class citizens, in spite of the race equality laws. Attitudes in key institutions remained very negative and they faced, and still face, racial violence and abuse.[5]

It is also well established that the people who emigrated to Britain were often those who were physically fit and emotionally strong. Yet when they reached middle age, ethnic minority immigrants began to develop serious chronic illnesses. The hard lives they led have taken their toll.

Nevertheless, whilst it is very important to recognise the extent of discrimination that ethnic minority elders may have experienced, superficial generalisations about this issue are unwise, as Alison Norman reminds us in her book *Triple Jeopardy: Growing old in a second homeland*:

> Too often they [ethnic minorities] are living in conditions of loneliness, fear, sickness, and privation in inner cities. This of course is not the plight of all elderly settlers in this country and it is the plight of many indigenous elderly people who also feel themselves to be 'strangers and afraid' in a hostile world.[6]

## Ethnic minority elders: treated as aliens

Most ethnic minority elders have been continuously reminded that they are considered somehow alien, a burden, not really British.

Here are some comments that were made by various interviewees about the problems they have faced.

■ An elderly Asian woman who lives alone in a council house asked for temporary help from social services when suffering from shingles. The white care assistant told her:

> It is very difficult in our department. We can't even help our own elders. You are lucky living in this country, Mrs Desai.

■ A Nigerian woman who worked as a nursing auxiliary for 40 years described what it was like:

> I was always kept down, laughed at and excluded. So I got angrier and angrier and became like a sore lion. They made me like that. Sometimes patients were racist towards me and I was told it didn't matter. I felt like a human being again, like the warm person I was, the day I retired. But now you get it from the other end. Always being asked whether I am a legal immigrant or not, even in hospital.

■ **Mr Gurdial Singh** again:

> My workmates used to call me such names – curry face, wog, smelly, tea cloth. Some of them were young men. I just smiled and kept quiet. Why make trouble? The only time I complained was when one of them urinated on my feet in the toilet and they all laughed. But the supervisor said not to worry. Now these young men on the streets tell me I am a Paki and I must go home. It hurts me so much.

These experiences have justifiably made many ethnic minority elders bitter.

## Successful ethnic minority elders

There are good stories too, of course. This is why it is dangerous to assume that all people from ethnic minorities regret coming to Britain or feel let down. Some ethnic minority elders say that this country gave them opportunities. Many of them were self-employed and therefore did not rely on employers. They are proud that they were able to make something of their lives through sheer hard work and their skills.

**Mr Patel**, a retired businessman:

> I came here when I was 45 as a refugee from Uganda. We came with nothing, paupers, to a country we did not know. Look at us now. We have 20 shops around the country. I live like a king, no worries. The British people have given me more than I imagined.

But even Mr Patel is of the opinion that the contributions people like him have made to this society, culturally and economically, remain unknown and unrecognised by the majority population.

Ethnic minority elders have also been very successful at organising their own community day centres, sheltered housing and residential homes. These have become a lifeline for them. As time has gone on, the elders, through meeting and having key workers from their own communities, have become more conscious of their own rights and have started to use the system to cater for their needs. Even in the Jewish community, where such initiatives are among the most developed, care homes have been opened to cater specifically for elders who were victims of the holocaust, because they needed a place of their own. In Leicester, for example, there are places such as the Roshni Centre, Scope and Preston Lodge.

## Changing values and circumstances

As we have seen, immigrants from all kinds of communities have to confront threats to their value systems when they move into a new environment. Many of them, including those from other European countries, grew up with very different attitudes towards old age from the ones they now see around them. They would have expected increased respect and better status within the family as they got older, because they would have been seen as sources of experience, wisdom and stability. They would have known that their own families, and not 'strangers' or the state, would, as a matter of pride and obligation, support them within the family network until death.

These people now have to cope with the erosion of these values and the anxieties of what will happen to them if their families cannot or will not look after them.

**Mr Singh** again:

> My sons are better than my daughter, who I hate. They married with our permission. But now they don't like us living in their homes. They don't like the joint family. We are treated like rubbish. You know, I don't mind if I don't have the food or clothes. But no respect at my age, it is better to die. And they are talking about us going into a council house or a home. It is the biggest shame for us.

Even in communities where, in the past, elders would never have been put into institutional care, it is now happening across the country. Sometimes the decision is taken because there are economic problems. In other cases there are social reasons: the extended family is going out of fashion, young people prefer to live in nuclear families (two parents and their children) and tensions between the older and younger generations are growing.

### Family values

These splits within families and other realities such as high unemployment among the younger men of the family mean that it is no longer right to expect certain groups to live up to the convenient stereotype that they 'look after their own'. As ex-Deputy Chairman of the Commission for Racial Equality, Ranjit Sondhi, pointed out during a speech delivered to the Standing Conference of Ethnic Minority Senior Citizens:

> Research shows that not all elders are in poverty or are suffering disadvantage, but equally it shows that not all are adjusted to life in Britain. In some communities there has been an adaptation of traditions and family structures without losing sight of core values, of which caring for elders is one. In other communities, inter-

generational conflict and loss of community identity have eroded care for the elderly as a basic value.[7]

## Economic pressures

Even if children do want to look after their elders in the minority communities, it is becoming more and more difficult for them to do so unless they have done exceptionally well economically. We must remember that the number of elders in these communities is rising rapidly. There are other reasons, too, why elders are having to depend more on state provision. In some families, as with Mr Harrison, the children have moved to other countries. This seems to be happening a great deal in the Afro-Caribbean community, partly because many young people no longer feel they have a future in Britain. In other cases, parents have not been allowed to be united with their children until it is too late. This is what happened to Mr Uddin.

**Mr Uddin**, a Bangladeshi elder:

> I came in 1975 and work in the restaurant. My sons and wife were still in Dacca. They could not come over; now the boys are too old, so they cannot even visit me without the visa. I stay with my brother's family in a small flat. Like a beggar.

## Structural and institutional problems

HOUSING

Another obstacle, which is touched on by Mr Uddin, is that there is little public housing that is big enough to accommodate extended families. Large privately rented or owned properties cost enormous amounts of money, which many simply do not have.

Research has shown consistently that ethnic minority people do not understand the system and end up with less than they are entitled to. The 1991 English House Condition Survey[8] revealed that there is low take-up of housing services by ethnic minority elders. There is also evidence that the number of ethnic minority elders who live in poor housing conditions is disproportionately high, even when they are living with their families.

The General Household Surveys in recent years have clearly shown that Bangladeshi and some other ethnic minority groups live in overcrowded conditions. Enquiries in particular local areas reveal that many ethnic minority elders would prefer to move out, and some were willing even to go into sheltered accommodation. Other research around the country confirms this but also indicates that most black and Asian elders have little information that they need and that most sheltered accommodation does not cater for the religious and other needs of minority groups.

All elderly people have similar housing needs: to be warm, secure in decent accommodation and within reach of family and other members of their community. If Asian and black people are housed by councils in predominately all-white estates, not only do they feel more vulnerable and isolated but they cannot get the food they like and meet other basic needs either.

**Zohrabai,** an Asian elder, describes her life on one such estate until she begged her housing officer to let her move:

All these young boys and girls, children, call me 'Paki' and tell me to go home. I live with my husband who is taking the tablets for depression. I am so scared. Sometimes they throw the banana skins and we cannot get our food in the shops near us. So now I live in Southall and we are so happy. The flat is not so nice, but I feel safe with our own people.

Many, however, feel that they have no right to complain.

**Mr Khan,** a widower from Bradford:

What right do I have to say anything? I am not accepted as really British, and then I know that there are many white pensioners who are also living with no food sometimes, no heating. It would be insensitive to moan about people like me. So just keep quiet, I say.

## INCOME

The 1991 Census revealed that a large number of black and Asian people hold low-paid jobs, so elders who are entirely dependent on their children are hard hit and live in considerable poverty. Home workers and people who arrived in Britain late in their lives do not get state pensions. They have to rely on their children or other relatives, which can lead to family tension and sometimes abuse of the old.

**Savitaben**, an East African Asian widow, who speaks only Gujarati (the quote is translated):

> I have nothing, no money. My son and his wife work all day in the shop. They get up at five in the morning. I am getting old, I have arthritis and I cannot help much any more with the cooking and the children. So I am like a big burden. They don't want me, it is just one more problem. But where can I go? I don't speak English, the house is small, and my son can't pay for me to go to the home.

Research into the problem shows that unequal access to incomes is a particular problem for elders who have entered Britain as sponsored dependants, because they are not entitled to most state benefits. This also is the case when their sponsors, who might have been able to provide for them at the time of entry, can no longer do so because of unemployment, sickness or their own old age. Age Concern in Lewisham discovered that one-quarter of black elders were not receiving full pension entitlements. Black people's low earnings levels mean they are also denied the possibility of saving, purchasing private pension plans and so on.[9]

Black men and certain other groups of ethnic minorities suffer from disproportionately high rates of unemployment or have to work in the informal economy. According to the Labour Force Survey of 1995, 60 per cent of young black men (aged 16–24) in the London area in 1994/5 were unemployed.[10] They and their parents have not been able to acquire the funds and assets that they need to support the elders in their family.

**Raju Patel,** who runs a small corner shop in the Midlands, still cannot forgive himself because he failed to provide a home for his elderly parents:

> I came here from Uganda in 1972, as a refugee. I had a British passport so I could come over here. But my parents had Ugandan passports so they had to go to India. I worked so hard but it was only after ten years that I had the money and the house to bring them over. But before that time both died [*he cries*]. I can never sleep easy because I was the only son and I did not look after them.

Dr Mark Johnson confirms that there is a web of limitations and problems that affects the lives and obligations of ethnic minority families:

> The occupations which the minorities and migrants enter tend to be low paid and insecure. Their children in these areas often obtain a marginal and unsatisfactory education which in turn only suits them for low paid marginal jobs . . . not all will fail in this way, but will have overcome the handicaps and get a better education . . . An obvious consequence of this is that when they retire they will not have high enough savings to allow them to buy an easier life.[11]

### Continuing disadvantages

Many ethnic minority elders will have lived through all kinds of iniquities and unfair treatment while they were working, and they now face further humiliation. Because many do not have an adequate occupational pension, they must apply for means-tested discretionary benefits. If they have worked in harsh conditions, they will often have had to retire early because of chronic health problems or disability.

When they apply for benefits, language barriers and a lack of information about their rights often mean that ethnic minority elders do not get all that they are entitled to; they are often humiliated and confused by the attitudes of counter staff or those providing services in social service departments. And if you don't know what services and benefits exist, how can you ask for them and assert your rights? They also have to accept the impatience and irritation of staff who are hard pressed and do not have time to spend on 'problem' clients.

**Nirmal Kaur** is a social worker who speaks many of the Asian languages. She describes the kinds of encounters she has witnessed:

> They come and sit and look around as if they are in another world. With so many cutbacks, social service departments have no translators. It is hard enough for someone like me, because we are made to feel as if we have no right to claim anything because this is not our country. But for our elders, the workers make so little effort. They treat them like they are idiots because they are old and also because they don't speak English. I often have to pull them up. This social worker who was doing an assessment of a Sikh widow's needs said to me 'God, I wish they spoke some English. It's like getting blood out of a stone. No offence, but why doesn't she go back to her country? At least it is warmer there. I would.' When I checked with the client, it was clear that the social worker had not given her any information at all.

The story is the same in health care and housing, and even in transport when ethnic minority elders apply for their travel cards. There is an irony in all this. Many ethnic minority elders came over here to fill low-paid jobs in the caring sector or in transport. They had to learn how to provide services to a majority group that was culturally very different from their own. But now, when *they* need care, their cultures and values are not catered for.

One could argue that this is now being addressed, mainly because the training for National Vocational Qualifications for care workers and social work includes good anti-discriminatory practice. Anti-Racist Social Work Education by the Central Council for Education and Training in Social Work (CCETSW) also deals specifically with these issues. But much more work is needed to establish and improve such good practice.

## The numbers game

Serious problems can arise if we concentrate on bald statistics when we look at the needs of ethnic minority elders. They are indeed a minority within a minority, although the numbers are expected to double over the next decade. But the absolute numbers we are talking about are still a very small proportion of the total British population. The 1991 Census figures revealed that white people form nearly 98.9 per cent of the older population of this country. Ranjit Sondhi describes his concerns: '[we] run into the numbers game with the phrase "minority within a minority" being used to justify lack of action . . . we must dispel the myth that need is linked to numbers.'[12]

The lack of substantial numbers of ethnic minority elders has other consequences. As Vivienne Coombe wrote in *Race and Social Work*:

> At the present time, social workers are unlikely to have a large number of elderly people from the ethnic minority communities on their case loads . . . the black population in Britain is basically a young one with most of its members economically active . . . It is precisely because the black elderly do not make huge demands that social workers may have difficulty in assessing and interpreting their needs appropriately. This may be compounded by the fact that few social work departments have reached policy decisions on certain aspects of the care of their black elderly. In the next ten years the number of black elderly is expected to rise fourfold . . . Some forward planning is necessary if these clients are to be helped sensitively.[13]

# Myths about culture

Every one of us has a 'culture' that is informed by history and by present circumstances. Somehow, though, the culture of minority communities is seen as strange, exotic and pre-determined. And assumptions in this area are rife. One is that the older people are in some kind of unchanging cultural state. This is not possible for any minority that is surrounded by a more powerful majority culture.

The longer they live here, the more impossible it is for elders even from the most conservative communities to live the way their fore-fathers did.

**Salim Dawoodi** is a mullah in a small mosque. He watches the changes that are taking place among the elders in his congregation:

> They think more about what they are eating, for example, and whether it is healthy, or their weight, things that they would not have worried about before. Many of the women have had small but inde-pendent incomes through these years in Britain – working as home workers mainly. They have become more assertive and fight for the rights of their daughters. One old man came to me the other day and told me that he did not wish to visit his extended family in Pakistan any more because they were too old fashioned in the way they thought about things. So culture changes and moves even for the old. I never used to speak to my father because of fear and respect. Not until he spoke to me. Now my children are very free and open with me and that is better.

But the more damaging assumption – and this particularly affects the way ethnic minority elders are planned for and treated by ser-vice providers – is the persistent idea that certain communities 'look after their own'. This may be the case for some families, but it is dangerous and unfair to base care on such assumptions. An article in *New Community* showed this clearly:

> One of the convenient stereotypes applied to the Asian and black populations in Britain is that, when it comes to caring for the elderly, 'they look after their own'. A health authority gave this as a reason for not catering for Asian people in residential care in a London borough where one out of four people is Asian . . . the same reason was given to explain to us why a health-related agency in Bradford was only now beginning to consider its responsibilities under community care legislation to the Asian and black communities, and a voluntary organisation gave it as a reason for having no contact at all with elderly Asians and black people.[14]

It cannot be taken for granted that everyone has a family who feels an obligation or is in a position to look after their elders. As the same authors explain:

> Informants identified Asian and East European widows as being especially at risk of isolation, because many of them have acquired little English or lose whatever they have with advancing years. Divided families, elderly people on their own, and limited entitlements and negligible support from statutory services all emerged as significant issues.

The most damaging myths are those that try to justify inadequate service delivery. A low uptake of services does not mean that there is a lack of need or that numbers are too small to merit serious consideration.

## Assumptions about cultural hierarchies

Most people who work in the health and social services do so because they care about human beings. But even among them there are problems that are not recognised by the individuals concerned or their managers, precisely because it is assumed that these are caring people. This was pointed out in an Age Concern research report carried out in the London borough of Brent:

> Generally speaking, there is goodwill towards black people by members of the caring professions. However, goodwill alone is not enough . . . white people often hold negative stereotypes of black people and their cultures. The caring professions can develop quite sophisticated negative perceptions, based on their work with people who are in difficulties . . . more seriously, a white social worker may apply white perceptions and values to a problem faced by a black individual, which could result in a total misunderstanding and escalation of underlying problems and undermine the client's cultural and racial identity.[15]

# The dangers of stereotyping

In the past 50 years there has been some change in the way we treat ethnic minority people using public services. Many local authorities and organisations have tried to move away from the 'colour blind' approach and to look at different needs by getting relevant background information. The problem is that the information is often used in simplistic ways and care workers readily stereotype people from the different groups on the basis of the little they know instead of treating everyone as an individual. This is intensely annoying to many in the minority communities.

**Doris**, an active Caribbean woman in her late 60s, puts this argument succinctly:

> Why you want to write about us, eh? I am me, Mrs Doris Phillips to you my dear. Just me. I am black, but I don't go to the black church. There is far too much gossip there. So I go to the white church. I don't eat rice and peas, and I love the cold weather. But yes, I love to chat with my friends about St Lucia, where I came from, and I know that when I am in a room with West Indians I don't have to try to be understood. Don't put us in one basket like all these social service people do.

What is needed is knowledge of sufficient breadth and accuracy to cut through the stereotypes. This means information about the ethnic minority populations of Britain generally, including the diversity within groups, age structures, proportions born in Britain, why they came as immigrants, religions, etc. It means other facts such as unemployment levels, access to benefits, housing and health care. It must also be linked to their experiences of discrimination, self-help and aspirations.

# Specific areas of concern in the caring services

## *Health care provision*

The Commission for Racial Equality says on this issue:

> In terms of health and income, Black and Asian elders are clearly disadvantaged. Where there is a lack of sensitive and high quality health care for elderly generally, ethnic minority elderly face additional problems. Difficulties in communication is one, but the failure of the health service to adapt quickly to the realities of a multilingual, multicultural society is a significant problem.[16]

The following are the major areas of concern.

- Most health care providers have not taken into account the needs and lifestyles of ethnic minority elders.
- Except in a few areas, research of health care needs in the minority communities has not been translated into better practice.
- Communication problems are inadequately understood by providers and practitioners, and there is a lack of health information in various community languages. Even for basic needs such as eye tests and dental hygiene, most of the information and processes assume literacy in English. Often because they do not want to seem demanding, ethnic minority elders do not complain or even say that they have problems with understanding care workers and other experts.
- Elders from various ethnic communities are bewildered and insulted by the jocular and patronising attitudes that are often displayed towards older people by care workers. Most would prefer but do not get same-sex care workers.
- Health education campaigns that target particular problems within certain groups have worked well in the past but, as the health service goes through major structural changes, such approaches are becoming more difficult to co-ordinate.
- Instead of looking at discrimination within the health service that results in an inferior service to ethnic minority patients, the tendency is to seek cultural explanations. If, for example, health centres are not succeeding in imparting new information on diet,

they may blame 'cultural habits' rather than the fact that the information is not accessible because it is available only in English.

■ Although consumer choice within health care is being encouraged, ethnic minority elders are often denied the choices because they lack access to information and facilities.

■ People providing health care are often hostile to patients with communication difficulties, because they need longer consultation periods. Elders suffer most from these attitudes, especially as clinics and hospitals do not, as a matter of course, employ interpreters.

■ With increasing pressure on health service providers to cut back, ethnic minority patients are often checked up on and made to feel as if they don't deserve consideration. One black elder was told by a harassed nurse in hospital: 'You people are so demanding. Don't you understand that things are changing? That we cannot be there to do everything for you?'

■ Sometimes even professionals from ethnic minorities have negative attitudes. One Asian GP told the daughter of a 75-year-old Asian woman from the same community: 'I know that your mother will want to see me all the time. I know our people, they can be such a nuisance. They come for the smallest things. Tell her that I will not do special things for her.' This attitude has been confirmed by researchers. Even when there are no language barriers between the doctor and the patient, there are often others of class, educational snobbery and status.

### Attitudes to illness

People from non-western cultures have different concepts and beliefs about health and illness from those from the West. Immigrants retain many of their original beliefs and incorporate what they pick up in their new homeland as well. Often these non-western cultures believe that illness is due to more than just a malfunctioning of the body. They may attribute ill-health to bad luck, God's punishment for misdemeanours in this or a previous life or a spell cast by an enemy. For elders these may be very deeply held beliefs, which should be understood and not mocked or disregarded.

## Domiciliary services

Meals-on-wheels, day centre services, luncheon clubs and home care assistants in the main are geared to meet the needs of the indigenous population. These days it is more or less accepted that many Jewish elders require kosher food, and some areas now also provide halal and vegetarian food. But, in general, not enough thought is given to the specific needs of different elders as a matter of policy. Studies show that such people tended not to use certain services because they were not appropriate.[17]

Many ethnic minority groups simply do not know what is available or how to get what they need. A study in the Midlands found this to be true: only 16 per cent of Asians, for example, knew about care assistants.

## Statutory changes in health and social service provision

The Patient's Charter, introduced by the Department of Health in 1991, says: 'All health authorities should make provision so that proper personal consideration is shown to you, for example by ensuring your privacy, dignity and religious and cultural beliefs are respected.' But go into almost any hospital where there are large numbers of ethnic minority patients and these basic guarantees are rarely respected. It is little wonder that most black and Asian people regard such charters as something for the white population and not for them.

The main social services aspects of the NHS and Community Care Act 1990 were implemented in 1993, and have many serious implications for ethnic minority elders. The major aim of community care is to provide, through careful assessments, appropriate care to people who cannot manage to look after themselves and, where possible, to cater for them 'in the community'. In fact, the two pillars of the legislation are 'needs-led services' and 'choice'.

Potentially these open up prospects for all elders but in practice almost all authorities are largely failing to provide the kind of care that is required by elders in our community because of a lack of resources.

In an article in *Community Care*, Josephine Kwhali, Assistant Director of Quality Assurance and Planning for Hammersmith and Fulham Social Services Department, wrote:

> It is impossible to have credible progress unless efforts have been made to establish what different groups of black users are saying they want in respect of their community care needs. Black people do not speak with one voice. They have different life experiences, different levels of consciousness, different strategies for addressing racism and discrimination and different beliefs. However, there is enough uniformity in the black message for local authorities to be aware of black people's collective desire to have services where they can eat the food they like, follow their religious and spiritual beliefs and converse with others who share their language: and not be discriminated against by staff or other service users.[18]

The White Paper that led to the community care legislation acknowledged the need to cater for people with different cultural backgrounds. It asserted that 'Good community care will take account of the circumstances of minority communities and will be planned in consultation with them.' The main elements of the legislation are:

- Consultation
- Planning
- Co-operation between different agencies and professionals
- Assessment/care packages

But none of this is really possible if resources are inadequate and there is a lack of proper knowledge or awareness of the needs of ethnic minority elders except at a basic stereotyped level.

**Mrs Patel**, 75, lives on her own in a council flat in west London. Her daughter lives nearby with her English husband and her family. She visits her mother three times a week. Mrs Patel has a care assistant twice a month and on the whole she manages very well. But in 1994, she developed severe arthritis down her right arm which left her unable to function at all. After an assessment, she was assigned a care worker who goes in every day for two hours. The person sent was Jamaican, on the basis that, as another 'black' person, she would be more appropriate. Mrs Patel found her impossible to relate to:

> I did not understand her English, she cooked food which I did not like – I am a vegetarian and she did not know how to make our food. She cut my hair off because she said it was a problem to comb it and then put Vaseline in it. But I did not complain because she was not a bad person and I did not want her to lose her job. She did not like me also because I was Asian and she thinks that we people don't like black people. But that is not true for me.

It is a false assumption that, when services are improved in general for the wider population, everybody benefits. What is more likely to happen is that, because the majority feel better looked after, the needs of the minorities cease to matter to any significant degree. The gap between these two groups then grows and inequality increases.

Finally, therefore, the prospects for ethnic minority elders are not good unless these issues are seriously taken on board. Most experts in the field, such as Naina Patel, are not hopeful: '… the Community Care Bill [now the NHS and Community Care Act] promises not only more of the same but a worse scenario of service provision in a highly restrictive, chaotic, and ever shrinking welfare society'.[19]

Nevertheless, whatever happens in the wider arena, care workers can do much to provide more responsive, sensitive and informed care to ethnic minority elders. And this book aims to help in that process. In the chapters that follow, information is provided on ten key ethnic minority communities. The main issues that affect their lives are discussed, and interviews with elders from those communities illustrate the facts that have been provided.

# 3 The Black communities

In this book 'black' is used to refer to Africans and Afro-Caribbeans. We look in general at the two categories and not at the individual countries or islands, although of course Africa is a continent with various nations and traditions and the different Caribbean communities feel a strong bond with the particular places they come from. Europe is not a homogenous continent, and neither are Africa or the Caribbean. But there is enough common ground to justify the broad categorisation. It is important, however, to remember that diversity and difference, even antagonism, are as common under this broad identity as for any other group. The main areas in the Caribbean that people emigrated from are Jamaica, Trinidad, St Lucia, Barbados, Guyana and the Dominican Republic.

Black Britons have a shared traumatic history: slavery. This binds them together and has affected them in the same way that Jewish history has deeply influenced Jewish people around the world. For centuries, black people have been oppressed, exploited, denied rights and judged on the basis of their skin colour. The painful history in both of these groups has produced people who are extraordinary survivors.

Black people have been in Britain for centuries, and were the first to arrive when substantial migration began after World War 2. There followed a long struggle in this country and many elders see what is happening to them now as part of that struggle. But the survival skills of these migrants were and continue to be profoundly impressive and part of their story of settlement.

Jeff Crawford, a senior community relations officer, wrote in 1978 about black elders:

> The ethnic elderly are the forgotten ones, the unheard ones . . . It is as if they have suddenly appeared from nowhere in spite of the fact that a number of them, especially the West Indians, have been living and working for nearly 30 years in some cases. They now find that, having substantially contributed to the rebuilding of Britain after World War II, and having taken less out of the state than they have put into it, they are probably among the worst off of the retired.[1]

# THE AFRO-CARIBBEAN COMMUNITY
## History

Most people don't know that black people have been here for nearly 500 years. Some were born in Britain as early as 1505. In the seventeenth and eighteenth centuries young black men and women were brought here as domestic slaves. Others came here later to escape slavery.

Even during these early years, official panic about the numbers of black people and whether they had a right to be in the country had already begun. Queen Elizabeth I issued an order on 11 July 1596:

> Her Majesty understanding that several blackamoors have lately been brought into this realm, of which kind there are already too many here . . . her Majesty's pleasure therefore is that those kinds of people should be expelled from the land . . .[2]

That basic attitude to black people as undesirable and a 'problem' and not rightfully here has persisted through the years.

There has been little acknowledgement in this country of how much Britain directly benefited from slavery. For example, in the eighteenth century, 20 million guns were made in Birmingham – creating thousands of jobs – to export to the African coast in order to facilitate the slave trade. Companies in that same city were actively involved in selling slaves in America. Liverpool, Bristol and other places owed their prosperity to the slave trade and related activities; these are also the places with some of the oldest black and mixed race families in Britain. Many black elders feel that this history needs to be acknowledged so that people can accept that black people have contributed to the advances made in this country for many centuries.

## Why does all this matter?

General awareness of this history is important because, as James Baldwin the black American writer once said: 'People are trapped in history and history is trapped in them.'

For **George Brown**, a black Briton who was born here in the 1950s, such facts represent more than just a hidden history:

As we move to the end of the century, as the welfare state begins to be dismantled, as white racism grows in Europe because it is encouraged by politicians who want to see a white fortress, these are the facts that will determine our rights to be here, to be European. The Industrial Revolution, capitalism across the continent, the wealth generated over the centuries, has come from our toil as much as it has from white Europeans. More, really, because we were exploited more. So when my father, who suffers from senile dementia, is denied respect and care, I fight for him as someone who is British through and through.

There are records from the nineteenth and early twentieth centuries of black servants who were abandoned by their masters or who left their masters because of cruelty, and of seafaring men who had been sacked and had no way of returning home.

The outbreak of World War 1 in 1914 created a need for black labourers, who were made welcome in the munitions and chemical factories. Black seamen were recruited into the merchant navy. By the end of the war there were 20,000 black people in Britain. In 1917, a colonial administrator, Sir Harry Johnston, wrote a book called *The Black Man's Part in the War*, describing the gallantry of black soldiers.[3] But this made no difference to how they were viewed in this country. In fact, even as they were recovering from terrible wounds, some of these black soldiers – many without limbs –were attacked in hospital by white soldiers.

By 1919, when a significant number of black people began to be seen in urban areas, this white hatred erupted on the streets. Unemployment among the black population rose and attacks against them, particularly in Liverpool and Cardiff, were rife. An editorial in the *Liverpool Courier* commented at the time:

> One of the chief reasons for popular anger behind the present disturbances lies in the fact that the average Negro is nearer the animal than is the average white man and that there are women in Liverpool who have no self-respect . . . it is true that many of the blacks in Liverpool are of a low type, that they insult and threaten respectable women in the street, that they are invariably unpleasant and provocative.[4]

Such views have not altogether disappeared even as we reach the end of the twentieth century.

## World War 2

World War 2 brought in a large number of black volunteers from the Caribbean islands. Most of them joined the Royal Air Force. They were proud to fight for king and country but, although they were accepted in some ways by their peers, it was rarely as equals. The following was published in a magazine in 1946:

> Colonial troops came to this country to help us win the war. But they are bitter because the colour bar still exists in Britain. They are shunned at service camps, banned from hotels and called intruders . . . At one RAF station, just before a detachment of West Indian airmen was due to arrive, all the WAAFs were called together and told that, though they had to be polite to the coloured Colonials, they were on no account to 'fraternise' . . . The West Indians were, in fact to be treated like pariahs in the community of the camp. Yet these men had come of their own accord 5,000 miles to a strange land and unfriendly climate to help us in the war.[5]

It was mainly men who had come over, and many of them married white women. Life was not easy for either partner, and there are some deeply moving stories that elders tell of such mixed marriages. To them this history is still very much alive.

**Ethel** was born in the north of England. She came to London after the war and ended up working as a prostitute. Then she gave birth to a black child. The father had been an engineer in the RAF. He married her and she lived with his family, scorned by the white neighbours. She now lives in an all-white residential home:

> Once when we were coming out of a club, a policeman, a big man, stopped us and asked me why I was going with a nigger. He would not believe that we were married and thought I was picking him up. So he came to check our house and I could tell he was more shocked that I was married to him than if I had been going with him. Frank died in 1967. Here in the home I can't tell these ladies about any of that, of course.

**Brenda,** the daughter of such a mixed marriage, knew many women like Ethel when she was growing up in west London:

> I think in spite of all the racism, they were women first, and on the whole women are more human. In fact, when black men were being repatriated after the war, some of these white women tried to protect them, hide them and help them. My mother married my father to stop his deportation. Many of the relationships which started in the camps thrived. But there were other problems. I am very religious and believe in the spiritual life but the churches turned their backs on black people. So my family never went to the white churches although my mother is white. Now of course it is just as bad. They live on an estate where other white elders ignore them and the young kids call them names.

When care workers hear these stories, it can make a difference to the way they interact with their black clients.

**Sebastian**, in Birmingham:

> You know my regular home help, Sandra, a lass from Yorkshire, when she started coming here, she was so distant, like she did not like someone like me. Then bit by bit I told her my story. How I came during the war, how I met my wife Maggie who was from the north, how we used to dance the jitterbug, how she died. I showed her pictures of me in uniform, and my daughter – beautiful she was just before she was killed in a crash. Now Sandra is like my daughter born again.

Some of the Caribbeans returned to the islands after the war; others, like Sebastian, stayed.

This history is fresh in the heads and hearts of many Caribbean people, not just because it reminds them of how difficult it has been for them to be accepted in this society, but because so many white people seem never to have acknowledged what they owe black people. This is not to say that all white people behaved in racist ways or that black immigrants were forever victims. The true picture of this time is full of struggle but also strength and support – often given by white working-class women.

## Forgotten contributions

In 1995, with the many celebrations and tributes to those who fought in World War 2, the contributions of Africans and Afro-Caribbeans barely got a mention.

This invisibility affects people's rights here and now, for in Britain those who fought in the two world wars are regarded as 'truly British'. For example, one lady from Surrey said on a radio phone-in programme in 1995: 'When you think of how people died for this country, it makes me furious to see what we have done to our beautiful land. With all this multicultural nonsense.' A young nurse who had been dealing with an angry and abusive senile black elder reacted thus: 'Look, this is my country. If you don't like it, just sod off.' Such experiences are commonplace and need to be understood by care workers.

## Black migration after the war

On 22 June 1948, the *Empire Windrush* brought 492 Jamaicans over to this country, the first of many to arrive and settle in Britain after World War 2. By 1958, the community of Afro-Caribbeans had grown to 125,000. Many had been actively recruited in their own countries. Newspapers ran headlines such as 'Welcome Home'. Besides the heavy industries, which were trying to renew themselves after the war years, the budding welfare state needed them in the National Health Service, as did London Transport and the service sector. Many were skilled craftsmen or small traders and farmers.

**EMPLOYMENT AND IMMIGRATION 1955–1960**

|      | Demand for labour | Arrivals from the West Indies |
|------|-------------------|-------------------------------|
| 1956 | 934,111           | 26,441                        |
| 1957 | 725,271           | 22,473                        |
| 1958 | 535,186           | 16,511                        |
| 1959 | 653,120           | 20,397                        |
| 1960 | 848,542           | 45,706                        |

Research reports indicate how, by the 1960s and early 1970s, black workers were concentrated in low-grade jobs with a 'a higher likelihood of experiences of unemployment, of physically arduous and hazardous work, of undesired shift work and of low pay'.[6] These people were British citizens: the 1948 Nationality Act had freely handed over passports to all ex-subjects. Most of the people who came were skilled and ambitious, yet most had to settle for poorly paid jobs which in time deskilled them.

School back home had given them the impression of Britain as a great country full of highly educated people and wonderful opportunities. It was also their 'motherland'. There was no official policy to settle these migrants, and most had to make do living with other black people in cramped and inferior accommodation while working in low-paid jobs. This did not discourage the migrants from wanting to mix with white Britons. Sadly, more often the favour was not returned and white people who tried to break the colour bar were themselves victimised.

**Mr Morton** was a bespoke tailor from Jamaica:

> I used to make suits for all the high and mighty back home. Even the whites. I had a name, they used to call me 'Lightning' because I would look at a design and make it up so quick. What did I end up doing here? Cleaning floors in hospitals. But it seemed worth it for the sake of the children. The only time I felt I had my respect back was when I went to church in one of my old suits, until they began to fray.

### Dispersal

There are about 750,000 Afro-Caribbeans in Britain today. Most of them live in inner city areas such as Brixton in London and Handsworth in Birmingham.

# The experiences of black immigrants

The problems experienced by Afro-Caribbeans were complex and different from those faced by Asians. In terms of religion and culture, black immigrants from the Caribbean regarded themselves as part of Britain. Everything they had learnt in school had taught them that, except for skin colour, there was no difference between them and white Britons. All the signs they had been given by the home country – the invitations to come here, the recruitment advertisements in the West Indian papers – seemed to suggest that white Britons too thought of Caribbeans as brethren. But the reality was very different. They could not get lodgings; notices on doors and windows often said: 'No Blacks or Irish'. A book published in 1960 describes how black people were treated in this country:

> Coloured people are feared as competitive intruders; they are thought of as promoters of crime and carriers of disease; they are resented when they are poor; they are envied when they are resourceful and thrifty. They are looked down upon; they are patronised.[7]

They pooled their meagre resources to buy run-down properties in inner city areas, where many of them still live and are getting old. They felt unsafe in pubs because often they would not be served and many of them were picked on, so they had parties in their own homes. At work, although some white people made an effort to welcome them and make friends, most of them recall how during breaks they would be isolated away from the white workers. Employers exploited them and discriminated against them; the trade unions were little better. Even the churches were hostile to black people in the congregation, so black churches had to be set up to serve their own.

Their sense of betrayal and disappointment was acute. Some got angry and organised into groups such as The Black Alliance, promoting black consciousness and fighting racism. Others took a more stoic view, kept their heads down and put their faith in God and their people to see them through. Some simply went mad.

**Trevor Holmes**, a black pensioner who came to this country as a young man:

> I remember a neighbour, a bright breezy young man he was, living near Ladbroke Grove. He was a snappy dresser, loved life. The only job he could get was as a cleaner. He just got ground down. Then he started getting that look in his eyes. One day we heard that he had ended up in some asylum after gouging his eye out with teaspoon.

In spite of the hardships, most of these black people kept their spirits strong. It is interesting to note that mental illness is less common among black elders than among their children who were born in Britain.

White Britons were shocked when black people, recruited to take on the essential but dirty jobs the whites did not want to do, demanded equal rights and opportunities. Even after the empire faded away, many white people hoped to keep the old world order going with their internal subjects.

**Veronica,** a white woman who uses the same day care centre as Mr Morton, is an example:

> I mean I have nothing against coloured people. Some of them can be quite nice. My friend Mary was married to one of them and he was a real gentleman. Mr Morton here is my friend and he will get me stamps if I need them. But why are they always complaining? This isn't their country, so why do they expect more and more? They have jobs here, over there they would be nothing. They should be grateful.

Knowing the real history of why black people came here and why they should have the same rights as white elders helps you to inform people with such views. This should, of course, be done with tact and patience. It is not helpful to abuse white elders for the views they hold; many simply don't know better. Others need polite but firm responses.

Unlike people from many other ethnic groups, most black elders rightly feel a strong consciousness of their rights in this country, and this is why they face such hostility from people like Veronica who are ignorant of the facts. There are others who feel strongly that the black communities should not pull back into their own ghettos.

**Antony Robinson,** an elder from Guyana:

> I have all sorts of friends. I think it is a big mistake for us to feel that all white people are racist or the best thing for us is to be with our own. We share problems. We should unite with others.

It is important to understand that in terms of religion and culture, except for food, black people are more similar to white Britons than most other ethnic minority groups. There are some differences, of course. For example, the fact that, in the Caribbean and in Britain, because of slavery and other historical reasons (such as the lack of work near where they lived) that took black men away from their homes, children are generally brought up by the women in the family. Family ties and expectations are strong, just as they are among many white working class communities such as the miners.

Remember that, if you can establish a rapport with these elders, the experience is mutually rewarding. And though life has been tough for many of them, they do not sit around moping. Laughter, teasing and story telling are part of their heritage.

Some specific areas that you should be aware of so that you can provide a more relevant service to black elders include the following:

- Although English is their language, like the Irish and the Scots, Afro-Caribbeans have their own accents and ways of communicating. It is much better to admit (politely) that you have not understood something than to pretend that you have.
- Sometimes elders in these communities seem quiet and subservient. Empowering them and giving them a sense that they have rights is very important.
- As with all older people, the key to understanding them is to relate to their own individual and collective histories. The past is often more real than the present.

In schools in the 1950s and 1960s, black children were taught nothing about their identity. They were taught to be English but were never accepted as equals. Their expectations that they would be treated as equals were higher than those of their parents, and their sense of outrage was inevitably greater.

Even caring teachers made false assumptions of how far black children should be pushed. They were encouraged in areas like sport but academically their potential was often neglected. Recent research shows that this is still a problem in many inner city schools. Black parents formed organisations to battle for better education for their children, even though they were discouraged from getting involved. Many were thought to be too hard on their children when it came to discipline.

**Hatty,** whose son is currently in prison, mourns:

> We were always told not to discipline our children the way we were
> disciplined. That it was wrong to stop a child from doing anything.
> Our children were told to report any actions they did not like by their
> parents. Our children were taught to look down on us. So they had no
> guidance, no religion, and then white people rejected them. They are
> the lost people in our community. And I will die – I am getting on –
> not forgiving myself or this country for where my young man has
> ended up.

**Mr Thomas,** another black elder, feels just as forlorn:

> You know all this violence in Brixton last year [1995] the kids were
> angry and they were right to be angry after the way the police treat
> them all. But the way they behave I don't recognise them at all. They
> even attacked shops run by older black people. Some of these kids are
> so hard, even I am afraid of them. Some of our kids did OK too, you
> know, and we are proud of them – Diane Abbot, Trevor Phillips. It
> makes me so proud. But too many have fallen into the ditches of life
> and I don't know who to blame for that.

Some Afro-Caribbean young people are angry that their parents
migrated to this country, and also think that, once here, they were
too compliant.

**Flora,** a 21-year-old unemployed hairdresser:

> Why did they come and take us out of our world? Look how crazy
> and mixed up we all are now. These whites treated them like dirt and
> they said nothing.

Others feel a sense of real pride that their parents managed to survive in spite of all the odds that were stacked against them.

# Important facts about the Afro-Caribbean community

- Most Afro-Caribbean elders have lived here for more than 40 years.
- They came to Britain both because they were needed by this country and because they needed jobs. There were also many myths circulating in the islands – encouraged by the British government – about how this was their motherland.
- The immigrants who came have worked all these long years, although mostly in low-paid, low-status jobs.
- Most of them live in council accommodation. Owner-occupiers and those renting properties are, like council tenants, concentrated in inner city areas.
- Afro-Caribbeans see their identity, at least in part, in terms of where they originally came from. There is a lot of variation in the foods of the different islands.
- Many Afro-Caribbean elders are practising Christians and the church is an important point of mutual support for them. Many are Pentecostalists, Seventh Day Adventists and Jehovah's Witnesses. Some are Baptists, Anglicans, Roman Catholics and Methodists.
- Seventh Day Adventists avoid pork and stimulants such as alcohol, tea and coffee. Jehovah's Witnesses do not allow blood transfusions.
- Rastafarianism is followed but mainly among the young. Very strict dietary restrictions apply to practising Rastafarians.
- Traditions from back home do survive among the elders. Some are felt to be extremely important, such as collective grieving rituals when someone dies. There is usually a Remembrance Night Service which allows this to happen.
- The incidence of both hypertension and stroke is high in this community.
- A disproportionately high number of young black men are in prison, and a high proportion of young black boys are excluded from schools.

■ Young black women are often better educated because many of them return to higher education as adults.

## Issues affecting Afro-Caribbean elders

This is not a comprehensive list and the points do not apply to all Afro-Caribbean people. Remember to treat people as individuals: never assume anything and always check information with the person you are dealing with.

### Income

Studies have shown that, besides the loneliness, poverty, ill-health and infirmity that may be experienced by many elders in Britain, Afro-Caribbean elders have added problems. Many have had a shorter working period in this country than the established population, so they will be getting only a partial state pension. Although those who worked throughout their time here – particularly in the public sector – would be properly protected, there are many who were employed in areas where work was erratic and so they had long periods of unemployment because of discrimination. Savings were therefore not accumulated. People who have come to join their families as dependants are usually not eligible for state benefits, and this stretches many families to breaking point.

### Racism

Many of those operating the benefits systems seem increasingly suspicious of ethnic minority people, whom the tabloid press often target as dishonest and 'bogus'. Black elders believe that what they are receiving is theirs by right because they have toiled in this country, but they also feel that they are treated in a way that demeans them.

**John Harvey**, 75, tried to go to a luncheon club near his home:

I heard there was such a place so I went along one day. Smartly dressed you know, with my newspaper in my hand. I walked in and

> you should have seen the way they stopped talking, looked at me like I was a lizard. No one came to say hello. After ten minutes, I just left.

## Crime

Fear of crime and abuse profoundly affects the lives of black elders. Home Office figures reveal that black and Asian people are disproportionately more likely to be the victims of crime than are white people. As many of them live in deprived areas where crime is more common, their fears are often justified. Added to this is the reminder they have to face daily that, in the view of many white pensioners, crime is carried out mainly by blacks. However, both black and white elders believe that, in general, the young are worse behaved and less respectful than before.

**Bill**, a black elder living in Brent, London:

> You don't know what it feels like to be black and be talking to some of these white people you know. After Condon made his speech about black muggers, this woman at the bus stop asked me why our kids are so out of control and mugging old white ladies. What am I supposed to say? I told her that I had been pushed around by some white youngsters that very day but I don't think all white kids are thugs.

## Media images

The media continue to create stereotypes of the black community. They are often reported as perpetrators of crime or misdemeanour – as muggers, rapists, rioters, drug dealers and suchlike; or they are 'sunshine' people fond of sport and entertainment, free and easy and more than a little interested in sex. More recent images are those of black lone mothers, drop-out school children, aggression and anti-social behaviour. Rarely do we get the picture of a community with profound religious and moral beliefs, of people who have worked incredibly hard to survive and the huge array of talent that black people can rightly feel proud of. White care workers often unthinkingly take on these stereotypes.

# Religion

Many Afro-Caribbean elders are practising Christians who go to their own churches. Some are members of Seventh Day Adventist or Pentecostal churches. In general, the faith of black Christians is deep and their religion, some would say, has kept them going all these years. The black churches have services that tend to involve active participation from the congregation. Singing and vocal shared praying are fairly common. When there are family events, the congregation participates fully and the sense of a Christian community is very strong. Although each black elder is an individual, the sense of belonging to a strong community of faith is stronger perhaps than you would get in most urban mainstream churches.

# Diet

Afro-Caribbeans often feel that their dietary needs are not generally understood or met. In some ways this has been more difficult to argue for than for some Asian groups because there are cultural meeting points between the white and the black communities. But Afro-Caribbean food is distinct and there are also important differences between the islands, and elders would like at least to have a choice.

Food tends to be spiced up, sometimes hot with red peppers and chilli, and the staple preference is for rice, yams (sweet potatoes) and green bananas. Dried fish is popular, as are rotis which are like flour tortillas rolled up with different fillings. There are all kinds of different ways of cooking meat, chicken and especially fish. It is now possible to buy most Caribbean food in Britain. The cooking has been influenced by the food of many different countries, including Britain, Spain, India and Africa.

# Festivals

Christmas is of course celebrated. The days when the different Caribbean countries became independent are also very important, as is the August Carnival time when the entire country joins Caribbeans in what has become one of the biggest social events in Britain. There are many elders in the Notting Hill area of London who started the Carnival in the 1960s because they were so homesick.

## Clothes and appearance

Although most Afro-Caribbeans wear western clothes, the elders like to dress 'properly'. Home care assistants need to know how to take care of Afro hair and what products to use on the skin to keep it from drying up. On the hair, for example, coconut oil or Vaseline products are used in order to make combing easier. Hair-straightening products are also used by older women. Specialist skin creams suitable for black skin tend not to be stocked in ordinary chemist's shops but cocoa butter, which is easy to find, is a popular choice among most black women. In areas with large black populations (eg Tottenham in London), there are now many hairdressing salons and beauty shops that cater for black people, and further information can be obtained from them.

## Language, culture and values

All Caribbean people speak English, but they have made the language their own. Some speak a patois, and there is a wide variety of accents and also vocabulary and structures that you would not find in standard English. There is nothing offensive about asking black people to repeat or explain something you have not understood. It is the way you ask this that makes the difference. The impact of the following two sentences would be completely different, for example.

- Come again?
- Sorry, I didn't quite understand that; would you explain/repeat it please?

Many black people feel that they have lost the kind of respect they would have had in their own countries, where old age is viewed not as a problem but as something inevitable and to be valued. They crave respect from society in general and from their families in particular. Some are lucky enough to get the latter at least. A third have no families in Britain at all. They might also feel a growing hostility towards the values of the place they have made their home and which they once idolised.

**Mr Thomas** again:

> When you are young and ambitious and go-getting and innocent, England seems like the place to be to move forward into the modern times. When you get old you see the flaws in the values of this country. The way they throw their old on the rubbish heap, the total lack of respect for age and for experience even for their own old people. So you feel regret.

Cultural misunderstandings often arise between care workers and their black clients, which is why it is so important to ask and to check assumptions. Many black elders are very direct in the way they express themselves. They do not use the indirect and understated forms of communication that many middle-class white Britons use. This can seem impolite but it is rarely meant to be. If an elder says 'Give it to me, girl', for example, without 'will you?' at the end or 'please' at the beginning, it sounds abrupt but this is not intended.

Ask 'how', 'why', 'what', 'when' questions as you go along. It is the only way you can build up knowledge about how different groups and individuals in those communities see the world and live their lives. This needs to be done with respect and a sense of humour.

**Hatty**, who used to be a care worker:

> You get these conflicts. We always pick at lentils before we cook them; one social worker thought this black woman was going mad

when she saw her doing this. Most of us keep cleaning cloths for the kitchen separate from the ones we use in the bathroom and we rinse all our dishes; so many home helps don't understand such things and it can be very annoying.

## Family life

Many black elders are experiencing other unique problems within their families and communities. On the whole, in terms of opportunities, black men face more discrimination than many other groups in this country. Far too many of them are in prison; many others are deeply disillusioned. Lone parenthood among young black women is high, although it is equally true that black women are entering higher education as adults in impressively high numbers. Although Caribbean family structures have never really conformed to the white nuclear model of two parents and their children (this is also true of more than half the world), with the break-up of the extended family networks that served people so well in the Caribbean there is concern that the black family unit in Britain is under terrible strain. Many black elders are deeply worried about this, especially as it means that in many ways their expectations of family support are no longer feasible. It is important not to blame the families or to see them as somehow deviant. What has happened is often a result of the negative experiences many black people have had in this country and the economic hardships they have had to endure.

Many Afro-Caribbean elders feel a sense of guilt, loss and deep sadness at the way things have turned out. They also have mixed feelings about 'back home'. But probably just as many are resilient people who will not let all this get them down. It is important to realise that in certain aspects black elders consider themselves to be much more fortunate than their white peers. The mutual comfort and support they provide each other, especially in the context of their churches, is something they are very proud of. In some ways they feel that they survived better than the younger generation sometimes seems to.

**Hatty,** again, says:

> We have so little, but we will always share it, you know? If we know one of us is ill we will take some food, visit, make sure that they know we are there. I can still bake, so I take a little something to church on Sundays for those who can't. The older men will help sometimes with things in the homes of the widows. And I think we respect each other. And when someone dies we are there with the family, grieving properly for days, seeing the people off like they mattered to us. And not leaving families to cry alone. And our faith is so strong and living, you should come to the church and see the feelings and the singing. We can then cope with death better. You know, we black people should be more proud. I would rather be a black and old than white and old.

## Return: myth or reality?

There are indeed black people who are thinking of going back – many for negative reasons, but others because they wish to end their lives in a warmer place. (Many white Britons have retired to Spain for similar reasons.) At present it is not possible for black elders to return to their countries and get the same amount of financial support they are getting here, inadequate as it is. For many, though, it was always their intention to go back.

**June Robinson** worked part-time in hospital catering for 35 years:

> We all came for a few years, but there were so many problems that money in our pockets never stayed there long enough for us to go back. It was a losing battle. Like a sack with a hole. Now with this small pension in our pockets, how do you go back? I would be so ashamed that all this time and this is all I got to take back. The relatives would just laugh at my foolishness.

They also feel that the country they left behind has changed so much that they would feel as alien there as they do here.

**Mr Thomas** again:

> Jamaica had problems but now it is a hard cruel place. I felt so upset when I went there to visit. All the dirt, pollution, violence, industries. Better the evil you know, I think.

## Illness and death

Attitudes to health and remedies are different from those in the white community. Elders will tend to use a combination of faith and prayer, home and herbal remedies and mainstream medical facilities.

There are some conditions that Afro-Caribbeans are particularly prone to. Sickle cell disease is one of these. It is a very painful and debilitating condition that can be managed but never cured. Fatigue is one effect, which makes life very difficult for Afro-Caribbean elders. It has also emerged in recent years that this community is prone to heart disease, chronic conditions such as rheumatism and also mental illness, though this last problem is more common among the young. Many of the problems are the result of physical and mental stress over many years.

As Hatty says, the main things that distinguish the community are the family and the support that is offered to the dying and their relatives. For at least two weeks, families, friends and neighbours offer their support to the bereaved family. They will do the cooking and cleaning and look after the children. There is no expectation that bereaved people should keep grief inside themselves. Communal crying and grieving goes on for days, but for those with faith there is also optimism that the person has passed on to a better world.

## Appropriate services

Many black elders feel a need for day centres where they can meet, reminisce and share a sense of history and community with others who have been through similar experiences. This should not be interpreted as reverse racism. As they get older, people with similar personal experiences need to meet and communicate with one another. This is as true of ethnic minorities as it is of the wider white community.

According to local studies, Afro-Caribbean elders seem to be generally well informed about the services available to them. A study in Coventry showed that 80 per cent knew about the range of provision in the area to cater for elders. But, interestingly, at most only 32 per cent made use of some of these services. In Nottingham, it was found that 84 per cent rejected homes for the elderly and 72 per cent failed to use meals-on-wheels.[8] This is probably because the services are centred on the needs of white people except where there are large numbers of black elders involved and where either the local authority or (more likely) the black voluntary sector is providing the right food, for example.

Remember that black elders are individuals. There are atheists, those who would argue that life in Britain has been more than gratifying, and those who say there has been no discrimination against them in this country.

**Marcus**, an ex-train driver, breaks every general point we have made in this chapter so far. He and his wife live in Pinner (north London), and he has this to say:

All this talk about racialism and all that. Our people don't know a good thing. When in Rome do as the Romans do, I say. Go to Jamaica, they kill you for a few chickens. No benefits, nothing. Dirt everywhere. I worked hard, saved my money and bought this nice house. We do the garden, our children are well educated and they care for us. Don't think we are all sorry people. I am proud to be British.

# Rastafarians

This is a distinct group within the Afro-Caribbean community, with its own religion and strictly prescribed dietary and other rules. They believe that Haile Selassie, once emperor of Ethiopia, was the son of God.

Rastafarians believe very strongly that you are what you eat. They try to eat only 'uncontaminated' foods that do not contain additives and preservatives. Most do not drink alcohol, and are vegetarians. Those who do eat meat would never eat pork. (This is also true of Seventh Day Adventists.) Rastafarians do not cut or brush their hair and wear it in dreadlocks, which they wash and oil regularly.

Rastafarians are among the most misunderstood people in this country, and many of them have had to learn to live daily with racism directed against them.

**Patrick**, a young Rastafarian:

> We are just regarded by the police, housing officers and social workers as dangerous, because we have dreadlocks and because we do smoke ganja [marijuana]. But what they don't know is how self-controlled we are and how we look after ourselves and our children and how much we respect life.

# THE AFRICAN COMMUNITY
## History, origin and dispersal

At present there are only a few thousand African elders in Britain. This is partly because they arrived much later than Afro-Caribbeans, often in the 1960s as adult students who did not return home. Most are from West African countries, although there are some who came from southern Africa and also East Africa. They tend to live in our larger cities.

Most Africans have a particularly strong national or continental identity. They too have been colonial subjects and victims of racism and indifference, but in some ways their expectations when they came here were more practical and less idealistic than those of the Afro-Caribbeans:

**Alphonse Otiengo**, originally from East Africa:

> I came here as a political refugee when I was in my thirties. I never thought then that I was coming home. My father had fought for independence and had been punished by the British. So I came here quite cynical. Life has been hard, and for us our countries are still in turmoil so it is not really possible to go off home. But before I die, I do want to go back, to return to all those ancestral spirits. With all the changes in Social Security payments for burial, our bodies can't be sent back the way they were once. You feel very worried about things like that.

## Equal opportunities

In other ways, though, the experiences of African elders are very similar to those of Afro-Caribbean elders. Many Africans fought in World War 2. Yet, like other black people, they are also often denied equal opportunities. But because they are so few in number it has been difficult to argue for special provision for this group. Nevertheless, it is important to remember that Africans generally have high educational qualifications and some in Britain have done very well indeed, particularly in the professions.

## Confused with Afro-Caribbeans

There is a problem of confusion, too. Often all black people are assumed to be from the Caribbean Islands. Africans constantly have to explain that there are massive differences, not only between those two areas but also of course within different groups.

**Isa,** a young painter from Nigeria:

> Even for a Nigerian, it is what part of the country you are from that matters. Most people from the East African countries would be Christians whereas in West African countries so many of us are Muslims. And yet when my father was in hospital, people kept talking about carnival and all that. He told them he didn't eat pork, and my God that really blew their brains. But, you know, when you are in a vulnerable position, it isn't easy or polite to point out mistakes to people who are taking care of old relatives.

This story is important for several reasons. It shows the dangers of stereotyping and generalising from basic information. A little knowledge is indeed a dangerous thing, perhaps sometimes more than not knowing anything at all because you are less likely to ask the questions that need to be asked. Another point is that ethnic minority elders or their families do not find it easy to correct carers who think they have an idea of the 'culture' of a certain group. It feels wrong. What is clear, however, is that there are profoundly important areas that are very different within the various black communities living in Britain and that these need to be checked out by you as a care worker.

# Religion

Many Africans believe in the after-life, and there are rituals connected with this that are impossible to follow when people are living in Britain. Islam as practised in many African countries is infused with certain pre-Islamic practices. This means that no casual assumptions can be made about people just because they say they are Muslims or Christians.

# Diet

Food preferences would include at least in part the food they ate back home. In many African countries, for example, cassava is the staple vegetable. It is now possible to buy this fresh and frozen in Britain. If you are helping elders in their own home, such information about what is available in ethnic food shops is invaluable. Yam, green bananas, goat meat, okra, maize flour products, fish, corn, red beans and spinach are some foods that are eaten in many African countries. In West Africa, spices and hot pepper are added, but East Africans in general have plainer food, although the influences of Arab and Indian cooking have crept in.

## Language, culture and values

Many different African languages are spoken in this country, and they can be completely different from each other. English or French is also spoken, as is Portuguese; these were the languages of the colonisers. Africans have adopted these languages and made them their own. Sometimes unusual accents may make it difficult for care workers to understand a person. Asking politely for clarification will not be offensive.

Only women are present at birth, and showing emotions and expressing pain loudly are not considered taboo in African societies. This should not be judged or misinterpreted by people using British values as yardsticks.

**Isa,** the Nigerian painter, who was asked to interpret for another patient:

> They asked me to translate Swahili the other day at a surgery. I just laughed. I come from West Africa and they ask me to speak the language of Kenya and Tanzania.

All over Africa, family relationships across the generations and large networks are well defined and considered deeply important. The fact that African elders are growing old in a country far away from this may have a strong effect on their sense of well-being. Many African elders are living either in small family units or alone.

# Illness and death

Although most Africans believe in modern medicine, faith healing and traditional cures also feature in their lives. Organ transplants and abortion are not accepted by some Africans, though these are not a problem for others.

Belief in spiritual life after death and the importance of proper grieving are central to many African people. Grief is displayed openly and shared with members of the community. Forty days of mourning are common among some groups but it is always important to check, as many Africans also follow Christianity or Islam.

Africans' emotional bond with their country of origin is more complicated than many people realise. Whereas many Caribbeans have openly dreamed of going home, for many Africans it is often the opposite. If they escaped political turmoil or starvation or other disasters, they are often reluctant to talk about where they came from. The increasingly hostile immigration and refugee laws also affect them, and they might not always approve of changes that have happened in their own countries. At a deep level they may long for their homes, but the circumstances of their departure make them less obviously nostalgic than many Caribbean elders.

Finally, it is essential to remember that there are exceptions to all of these general facts and observations, and it is not hard to find them. Simply talking to black elders in one week brought out the following comments.

> I was brought up as a Christian but I don't believe in that religion any more. I think black people have allowed themselves to be kept down because the churches gave them all this nonsense about the better after-life. I want to have a better time *now*. This is just giving backup to the rich. As long as the oppressed believe that their lot will be better in the next life, they aren't going to fight for too much now.

I eat only boiled and steamed food, not all that greasy fried chicken and that, because it may be good to eat but it is so unhealthy. And my favourite food is Stilton cheese on a bit of biscuit. My wife thinks I am eating fungus!

Nigeria it is hell, hell on earth. Not just now but always has been. The people are hard out for themselves, why would I miss it? I hope to die here in Lewisham with all my good neighbours to wish me away. As for family, all they want from me is something from England, they are so greedy.

The last word must go to **Doris,** the pensioner who simply cannot stand being researched, questioned or written about:

You don't need books, girl. We are all different and all God's children. Don't you go around putting us together like a basket of oranges now. I won't have it.

# 4 The Asian communities

British Asians form the largest visible ethnic community in Britain. It is also the most diverse and therefore the most complex group. Talking about 'Asians' therefore makes little sense in terms of service delivery, although Asians do of course share many common features and experiences. When it comes to racial harassment, for example, people do not distinguish between Pakistanis, Indians and Bangladeshis. But religious, class and other differences need to be taken account of because most Asians describe their identity not only in ethnic but also in religious and geographical terms.

This chapter deals with the general issues that affect Asians as well as the particular features of the three main religious groups in the community: Hindus, Muslims and Sikhs. Inevitably, the information provided is basic and only a starting point. Everyone, whatever their background, should be treated as an individual. It is their right.

## History

### Eighteenth to early nineteenth centuries

It is extremely important for anyone working in the care sector to know this early history because it helps to correct misconceptions both about what Britain once was and about what has happened to it. The personal histories of Asian elders are interconnected with the colonial history of this country, and the reason why people are here now is that Britons were in their countries for many decades. Many also went through independence and are haunted by the terrible events of Partition: immediately after independence, there was a bloody confrontation that came out of the division of India into two countries of India and Pakistan.

Although large-scale migration from the Indian sub-continent to Britain did not happen until the 1950s, there were Asian people here much earlier, and the relationship between India (then an undivided country) and Britain go back to the beginning of the seventeenth century. The East India Company sent out the first trading ship to India in 1608. By 1757, following territorial battles in some areas, the East India Company ruled India. Eighty years later the British government took control. Besides the huge amount of wealth that was imported back into this country, servants and sailors from India also arrived in Britain, as did the occasional prince. In fact, 'Indian domestics provided a cheap source of labour and, like African servants, Asian valets and footmen came to be quite in vogue for fashionable British families in the eighteenth century.'[1]

In 1775 the following advertisement was placed in the *Daily Advertiser* by a lady who wished to pass on a servant girl:

> She is a Slave Girl and the mistress who brought her over having no occasion for her will give her over to any lady to attend her in the passage to India and to serve her for three years after the arrival there without wages, provided the lady engages at the expiration of the Term to give her freedom. She is a good servant, perfectly good natured, and talks English well . . .[2]

Indian sailors worked both in the merchant navy and in the East India Company ships. They were paid far less than white sailors and were often abandoned in this country by their employers. In the early 1800s, thousands of these destitute sailors were found in appalling conditions. They were beaten, left cold and starving, and many died. Their plight finally stirred the conscience of some, and in 1856 a strangers' house was set up to house them and find ways of repatriating them. This kind of exploitation continued for decades.

**Haji Shirajul Islam,** a Bangladeshi elder who eventually settled in the east end of London, told this story in 1987:

I was born in 1912, that time it was British India, in Sylhet. [When I was 24] we found these people talking about the English ship and they were getting quite a bit of money . . . the ship I found was the *Clan Baxter* – it was very hard work, just like slaves we worked. When the ship came to Tilbury, five or six people ran away from the ship. We were lucky, no watchmen and we just walked out free . . . cold . . . in 1937 in December . . . ordinary clothes we got . . . I had no money . . . Things have changed here; in the old days, our people we were all one. I remember once I came out of South Kensington station and I asked a lady the way to Chelsea. She told me, and she said 'Have you got the bus fare or shall I give it to you?' Can you imagine anyone doing that now? All they want now is bashing and stabbing and beating. But there is some fault with our people, too. The young boys who have come here behave badly, they go around the streets and do bad things; they don't understand the way to live . . .[3]

Hand in hand with economic exploitation went the ideology of European superiority and Indian backwardness. Christians played their part in this. The following extract is the kind of thing missionaries wrote in the nineteenth century:

They are the senseless worshippers of dumb idols or the deluded followers of the licentious doctrines of a false prophet . . . ignorant, darkened and deceived through the blindness that is in them.[4]

And this is what a health worker in Tower Hamlets said to a Bangladeshi interpreter in 1988:

These women are having all these babies because their religion is so backward – it tells them to keep reproducing for Allah or some such thing. It is difficult to feel they are living in England in the twentieth century.

In the nineteenth and early twentieth centuries Indian students came to study law and medicine. Three Indian MPs were elected to the House of Commons from these intellectuals. Indians also fought in World War 1 and had a special hospital set up for them at the Brighton Pavilion. Hindus and Muslims had separate kitchens provided to meet their needs!

## World War 2 and forgotten contributions

Over 3 million Indians volunteered to fight in the war. Many British people do not know this, and it does matter. This history is alive and part of the way people think and feel today. There are, for example, white elders who feel that they have more rights because they fought in the war and that immigrants did not.

**Hardial Singh,** 76, a war veteran:

> Do they remember anything? This old man at the centre said loudly, 'We fought in the war. Why do these coloured people get everything?' So I talked to him for a very long time and showed him my pictures of the regiment.

These memories are all the more powerful as people get older and they realise that much of their contribution has simply been eradicated by those who write history books and the media. When the former MP for Stretford, Winston Churchill, made disparaging remarks about black and Asian Britons, the people at a day centre in Southall where many war veterans spend their time wrote a letter reminding him that they too had helped to fight fascism.

**Hardial Singh** again:

> I feel so depressed. I fought in the war, we have medals to prove what we all did. The King said at the time that without people from India the war would not be won, and now not only do they forget, they treat you so badly they take away your dignity. Where is their great civilization?

## The 1950s, 1960s and 1970s

The major migration of Asians into this country from India and Pakistan took place in the late 1950s and 1960s. The bloody partition of India and Pakistan, the poverty that ensued and Britain's need for labour in heavy industry were the factors that led to the migration. Like the black community, Asians were needed for the low-paid, less desirable jobs that white people did not want to do after the war. It was mostly the men who came over first and then, as they began to settle and tighter immigration policies began to be introduced, they sent for their families before the doors shut.

Although they did not nurture the same emotional hopes of a motherland the way that the black migrants did, there was a belief that the English were supremely civilised people – but many were to be sadly disappointed as they settled here. The overt racism many experienced in their homes, in the streets and in the factories affected their views. There were others of course who were not racist towards Asians, but few close friendships developed between whites and Asians, and sometimes the problem lay with language and cultural differences between the two.

**Musa Ahmed,** an Asian elder from Bradford:

> It was so easy to get the work in factories. The supervisor used to say 'Bring your relatives, we like your work. You don't complain.' So we all got the jobs. But the other workers did not like us. But you have to sacrifice and suffer. And never we got the time off for Eid or Hajj.

This immigration continued through the 1960s and 1970s, although by then it was mainly family members joining settled immigrants. Political problems as Bangladesh became an independent nation led to immigration from there, and in the early 1970s East African Asians with British passports were forced to come to Britain as African leaders such as Idi Amin took against them. In 1972, 30,000 of them were expelled by Amin. Many came with nothing and are now one of the most successful groups in this country.

## Some important facts about the Asian community

- Older Asian women (which includes Sikhs and Muslims as well as Hindus) outnumber older men.
- Larger households are more common among south Asians than among black or white families.
- There is a high rate of home ownership in many of these communities.
- Some groups experience high levels of overcrowding and a great lack of housing amenities.
- There are significant differences of class between the Asian communities.
- South Asians, even those with high qualifications, have higher unemployment rates than white people and are usually employed in lower positions.
- There is a higher rate of self-employment among some groups than among white people.

## Issues affecting the lives of Asian elders in general

### Values

Many people who emigrated to Britain came with unrealistic expectations that it was going to be possible to retain cultural and religious values absolutely. This has been one of the biggest shocks for the Asian elders. Even those who have happily adjusted to life in this country have conflicting feelings about ageing and dying in Britain.

**Altab Ali**, a Muslim elder from Bolton:

I came after all the problems in Pakistan following Partition. My cousin was already in Bradford. He had a hard job in a foundry but he was making good money. I came with my wife, who was pregnant. We had four children – three boys and a girl. The boys are fine, they still obey us, but our daughter married a Hindu. I do not see her. She does not cover her hair. We just lost her. And our grandchildren are just totally English, no care for the elders, no manners. They laugh at us.

Studies show that changing values are creating problems for Asian elders, especially as the young seek more individualistic lifestyles. But it is equally true that, in most Asian family homes, there is a good deal of support and warmth and mutual respect.

### Class and gender

As in society generally, class makes a big difference to how people live and think. Many middle-class Asians find it easier to integrate than do working-class Asians. This is because often (though not always) they take on more western lifestyles and also retain a degree of power over their lives. But they are not totally immune from discrimination or abuse. In fact, their success can make them a target. Strong gender roles make it difficult for Asian elders to cope with the death of a partner. Asian men, for example, often have difficulty with housework and women cannot easily learn to manage bank accounts, paying bills, etc. Within matriarchal families, women gain in status as they get older. They also seem to remain more involved in family life. In many families, elders are given enormous respect and even power to influence decisions in ways that you would not usually get in white British families.

Women in some communities, especially those from rural backgrounds, may still observe seclusion from men, and older women find it very difficult to adapt to more 'modern' ways of behaving. They may also find it hard to see their daughters moving away from those traditions. In all the Asian communities, in general, women prefer female doctors and care workers whilst men prefer males.

In some families the mother-in-law seems to dominate her daughter-in-law, and this is one of the causes of family discord both in Britain and in the sub-continent. Because family problems are not meant to be discussed in public, these tensions often remain unseen. Asian counselling services are not yet widely available.

Many older women do not speak English because, after migration, they either did not go out to work or formed part of the large low-paid home-work labour force where there was no need to learn

English. Resources to teach English to immigrants have seriously diminished over the years; where once local education authorities provided 'English as a second language' teaching in the home, the workplace and community centres, this service has almost totally dried up.

## Sub-continental connections

Sub-continental politics are still very important to Asians in general but to Asian elders in particular. There are many ethnic newspapers that give them the information they need in order to maintain their bonds with the home country. There are also very popular British Asian radio stations that the elders love to listen to. Many of the programmes are in community languages, with news of India, Pakistan and Bangladesh. Festivals are celebrated and Hindi, Urdu and Punjabi music is played. One of the favourite stations is Sunrise in London. BBC local Asian networks in Leicester and Manchester are also very popular. There is also a cable Asian television station – Zee TV – which has many Asian elder subscribers because the station shows Hindi movies and news about India, Pakistan and Bangladesh.

**Mrs Ramji**, an Asian elder in west London:

> It is my whole life. I live alone. So the radio is on, I feel I have the company. I can find out about my country, listen to the songs and feel as if I am not a stranger in someone's country.

Unfortunately, there has, in recent years, also been a tendency for antagonisms from the sub-continent to be imported to Britain. Indian–Sikh relationships have become strained since Sikhs started demanding a separate state and Indian troops stormed the most important Sikh shrine, the Golden Temple, in 1984. In recent years Hindu and Muslim fundamentalists have clashed across India and this has created tensions in Britain. Indians and Kashmiris are also struggling with the issue of an independent Kashmir. This is human nature. Irish people living in this country have been abused by

English people following violence on the part of the IRA in Northern Ireland and the mainland.

## Discrimination

Some groups are more discriminated against than others, although this tends to change over time. In recent years, for example, because of the image of Islam as a demon religion – which is how it is often portrayed in the West – and since the war in Bosnia, British Muslims feel a heightened sense of themselves as a religious group that is under threat in Europe.

Various reports reveal how much racial discrimination is experienced by Asians and also how they face racial harassment. A report by the Institute of Public Policy Research indicated that white people felt that Pakistanis were the group most likely to suffer prejudice in this country. The word 'Pakistani' is often used by white people to mean Asian but it is inappropriate and sometimes offensive because 'Paki' may be used indiscriminately as a term of racial abuse.

## Media images

The Asian community is often portrayed by the media as culturally 'backward' or passive. Asian women are all presumed to have appalling lives, and in general it is the image of the corner shop that is most commonly portrayed.

## Housing

Most Asians own their homes. As Alison Norman points out:

> Another point of contrast with Afro-Caribbeans is that the Asians have made very little use of council housing . . . Age Concern found that 63 per cent of their sample of Asians were owner-occupiers . . . One consequence is that the Asian population have retained greater opportunity for mobility, and the indications are that the 'outward movement' of the more prosperous members of some communities has already begun.[5]

More recent research indicates that some housing needs are changing in the Asian community and that many of these needs are not
being met.[6] For example, growing numbers of grandchildren may
make joint family set-ups more difficult to accommodate because
suitable housing is not always available in the area.

## Employment

From the 1950s onwards the employment of both Asians and
blacks was infected with negative attitudes. By the 1960s employers were starting to say:

> There are circumstances when it is impossible to employ a coloured
> person, despite his qualifications . . . the higher the level, the greater
> the pressure and practical considerations that inhibit the employment
> of coloured people.[7]

As researcher Colin Brown says:

> Dark skinned immigrants were seen as undesirable but necessary in
> their allotted place and it was not just employers who took this view.
> Governments, both Labour and Conservative, in the 1950s wrestled
> . . . with the impossible equation of ensuring labour supply, support-
> ing free movement within the Commonwealth and discouraging black
> settlement.[8]

Many Asians at this time were involved in manual work, but a
number of them were self-employed and professional workers.
(People from the Indian sub-continent generally came from a much
wider variety of backgrounds than those from the Caribbean.)
Nevertheless, race discrimination was experienced in all areas of
employment.

In recent years Afro-Caribbeans, Pakistanis and Bangladeshis have
suffered higher rates of unemployment than Indians. But a quarter
of 'economically active' Indian men in this country are self-
employed, a rate almost double that for white men in the same
category.

## *Identity*

Identities in all cultural groups – whether white or black – are constantly going through changes. Few of us are born with a fixed identity that lasts us into old age and death. You only have to look at how, for example, curry is now one of the favourite foods in Britain, different cultural groups of people watch Hollywood films and attendance at church has fallen to see that all cultures change and move on.

**Mrs Smith,** a 60-year-old white pensioner:

> I lived in Hove all my life, never met a coloured person. Then my son, who was in his 40s, never married, turns up with this Indian girl who was to be his wife. I think we were all taken aback. I mean I don't have anything against them, you do understand? Now there are two lovely granddaughters, and my daughter-in-law, Rani, is a gem. I stay with them for days on end, and have even learnt to eat with my hands and am learning just a few Hindi words.

It would be fair to say that in recent years some groups have either panicked about the loss of an identity that is connected to their ancestral roots or tried to reclaim it because of the pain of immigration and racism. You can see this among Hindus, Sikhs and Muslims. Many white Britons are similarly anxious, not only because they have watched their country become multicultural but also because of the European Union. Nevertheless, it would be wrong to assume that Asian elders are all deeply unhappy. On the contrary, many feel more than happy to be part of this country, and to have safety nets available if they need them.

**Mr Rooparel,** 65, puts it like this:

> I am much better off here than in India. We have what we need, we can be free of obligations and people are good to us. It is up to us sometimes to try harder to mix.

## Languages

Several different languages and dialects are spoken by British Asians:

- Bengali – spoken by some people from Bangladesh and India. Those from Calcutta often speak this language.
- Gujarati – spoken by people with roots in the Gujarat. Many East African Asians speak this language or a dialect – Kutchi.
- Hindi – the administrative language of India and the language of popular Bombay movies. Most older Asians understand this language. Hindi songs are very popular among Asians around the world.
- Pashtu – spoken by people from Afghanistan and northern areas of Pakistan.
- Punjabi – spoken by people with roots in the Punjab. This includes Punjabi East African Asians.
- Sindhi and Kashmiri – spoken by some people from Sindh and Kashmir.
- Sylheti – a dialect of Bengali that is spoken by most British Bangladeshis.
- Urdu – similar to Hindi but more formal and complex. It is spoken by most Pakistanis. Elders in this community love listening to Urdu poems, called ghazals. Many even write them and then recite them to friends who gather to listen.

## Food

Most people in the Asian communities believe in the humoral theory of food: that some foods are 'hot' and stimulate, while other foods are 'cold' and have a calming effect. Hot foods include wheat, potatoes, meat, lentils, carrots, garlic and eggs. Cold foods include rice, milk, yoghurt, peas, beans, onions, spinach, lemon, mango and banana.

The list below is a basic guide on dietary restrictions among the different religious groups. Remember, though, always to check with the individual.

- Beef – not eaten by Hindus and Sikhs; Muslims eat halal beef.
- Cheese – some cheeses containing animal rennet are not eaten by Hindus; in general, curd cheese is preferred to strong hard cheese.
- Eggs – most Hindus and some Sikhs do not eat eggs.
- Fish – not eaten by Hindus, but eaten by the other groups; shellfish is not eaten by some Muslims.
- Lard – not eaten by any of the groups.
- Milk, butter and yoghurt – eaten by all groups.
- Mutton – most Hindus and some Sikhs do not eat mutton; Muslims eat only halal mutton.
- Oil and ghee – eaten by all groups; people generally do not eat olive oil.
- Pig products – not eaten by Muslims; some Sikhs may eat pork.
- Poultry – not eaten by Hindus, but eaten by some Sikhs and all Muslims; for Muslims it must be halal.

## Illness and health

The incidence of diabetes and coronary heart disease is higher than the national average. Alcoholism is high in the Sikh community, though not as high as among white Britons. Tuberculosis is a problem in some Bangladeshi communities. Traditional medicines are often used by Asians, and indeed for some chronic conditions they can be very effective.

### Health care

There are many beliefs about what to do in order to promote and maintain good health. Vaids and hakims – traditional healers – practise aryuvedic and other forms of medicine which go back centuries. Many Asian elders will go to these practitioners. When they use the National Health Service they tend to feel better looked after if they are prescribed medicines. Mental illness is considered a stigma or a curse. Asian people with depression are often misdiagnosed because of the way they report their symptoms. Little suitable psychotherapy is available to this community, which is anot.     nple of their unequal treatment. Many Asians are fatalistic v     faced with long-term problems or illnesses they do not understand.

There is evidence that Asians are particularly prone to heart disease, diabetes, iron deficiency (in some groups) and arthritis. Some researchers have argued that eating clarified butter and too much sugar – something that is fairly common in the Asian diet – is causing some of these chronic problems. Hindus are vegetarians and most don't eat eggs, so iron deficiency can sometimes be a problem.

## Attitudes to old age

The attitude to age in all Asian communities is complex. In some ways the status of the elderly is taken on by Asian people at a much younger age than in the white community. Being grandparents means a lot to Asian people and they psychologically take the birth of a grandchild as the time when they regard themselves as elders. But there are also other indications that there is premature ageing in the community, caused by the shock of migration, hard toil and the physical environment.

## Family

As with other Eastern peoples, families are expected to look after each other and especially elders. Extended family connections are very important and there are different titles for each different relationship. There can be up to six different words for uncle, for example.

Modesty in dressing and behaviour between the sexes is extremely important in all Asian communities. In many communities, legs and arms are covered, and, in some groups, the hair also. A married woman becomes part of her husband's family and is expected to take this responsibility very seriously. The shame and pain that is felt by elders when this does not happen is acute, and people will often not talk about it openly.

The 1991 Census has shown that the extended family is no longer a norm in the Asian community and that, for the reasons we have seen in Chapter 2, all kinds of family formations are beginning to emerge. However, it is still common among many Asian families for all the incomes to be pooled. Joint decisions are then made about expenditure, the elders having been consulted.

In many families grandparents play an important practical and emotional role in the care of the grandchildren. This includes taking them to and collecting them from school, some cooking and child minding. Teaching the mother tongue and about their religion is often done by Asian elders. Certain practices, such as a dowry to be given by the family of the bride, continue in Britain and sometimes create tensions. Elders have certain expectations and are often unwilling to change.

## Expectations of care

Research has consistently shown that local authorities make little effort to cater for the communication needs of Asian elders. Bilingual GPs, pharmacists, nurses, social workers and other professionals can make a difference, but there are not enough of them around the country.

Unfortunately, most service providers blame the cultural or the language problems instead of examining how their services can be made more accessible and fair. Many Asian elders feel uneasy complaining, even when they are victims of racism in the way they are treated, and few will discuss this openly with carers. They feel vulnerable enough and don't want to create greater hostility. Many Asians do not know what services are available and what they can claim; moreover, they find that their lives are not understood by policy makers and practitioners. In a study done in Middlesborough, 41 per cent of the Asians had never heard of the social services department.[9] In another study, in Birmingham in

1988, researchers found that there was a serious lack of information but that, once people knew what was available, many said they would use the services.[10]

# THE HINDU COMMUNITY
## Origin and dispersal

Hindus make up about 30 per cent of the British Asian population. They came to Britain either from India – mainly from the western coastal area of Gujarat – or (those who arrived much later) from the East African countries Kenya, Tanzania and Uganda, which is where Gujaratis had emigrated to in the nineteenth and twentieth centuries. A few come from the Punjab. Hindus are likely to be self-employed, and as a group they offer enormous support to members of their extended families and also to their communities at large. Many have done very well indeed here with their small businesses. In areas such as Leicester and Alperton (in London) you can see evidence of this success. Their children tend to be high achievers and they have entered many key professions such as pharmacy, medicine and accountancy. Hindus from East Africa tend to have more in common with other religious groups from East Africa than with Hindus from, say, a rural part of India.

As with any other religious group, there are sub-divisions within the Hindu community, but the underlying principles by which a practising Hindu leads her or his life remain common to them all.

## Religion

Hinduism is believed to be the oldest religion in the world, and has evolved gradually over thousands of years. The main religious text is the Bhagvaid (or Bhavagad) Gita. Unlike the Qu'ran, this is not a definitive scripture. The Gita gives moral guidance. The book should be handled only after proper ablution.

Shoes are taken off before entering a temple or a room with a shrine. Women cover their hair when they pray. Hindus believe in different manifestations of God; for example, Bramah the Creator, Vishnu the Preserver and Shiva the Destroyer.

Hindus believe in reincarnation, in a cycle of birth, death and rebirth until the soul finally becomes one with God. What you do in this world determines what is likely to happen to you after death. All living things are considered sacred and inter-dependent and it is considered wrong to kill another creature in order to sustain your own life. Some animals are worshipped. The cow is particularly sacred, representing the gentle, giving qualities of motherhood. Cows are also revered because they provide milk, which is central to the Hindu diet. Eating beef is strictly forbidden in the Hindu religion. Killing a cow is a grave sin.

Hindus, mostly women, fast a few days of a month. Sometimes this ties in with the times of the full and the new moon. Sometimes it is to do with a special situation or worry that might be plaguing the family or the individual. The fasts usually consist of eating only fruit and drinking liquids. Hindus believe that fasting and praying can affect events.

The Hindu community, in common with other Asian groups, are keenly trying to revive pride in their religion, especially among the young. A magnificent temple in Neasden in London, built entirely with funds raised from within the Hindu community, is fast becoming a symbol of that renewed pride and identity. And the young are indeed returning to their roots in ways that the elders find reassuring. A fear that has dominated their lives is that their young will abandon their religion and values and become so westernised that their ancestral connections will be lost.

## Prayers

Pooja, personal prayers, are very important to Hindus. There is often a small shrine in the home, and this is where pooja take place. The shrine faces eastwards, towards the rising sun. Lamps are lit and sometimes tinkling bells are rung to drive out other thoughts and noises so that the worshipper can concentrate. As people get older, they tend to concentrate more on the spiritual side of life.

Non-believers should not touch the family shrine. Menstruating women are not allowed to go near the shrine or, in some families, into the kitchen.

## Diet

Most Hindus follow strict vegetarian diets that exclude eggs and seafood. Some Hindus, though, are non-vegetarian and do eat some meat – though never beef. Food is never cooked in utensils that have previously had meat in them; they are kept separate. Alcohol is forbidden. Western cheeses are not generally liked because the taste is too strong for anyone not used to it. Some people do like eating curd and cottage cheese because it is similar to the curd cheeses they make.

Food is believed to affect the body and the mind. The categories of different foods cannot be deduced by using western 'logic'; these are belief systems handed down through the centuries and make sense in their own context. Some foods are considered 'hot' in that they raise the body temperature and excite the emotions; onions and garlic are in this group. Yoghurt, on the other hand, is a 'cold' food. Turmeric, garlic and ginger are thought to have medicinal properties. Some Hindus do not eat anything that is pulled out of the soil, because insects will have been killed in that process. Indian vegetarian cooking is very sophisticated and highly skilled. Most Hindu women elders, unless seriously hampered by illness or disability, are able to demonstrate impressive culinary skills.

The staple diet is rice and different unleavened breads such as chappatis, puris, parathas and rotis. A meal will usually include a couple of vegetable dishes. Ordinary vegetables such as potatoes, peas and carrots might feature but what makes British Hindu cooking so exciting is the variety of Indian vegetables you can now buy in shops throughout the country. These include bhindi (okra), fresh coriander, and many other vegetables that are not eaten even in Indian restaurants. Dhal (lentils) usually accompany every meal, as does freshly made yoghurt. Spices are used in all dishes, although many families living in the West eat food that is made with less fat, spices and chillis.

**Mrs Kanta Patel,** a volunteer community worker:

> We eat more healthy food now. Sometimes even boiled things, which we did not like before. Our grandchildren like too much chips and that kind of thing. So we tell them our food is better for the body. But maybe not with too many chillis, bad for the stomach, and not so much ghee and oil. I had a heart attack so I have to be careful. We have to change a little bit. Our sweets like ladoo and jalebi are so sweet and too much frying.

On the other hand, the normal Indian vegetarian diet is considered by nutritionists to be healthy and better than a diet with a very high content of meat and fat. The only problem has been a lack of vitamins D and $B_{12}$. Many Hindu elders need to take extra vitamins to supplement their diets because really fresh foods are not easy to obtain. Many vegetables used in Asian cooking, now found in most good supermarkets and in Asian foodstores, have travelled long distances and this affects their nutritional quality.

Contamination of their food by forbidden ingredients is one of the greatest worries for Hindu elders when they eat in unfamiliar places. The least they would expect is reassurance that the food has been cooked in pans that have been thoroughly cleaned after they have had meat in them. Some, on the other hand, will not eat food that has been cooked by anybody outside their immediate circle. This can be offensive to care workers, and the situation needs patience and understanding. If you feel strongly that this attitude is not appropriate, you should try to explain politely why, while respecting the person concerned. Such incidents can obviously be hurtful or annoying. If there is a language barrier, the situation can become even more difficult. The way to deal with this delicate matter is to find someone within the family or organisation, or even a nearby temple, who can mediate and help achieve a satisfactory solution.

# Festivals

Hindus have many celebrations through the year, but the main ones are **Diwali**, the festival of light, which is followed the next day by **Bestuwarash**, New Year's Day. These occur some time over the winter solstice period. During Diwali, oil lamps are lit in homes, fireworks set off and sweetmeats given to friends, family, neighbours and customers. Unlike Christmas, expensive presents are not central to Diwali, although this too is changing and these days you even get greeting cards for Diwali. It is important to wear new clothes and to be generous towards those in need at this time.

**Holi** is a springtime festival. This is when water mixed with different colours is thrown over people and there is joy as good triumphs over evil.

**Rakhsha Bandhan** is a celebration of love between brothers and sisters. Sisters tie a special bracelet made of string and coloured threads and glitter on the wrists of their real or adoptive brothers, who in turn give them a present or some money.

In the autumn, or sometimes in spring, comes **Navratras**, a festival of nine days when girls and young women dance special dances and celebrate the power of devis – female goddesses – and especially Veshnu Devi, the goddess of wealth, wisdom, learning and power.

Other festivals include **Mahashivaratri**, the birth of Shiva, and **Ram Navami**, the birth of Ram.

# Ablutions

Washing is very important in the Hindu religion and not being able to wash can cause distress. Cleansing the body is essential before prayers. Hindus prefer to use running water and not to lie in a bath; a shower or a bucket with a mug that they can use is what most people want. They also wash themselves after using the toilet. Elders clean out their nasal passages and tongue and prefer to wash out their mouths after a meal. At home, food is usually eaten with the hand and sometimes a spoon. Feet are considered dirty.

Cloths, mops and sponges that are used to clean the kitchen are kept separate from those used in the bathroom. Plates are rinsed thoroughly after washing so that no suds remain.

## Clothes

Most women elders wear saris; they cover their heads when praying, and some also when in the company of men or priests. A sari is six metres of material that is wound round the body and tucked into a long skirt (ghaghra) which ties round the waist. A fitted blouse is also worn. The sari is pleated in the front and then a length is thrown over the left shoulder or brought forward on the right shoulder. Sometimes pins are used to keep these in place. Care workers may need to learn this in order to help dress Hindu women. Any sari shop will demonstrate how this should be done.

Most elderly women use oil in their hair and then tie it up in either a plait or a bun. They do not usually cut their hair, although this is becoming more common among the younger generations.

Jewellery is very important even to older Hindu women, especially the items that they were given when they got married. Some jewellery may have religious significance, so it is important to ask permission to remove any. Most women wear a necklace with gold and black beads and bangles, which they wear until either they or their husbands die.

Some Hindu men and boys wear a sacred thread on their wrists, which must never be removed.

Modesty is very important to Hindus, as it is to the other Asian groups. Hindu women do not generally cover their heads unless they are praying. Traditionally it is very important to cover the breasts, upper arms and legs. Undressing can be deeply embarrassing for women and they prefer to expose only parts of their bodies rather than getting completely unclothed.

# Language, culture and values

Hindus who come from the Gujarat or East Africa speak Gujarati and/or Hindi, both of which have written scripts. Hindus from other areas may speak Punjabi and/or Hindi. Newspapers and books are available in these languages, and these days some public libraries stock books and newspapers in Asian languages.

Weddings tend to be the time when parents can display their love for their children. Gold is bought in large quantities and given to daughters, and dowries are commonly given to the new husbands and their families.

At birth, the mystical symbol 'OM' is written with honey on the baby's tongue. Mothers do not go out for 40 days after the birth. Women are regarded as the custodians of the moral values and reputation of both the family and the community. Social shame is very important and one way that behaviour is regulated. It can also become a way of hiding what is going on. Many elders prefer to suffer than spoil the family name.

**Mrs Devsi**, a Hindu woman from London:

> I left my son's house because I was so unhappy. Please don't say my name. My daughter-in-law, who is a lawyer – can you believe it? – sent us out of the house at eight o'clock and we were not allowed to come back into the house until half past three when her children come home. They have the keys. We did not. So we have to walk around, go to see the people, go to the temple or just travel around in the bus. It was terrible for us. But we cannot tell anybody. Our name will be spoilt. Then my husband died, I could not live there and one lady she helped me to get this flat.

Widows, especially elders, generally do not marry again and tend to live simple lives. Widows dress in white and wear no jewellery or make-up. They have withdrawn from the world as they knew it.

**Mrs Devsi** again:

> I feel I am just waiting for my death, which I hope will come very quickly. I am 60. If I have 20 more years of this life without my husband, just a nothing, just a widow, I think I will go mad.

Divorce used to be rare within the community but all this is changing the longer people live in Britain and are influenced by the values of mainstream society. Men and women have demarcated responsibilities, although this too is changing.

Hindus are not supposed to smoke or drink, because both are considered harmful to the body. As younger people in the community take up these habits, it causes great anxiety to the elders.

**Mr Desai**, a Hindu elder from Brent:

> They are just learning the bad habits of this country. My son drinks so much his marriage is destroyed. Really what we taught them and what they learned are so different. I will die an unhappy man.

Many Hindu elders live with their families, and most still consider it a matter of deep shame to live on their own or in residential homes.

**Mr Desai** again:

> It would be better for my son to die than to think about putting us into a home. He will never do such a thing. Our religion teaches us to respect the elders, to care for them; that is your destiny. You are lucky if you can do such 'seva' [service] in your life to your parents and grandparents.

Unfortunately, the cultural changes that this community is going through, in common with all immigrant groups, mean that this support is falling away. As one elder interviewed for a Brent study said:

It is not because our children don't want to respect us. They want to live separately and can't see us every day. It is not practical for them. They have their jobs, home and children to look after. We can't do anything to help them; in fact, if we need bulk shopping or need to go to the doctor, they have to come with us. How can my son respect me like I did my father? Everything has changed so much.[11]

This is something that professionals need to remember: the Asian family unit is changing and assumptions of support should not be made. You need an open-minded, non-judgemental and empathetic approach to find out gently what the exact situation is and how the elders *really* feel about it.

## Caste and religious differences

Some other problem areas can arise with Hindu elders that require tactful handling. Elders are likely to be unsettled by challenges to their deeply held beliefs. Nevertheless, no culture should be absolutely sacrosanct. If, for example, a Hindu elder expresses hostility to a care worker on the basis of caste differences or religious antagonism, the situation will require delicate but firm handling. There is no doubt that the caste system exerts a powerful influence on British Hindus, just as class still colours life for many white Britons. In the case of the Hindus, because this influence has a religious basis, it can be very difficult to challenge by simply saying it is wrong or unfair. On the one hand, choice is increasingly built into the care plans of elders, but, on the other hand, we have race relations legislation and equal opportunity policies that forbid discriminatory behaviour. If you encounter such a difficult situation, you could say something like: 'I know it is your religion and it means a lot to you. But the laws in this country do not allow people to reject anyone because of their colour, religion or caste.'

**Jyoti,** a Hindu care worker in Brent:

In our community, I try to talk to the many elders who still speak about high caste and low caste and will not eat food prepared by people of another religion. I explain to them that this is simply wrong and then turn it round. What would they feel if an English nurse refused to touch them because they are Hindu? And they do listen and change. But you have to work with them. Of course, it is important not to use the same cooking pots used by those who cook meat. That is reasonable, I think.

Cleaning toilets is another one that makes some problems. You see, in India, it is the untouchables who still do it in many places. Here we all have to do it ourselves and our older folk find that very tough. So I tell them that Gandhiji cleaned toilets so they must be like him.

## Illness and death

Many of the customs described above become even more important for families during periods of illness. Coronary disease in this group is 30 per cent higher than the national average. There is also a degree of lactose intolerance: 50 per cent of Hindus have problems digesting milk products.

Patients in hospital may want to set up their little prayer shrine in their locker. Many Hindus use aryuvedic medicine, which has been known to help in many conditions (eg arthritis). Mixed wards cause a lot of distress to Hindu patients.

Beef-derived insulin may be unacceptable. Capsules with gelatine are a problem for this community.

Dying Hindus often ask for readings from their holy book, the Bhagavad Gita. Sometimes a priest may be called to sprinkle holy water and perform other rites. Some people ask to be put on the floor before they die. It is important for people outside the religion not to touch the body or any of the objects or the holy books.

Hindus are cremated after death and there are strict rituals about how the family is involved in the process. The eldest son is supposed to ignite the pyre; in Britain he usually presses the button at the crematorium. (If there is no son, a boy from the extended family or other male relative will fulfil this ritual.) Prayers and hymns are chanted at this time. Many Hindus ask for their ashes to be taken back and scattered in the holy river of the Ganges.

The period of mourning lasts for many weeks, and people from the community all help to support the family emotionally and practically. Often no cooking is done in the house, for example, so food is brought in by relatives and neighbours. Grief is expressed openly and, as a care worker, you need to know that this is what normally happens. Keeping emotions controlled is considered heartless. Touching and hugging someone in mourning is fine if it is by a person of the same sex.

## Names

People generally have two names joined up and then a family or sub-caste name; for example, Kirankumar Patel. The word 'behen', meaning sister, is often added to the end of a woman's name as a mark of politeness; 'bhai', meaning brother, is used similarly for men. So Leela becomes Leelabehen and Ashok becomes Ashokbhai.

Many Hindu men and single women use their father's names after their own and before the family name. A married woman uses her husband's name instead. It is important always to check that all three names are being recorded – in the same order and with the same spelling. (Confusion sometimes arises if a different spelling is given to different services, and the staff in those departments don't realise that two – or more – files relate to just one person.)

### Common Hindu names

MALE FIRST NAMES

Ajay, Amul, Anand, Anil, Anoop, Atma, Bhaskar, Bimal, Devendra, Dinesh, Ganesh, Gopal, Govind, Gautum, Haresh, Jayesh, Jitendra, Kishore, Krishna, Magan, Nirmal, Pajendra, Rajesh, Ram, Raman, Ravi, Shiva, Suman, Suresh, Tarun, Vijay.

FEMALE FIRST NAMES

Ansuya, Aruna, Bimla, Bindu, Ela, Hansa, Indira, Jayashree, Jyoti, Kamla, Leela, Leena, Manjula, Mira, Nirmala, Pushpa, Sandhya, Usha, Vanita, Vijay.

LAST NAMES

Advani, Amin, Ashar, Bhandaria, Chopra, Choudhury, Desai, Gohil, Hirani, Khanna, Patel, Rao, Sethi, Shah, Sharma, Vasani.

## Useful terms

**arti** offering to the gods

**bindi** spots worn on the forehead; red usually indicates that a woman is married. A widow does not wear bindi

**Brahmin** the highest caste in the Hindu religion

**ishta devata** the personal god chosen by the family

**janeu** sacred thread worn over the right shoulder

**karma** the destiny of a person, which has been determined by actions in the previous life

**Ram, Vishnu, Shiva and Krishna** the main Hindu gods

**sindur** red powder worn on hair partings, often only by newly-wed brides

**Sita** Ram's virtuous wife

# THE SIKH COMMUNITY
# Origin and dispersal

There are about 300,000 Sikhs living in Britain. Although some have come from East Africa, they are mostly from the Punjab, which is in the north-western part of the Indian sub-continent. In the main, Sikhs live in Leeds, west London and the west Midlands; a few have settled in Scotland. They speak Punjabi; it is written in the Gurmukhi alphabet, which is not used for any other language.

# Religion

Sikhism is a reformist religion, which came into being as a reaction against some aspects of Hinduism and, later, Islam – for example, against the caste system and the power of priests. Guru Nanak, founder of the faith, believed that an individual should make his or her own relationship with God. Through a process of evolution, other gurus developed the principles of Sikhism from 1469 to 1539. Their teachings are written down in sacred scriptures. The holy texts are considered deeply sacred. In essence, there are no caste divisions among Sikhs and there is a strong charitable tradition. Sikhism tends to be liberal and does not have priests, and caste hierarchies that have evolved are less important than among Hindus.

Sikhism emphasises equality between men and women and between the different races and castes. In principle. In reality, however, as in all religions, women do have lower status than men and social hierarchies have developed over the years.

**Mr Gurnam Singh**, an elder from Wolverhampton:

> You know, when I was a boy, we were taught that we should all be respectful of each other. No untouchables and that sort of rubbish things. Now some of us are rich so we treat poor people like less than us. Too many of us drink the alcohol. We are losing our way. I am very worried.

The five 'k's or 'kakkar' are religious symbols that define Sikhism.

- **Kesh** is hair, which is considered to be a gift from God. A practising Sikh is not allowed to cut, shave, trim or pluck any hair. Sikh men wear turbans, which are kept with great care. Over the years, owing to discrimination against Sikhs wearing turbans, some have given up wearing them. It is in fact illegal in Britain to discriminate against someone for wearing a turban, but the practice continues.

- **Khanga** is a wooden comb that is worn in the hair all the time. It is a symbol of cleanliness and tidiness, real as well as in the mind.
- **Karra** is a steel bangle that is worn on the right wrist. It links the wearer to the religion, and is a mark of identity and of simple honesty, restraint and virtue.
- **Kirpan** is a small symbolic dagger that is stored in a scabbard called a gatra. It represents power, resistance, self-respect and self-defence.
- **Kachha** is special cotton underwear that sometimes people wear on their own, like light shorts. It is a symbol of continence and self-control.

These symbols are very important and should always be treated with respect.

### Prayers

Sikhs pray in gurdwaras, their temples, which are found in different parts of the country. Usually Sunday is the day of collective prayer. Men and women sit apart, and prayers are led by lay people and religious teachers. There are no priests – anyone can read the sacred scriptures and lead prayers. Sikhs also pray at home early in the morning, using a string of beads to count on.

## Diet

Many devout Sikhs are vegetarian, but some eat mutton, lamb and pork. Sikhs do not eat meat that is killed according to Muslim rituals. Offering them halal meat, therefore, would be regarded as an insult.

Some Sikhs fast in the same way that Hindus do. These are traditions that remain because the original Sikhs were converts from Hinduism.

Punjabi food is famous for its robust taste and variety. There are countless ways of making breads, and the food is spiced quite differently from Gujarati food. Meat and chicken cooked with spinach, chickpeas served with potatoes and yoghurt are some examples. Punjabi rotis – unleavened bread – are large, and fairly thick and low in fat. Gujarati rotis are very thin, flaky and made with ghee. Punjabi stuffed parathas – stuffed with vegetables or with mince meat – are famous across the sub-continent. Sikh men are often good cooks. Asian cooking is more varied and exciting than you might think from the food that is usually available in restaurants.

Sikhs should not smoke or drink but younger people are taking up these habits, which many elders feel pollute the body.

## Festivals

The main festivals are **Baisakhi** (or Vaisaki) which is a spring festival, **Guru Nanak's birthday** and **Diwali**. Bhangra dancing, a robust folk dance, is one of the defining cultural marks of Sikhs. Both men and women dance, sometimes together, and the dances are performed during festivals and weddings.

## Ablutions

Sikhs have the same ablution practices as Hindus, and for the same reasons. They must wash before they pray. They wash after using the toilet and use their left hand for this.

## Clothes

Modesty of dressing is very important for Sikhs. Women usually wear shalwar khamiz – loose trousers and a long chemise over them, with a long scarf that is used to cover the front and sometimes the head. Men wear similar clothes but without the scarf and in subdued colours.

## Language, culture and values

Sikhs speak Punjabi as their first language. There has been a revival of the language among the young in Britain since Bhangra has become so popular in this country. Weddings are the focal point of social life. On the whole, family life is valued and the old expect strict respect from the young. In many ways the cultural expectations of Sikhs are the same as for Hindus, and in both communities there is some anxiety that these values are being destroyed in the West.

Marriages are still negotiated by families but these days the young people concerned have the right to choose. When young people in the community break from these traditions, elders find it almost impossible to accept and some do turn away from their offspring.

Sikh babies wear a thread on their wrists and midriff for good luck and to keep evil away.

## Religious differences and other problems

Since Partition, there has been a deep hatred between many Sikhs and Muslims. This is because so many of their families were involved in the violence as perpetrators or victims. Sikhs are well known as brave warriors. These enmities are more obvious among the elders. Interestingly, though, Muslims and Sikhs were the communities that fought in the British Indian Army and many have shared memories and deep friendships that even the horrors associated with Partition could not affect.

In the last few years many Sikh elders have been acutely affected by the political turmoil in India over Khalistan, a free independent Sikh state that many have been fighting for. There is continuing tension and violence, which erupts from time to time between government forces and Sikhs. When Indira Gandhi was killed by her own Sikh bodyguards, tensions here between Sikhs and Hindus and within the Sikh community were very high. The editor of a Punjabi newspaper was assassinated in 1994 over this issue.

**Anonymous** Sikh elder:

> I don't believe that this is happening in our beautiful Punjab. We are Sikhs and we are Indians. Many of us fought and died for independence from the British. Now there is all this hatred between us. I feel really very bad. I wish I was dead before to see such a thing.

## Illness and death

During serious illness or when a person is dying, hymns are read from the Sikh holy book. The final rituals are performed by members of the community. They do not mind bodies being touched by people outside the faith but all the rites are performed by those from within the fold, often the family. Sikhs are cremated after death: cremation must take place as soon as possible. Expressions of grief and periods of mourning are the same as for Hindus. Gurinder Kaur Gill, a widow, described how she felt when the nurses who were caring for her dying husband did not understand this.

**Gurinder Kaur Gill:**

> They told me no cry, be strong. Am I without a heart? This was my husband, even five years of tears are not enough. These people don't understand our feelings and how we feel dying in a strange country so far away from home.

## Names

'Kaur' is the title given to all Sikh women. It means princess. This was given as a title by the original gurus in order to equalise the status of women with men. 'Singh', meaning lion, is the title given to all Sikh men. You get a personal name, followed by 'Kaur' or 'Singh', and then the family name; for example, Balwant Singh Sahota. Male and female first names can be the same – it is the middle name that distinguishes them. In official records, sometimes only 'Singh' and 'Kaur' are recorded, which obviously causes confusion. Getting the surname is therefore very important.

### Common Sikh names

FIRST NAMES (MALE/FEMALE)

Ajit, Amarjit, Amrit, Avtar, Balbir, Balwinder, Daljit, Davinder, Harbans, Hardip, Inderjit, Jaswinder, Joginder, Kamaljit, Khushwant, Kulldip, Manjit, Mohan, Mohinder, Paramjit, Piara, Rajinder, Ranjit, Surjit.

FINAL NAMES

Bahra, Bassi, Bhumbra, Dhaliwal, Dhesi, Gewal, Gill, Kalsi, Mangat, Sandhu, Uppal, Verdi.

## Useful terms

**dupatta** a scarf used by Sikh women to cover their heads and torso

**gurdwara** Sikh temple

**gurpurb** religious or feast day

**mela** festival

**pagr** turban worn by most Sikh men

**patka** inner turban used by younger boys on its own or by older men to tie their hair under the main turban

**shalwar khamiz** loose trousers and long top worn by Sikh women, who don't usually wear saris

**vayid** traditional healer

## THE MUSLIM COMMUNITY

## Origin and dispersal

Most Muslims come from Pakistan and Bangladesh. Some are from East Africa and India. There are also Malaysian, African, Middle Eastern, Turkish and white Muslims in Britain.

Although they all believe in Islam, there is enormous diversity within the million-strong British Muslim population. Besides the two major sects, Shias and Sunnis, there are all kinds of sub-sects and groupings. Many Muslims came here from rural Pakistan. They have created strongly knit enclaves in the north of England in areas such as Bradford and Bolton, where their traditions have little to do with Islam and much more to do with rural village life in Pakistan. These people are Mirpuris, who often practise cousin marriages and tend to be suspicious of urban modern life. Bangladeshi Muslims are also mostly from rural areas. At the other end of the spectrum are Indians and other Pakistanis who live in highly desirable residential areas of London and have typically middle class lives.

# Religion

The Qu'ran is the holy book of Islam. It is believed to be an expression of God's will through Mohamed, and his teaching must be accepted without question. All Muslims must learn the verses of the Qu'ran. Islam rejects difference of colour, caste and race, believing in the universal brotherhood of humankind.

'Islam' is an Arabic word meaning peace. To be a Muslim is to follow a complete way of life. There are basic principles that all the different sects follow:

- Muslims believe there is one God, Allah, and that Mohamed is his last prophet. They also accept that Noah, Abraham, Moses and Jesus preceded Mohamed.
- Prayer is a duty of every Muslim.
- Giving to charity is also a duty.
- Fasting during Ramadhan is required.
- Muslims try to make a pilgrimage (Hajj) to Mecca once in their lives if possible.

All Muslims fast during the month of Ramadhan. During this time, from dawn to dusk, they are not allowed to drink, eat or smoke. This is to acquire self-discipline and to understand what it means to be hungry. Many people feel that there are physical benefits to this period of denial. Days missed have to be made up, and even elders who may have health problems will attempt to fast. Muslims who are ill or infirm, pregnant or menstruating women and very young children are exempt from fasting, although those who can't fast often feel guilty about it.

People are expected give to the poor, and this is done even in humble homes. Those who can afford it should make a pilgrimage to Mecca. Elders who have never been are often deeply distressed about their 'failure'.

**Mr Khan,** an elder dying of cancer:

> The day of judgement will be very hard for me. It is too late now; I never went on Hajj because there were so many money problems and too many family responsibilities. I was sending the money to my brother's widow in Pakistan. Now it is too late and I feel so bad, so terrible.

Muslims believe in individual responsibility, the day of judgement and an after-life. Angels are thought to be messengers from Allah.

### Prayers

Muslims pray five times a day. Men and women pray separately. The midday prayer on Fridays is especially important.

# Diet

Muslims do not eat pork, bacon or any other part of a pig because it is regarded as a scavenger and unclean. (This is just like Jewish people.) They do eat other meat but only if the animal has been slaughtered in a specified way. The meat is then called halal meat. Some Muslims do not eat shellfish because they regard them as scavengers, just like pigs. They are not allowed any alcohol, and some will not take liquid medicines that contain alcohol or capsules if they contain gelatine in case it comes from pigs.

# Festivals

The main festivals are **Eid-ul-Fitr,** which is the feast at the end of Ramadhan, and **Eid-ul-Adha,** which is the festival after the annual pilgrimage to Mecca. The near-sacrifice of his son by Abraham and the substitution of a sheep is symbolised by the sacrifice and cooking of a sheep or lamb. **Mawlid al-Nabi,** the birthday of Prophet Mohamed, is also celebrated.

# Ablutions

Before prayers, Muslims have to perform complicated ablutions. These involve washing the hands up to the wrist and rinsing the mouth, nostrils, face, ears, forehead and feet. The right hand is used for eating, holding the Qu'ran, etc; the left hand is used to wash after using the toilet. Intravenous drips and injections should be administered to the left hand or arm.

# Clothes

There are strict codes of behaviour and dressing that most Muslim men and women follow. They are expected to dress modestly. Many women cover their hair; others go further and cover a substantial part of their bodies and faces, too. However, there are Muslim women who do not follow these codes and dress as they please.

# Language, culture and values

Muslims speak a variety of languages, depending on where their families originally emigrated from. Forced marriages are forbidden by Islam, and the rights of women to their own property and to support after divorce are enshrined in the Qu'ran. Social traditions sometimes do not honour these rights.

Many Muslims prefer people to take off their shoes when they enter the house. Traditional men in the Muslim community do not

shake hands with women. In fact, there are strict codes governing the relations between men and women; usually, a dignified distance is maintained with those outside the family. (Women do not like male doctors or care workers for reasons of modesty and strict rules that govern interaction between the two sexes.) Men and women are often separated from each other during feasts and other celebrations. Menstruating women are not allowed to take part in some holy activities. The call for separate schools for Muslim girls in Britain is at least partly to do with anxieties that the young women will pick up the 'bad habits' of people in this society.

Prayers are said when a child is born and the baby is washed before being given to the mother. Like Jewish boys, Muslim boys are circumcised. Girls in Islam are not meant to be circumcised but in many North African countries this is what happens because of cultural practices that have nothing to do with the religion.

The largest immigrant group in this country, Muslims have often suffered the worst kind of discrimination in public services. Many of them are bitter about the way their religion is treated by the media and the way their beliefs are misunderstood. They are also worried about the growing extremism among the youth in their own community.

**Mr Ahmed,** an elder from Bradford:

> Our youngsters are always told that Islam is a bad religion and that we are all crazy. It is not fair. We expect our sons and daughters to be self-controlled, to be obedient, to care about Allah, to be afraid of God. Is that so bad? Do you want our children to do what other children are doing? Smoking, stealing, attacking old people, having babies before marriage. Our children will not do that.

Sometimes care workers can find it difficult to accept the different values that many in the Muslim community live by. In part this is because they have been conditioned to think about Muslims as dangerous and oppressive. But most Muslims are very happy being Muslims and don't feel that they are prisoners of their faith.

There are, of course, many practices that go against values that people in Britain hold dear. In some Muslim communities, girls are taken out of school and not allowed to go to college. But this is not what Islam demands. The Prophet himself worked for his first wife, who was a businesswoman, and education for women is an important part of the religion. No culture or religion should be above criticism or enquiry. And there are many Muslims who are rebelling against the authoritarianism of some leaders in the mosque.

**Malika,** a worker with a voluntary agency:

> Some social workers think it is racist to criticise any ethnic minority community, whatever they are doing. That is just nonsense. I am a Muslim, and I often tell the older people in the community that some of the things they are doing to young girls in the name of religion is wrong. But because many feel that people in this country hate them, they get more conservative themselves.

The other issue that sometimes comes up is that some ethnic minority elders themselves have deeply prejudiced views about white society. Some of these views can be quite offensive to care workers. These need to be discussed in a way that makes sense to the elders in order to establish an acceptable working relationship.

**Claire,** a district nurse:

> I just hated going in there at first because this old man, Mr Abdullah, just went on and on about how in this country we did not know right and wrong and how young girls were out of control. He wouldn't let his poor wife turn the television on. So then I started asking him questions about life in India, and the films he watched and then we would have these mock fights. I told him about my parents and how religious they are and how I was brought up a Catholic and it all became much better. I think if I had kept it all in, I could not have given him the care I needed to.

## Religious and other differences

The traditional enmities between Sikhs and Muslims have been discussed on page 112. But these days the problems that are emerging are likely to be between certain groups. There are inter-mosque rivalries and also emerging gaps between more militant Muslims and those who want Muslims to compromise and live as equal citizens in this country, participating more instead of separating themselves from the mainstream community even if that is the more difficult option.

**Mr Khan** again:

> I am dying, but Allah knows what is going to happen to us over here. After Bosnia, I feel very afraid. But our people are just getting too hot-headed and that is not helpful. The Qu'ran teaches us to be peaceful, merciful. When all this happened with Salman Rushdie, I was very upset. He was wrong, very wrong, to insult Islam, but all those people saying he should die, that is not our way.

## Death

When a person is dying, verses from the Qu'ran are read by members of the family. The person may be moved to face towards Mecca. The call to prayer is whispered into the ear of the dying person.

Muslims prefer dead bodies to be touched only by other Muslims. If this is not possible, it is a good idea to use disposable gloves. Only someone of the same sex may touch the body. The body must be turned to face Mecca.

After death, the body is washed and prepared for burial by people in the community. There are strict rituals. The body is wrapped in a plain white sheet and burial takes place within 24 hours. The mourning period is 40 days and, as in the other Asian communities, families are supported in their grief and encouraged to express their feelings of loss. Prayers in the home take place throughout this

period. Where there are no close relatives or other community people, care workers may have to play a more active part in listening and helping the bereaved elder through their grief and mourning, giving them understanding and respect.

# Names

Muslim men have two or three names, one of which is of religious significance; women have two names – for example, Ali Khan (male) and Ayisha Begum (female). The last name, which must be included in written records, is often *not* the shared family name, and husbands and wives can have different family names – which can be confusing to people who are not used to this. It is not polite to use only the first name. The 'calling' name is usually in two parts; for example, Mohamed Ali or Ali Khan (male) and Ayisha Begum (female). It is safer and more polite to always use two names. The religious name should never be used on its own.

## Common Muslin names

MALE FIRST NAMES

Afthab, Afzal, Ahamed, Akram, Ali, Amin, Arif, Aslam, Aziz, Badhur, Bashir, Farrukh, Fiasal, Hasan, Hussein, Ibrahim, Imran, Iqbal, Jamal, Latif, Mahmood, Malik, Mansur, Nadim, Nasir, Omar, Rafiq, Sadiq, Salim, Sharif, Sultan, Tariq, Yusef.

FEMALE FIRST NAMES

Amina, Ayesha, Aziza, Hamida, Jameela, Kulsum, Naseem, Nasreen, Parveen, Razia, Slama, Yasmin, Zainab, Zohra, Zubaida.

FAMILY/LAST NAMES

It is not really feasible to list a small selection here: there are 19 different nationalities with various family names.

# Useful terms

**Allah** God

**Bayram** feast marking the start of the month of pilgrimage to Mecca

**burka** and **hijab** head scarves worn by Muslim women to cover their hair and sometimes part of their faces

**chador** long body covering

**faquih** faith healer

**Hajj** pilgrimage to Mecca

**halal** meat slaughtered in the traditional manner, as directed by Islam: the animal is killed so that the blood flows out quickly, and prayers are said at the time of killing

**haram** forbidden by Islam

**khitan/sunat** male circumcision

**namaz** prayer

**quibla** direction of Mecca

**Ramadhan** month of fasting

# CONCLUSION

In all three communities – Hindu, Sikh and Muslim – post-mortems are considered a violation and disrespectful of the dead. When these are necessary, they must be discussed with sensitivity.

There is no problem with blood transfusions. None of the religions forbids contraception, but abortion is disapproved of.

## *Remember*

These are brief and basic facts about the three communities. They are simply a starting point for carers who then have to develop their knowledge of clients' needs by communicating with them and working out an individual profile.

**Malika** again:

> The people I work with know nothing about us. One asked me the other day why Muslims were vegetarians. Another said she was really surprised to find that Muslim men were circumcised because she thought only Jews did that. Another thought that I was circumcised because Muslim women are. I told her that this is a cultural practice in some African countries and nothing to do with Islam. Would they ever let us care for white people if we were so ignorant?

Malika keeps the quotation given below to show those of her colleagues who do want to understand. Someone speaking at a function organised by the Brent Indian Association said this a few years ago about what many Asian elders go through:

> The Asian elderly has witnessed his world gone topsy turvy. His family got scattered pell-mell all over the world. His physical environment was changed overnight. The economic platform upon which he stood was barbarously snatched from him. The secure cultural terrain upon which he built his psychological foundation began to totter and wobble unexpectedly. Unsteady, he stands with ebbing energies and strength; even the support of a walking stick thrust into his hands by local charities could not help him to balance.

But this too is only part of the story and does not apply to all Asian elders. Many are happy, strong individuals who feel proud of their achievements and also of how well their children are doing in Britain today.

# 5 The Chinese and Vietnamese communities

## THE CHINESE COMMUNITY

When talking about black people in Britain, the literature usually refers to Africans . . . and Asians . . . whilst the Chinese are excluded from the discussion. Thus, the Chinese community is in a difficult situation and more isolated because not only white British but also black activists seem to ignore their presence.[1]

This is what a Chinese researcher wrote in 1986. The situation remains largely the same today, especially when it comes to provision for ethnic minority elders. Ironically, although we have seen how wrong it is to play the numbers game, among ethnic minority groups themselves attention is largely centred on the two largest communities – black people and Asians.

According to the 1991 Census, the total Chinese population in Britain – mainly from Hong Kong, though there are some from Malaysia and Singapore – was 157,000. Of these, 13.3 per cent were in the 45–59 age group and 5.7 per cent were over the age of 60. This was the first time a detailed ethnic breakdown was collected and collated by the national census, enabling us to obtain statistical information about this community (among others). Yet the Chinese are Britain's third largest visible minority group and they have, over the years, contributed greatly to its economic, social and cultural life.

**Lee,** a waiter in central London:

> We are very hard-working people. We think it is a terrible shame to depend on the state if you are fit and well, so we tend to under-use the welfare system. Even medicines, we go to our own for small problems and pay for our care. So I would say that we cost very little to this country. But our elders have some needs which it is unfair not to give them any more. So this is something that we are coming to understand. But out there the social workers just say 'they don't need our services'.

Academic research backs this up. A study in the late 1970s commented:

> . . . the Chinese . . . retain their ability to pass almost unnoticed in the wider community . . . they do not compete for jobs with members of the host society. They rarely if ever avail themselves of the right to unemployment benefits or Social Security handouts and tend to avoid state medical services unless they require hospitalisation.[2]

Although this is still an accurate description of what is happening in the Chinese community today, we should be careful not to use this as an explanation for why 'they don't need our services'. Their history in this country has taught the Chinese, like the other visible minorities, how vulnerable they are. In part they do not seek equal treatment because the idea of equal rights for all citizens has not been promoted by the various governments of this country over the years.

**Mr Poon,** manager of a restaurant in Wales:

> We have always felt like guests in a home, many times unwelcome guests, although in our case because we keep away from the public eyes, it is not so bad as for other groups. Or maybe we just don't talk about it. I know when I was a young waiter in Soho, how many insults I heard from our customers – especially when they were drinking a lot. There were terrible fights. A man broke my arm once when he tried to escape without paying the bill and I stopped him. But you

know I was too afraid to go to the hospital, so one of our doctors tied it up! It still hurts me. My mother will not go outside alone, because she remembers this and she is afraid.

It is very important to remember that the Chinese people in Britain come from different parts of the world, speak different dialects and have class and social divisions like any other group.

# History

## *Early history*

Like Indians, the Chinese first settled here through the seafaring route. Many came here as very underpaid sailors in the British merchant ships as far back as the eighteenth century. They were often seen in Liverpool, Cardiff and London's dockyards. The employment of Chinese seamen was the direct result of the massive growth in trade with the Far East after the end of the Opium Wars when the Chinese, who lost the war, were forced by the British to open up the country for trade in opium and other commodities. The indigenous Chinese were poor and desperate after the turbulence in the area, and many took jobs on British ships. This started a tradition and a connection with the seaports of Britain. The sailors accepted low wages but their dream was to save up money and return home to a secure life in old age. They were not unionised and this made them more attractive to employers and a threat to British seamen. In 1908 and 1911 there were violent demonstrations against Chinese sailors and settlers in Liverpool and Cardiff. Some of these were provoked by the sight of Chinese men who had married or taken up with white women. The men were accused of sexually corrupting these women. In Cardiff, Chinese hand laundries were destroyed in the violence.

From 1905 to 1920 a number of laws were passed against 'aliens', which resulted in the deportation of many of these early Chinese settlers. A minority were allowed to stay on because they ran laundries and were self-sufficient. By the 1930s these hand-wash laundries were killed off by self-operated laundries.

The effect of this early history has not been washed away by time. The incidents revealed to the Chinese their insecurity as a minority and the latent racism around them. Their response was a silent one. They withdrew from competing with any sector of the host community, involving themselves in special kinds of business – initially hand laundries and then the current Chinese catering – which, by their very nature, were not a threat. They stuck together for protection and mutual support, as all people do when they go abroad. The growth of 'Chinatown' was the result of the need for security. Their self-segregation was also a protective mechanism against the possibility of hostility and persecution, which could recur if general economic conditions deteriorated.

### The 1950s and 1960s

Most of the Chinese who now live in Britain came over in the 1950s and 1960s. They came from the new territories in Hong Kong where they had worked in paddy fields. The USA had flooded the world market with its own rice, and made this farming uncompetitive. The farmers then tried vegetable farming which could not sustain them, especially as water was being diverted to maintaining expanding cities. Many of these people eventually made their way here. First the men in the 1950s, then their wives and children in the 1960s and later the elders. Families were brought in to help in the growing catering industry and also because of fears of tightening immigration laws. Most of these immigrants did not speak English and had little formal education. In the post-war years, cheap 'foreign' labour was in great demand and immigrants were welcomed. They did not experience the kind of overt hostility that had been expressed for the previous groups of Chinese immigrants, but the stories of past hostility were passed down.

**Mr Poon** again:

> My father used to tell me about the difficulties our people had all over the western world. In Canada, in America and in this country. How they helped to build up these countries but how they were never trusted and never given the equal respect. He used to tell me that words did not mean anything in these countries. Equality was not easy for our people and even now if we do well we are hated. But he also told me never to talk about this to anybody outside. He would be very angry if he heard me talking to you now. It is too dangerous, he said. Just look after your family and keep quiet. Happiness is in our home.

### The 1970s onwards

Many of the Chinese elders in Britain arrived in the 1970s to join their families. After 1980 the families had to sign papers to guarantee that they would support the elders, which means that most of these elders are not entitled to state benefits. When they arrived, they joined families who had gone through many changes since leaving Hong Kong. Most Chinese people in Britain are anxious about what will happen to Hong Kong now that it has reverted to China.

**Mrs Poon:**

> So many people we know are so worried about what the future holds. And of course the way some of the leaders in this country have reacted is so disrespectful of us. We have never been a burden and they were still panicking about Hong Kong refugees. How do you think it makes us feel? That, after so long, they still don't understand us or our people and how hard we work.

# Dispersal

Although there are concentrations of Chinese people in large British cities, like London's Chinatown, the main feature of this community is that it is scattered throughout Britain, many families living in some of the remotest areas of the country. This is the result of spreading their businesses into places where there would not be any competition. The main cities with substantial Chinese populations, besides London, are Manchester, Liverpool, Birmingham, Glasgow and Cardiff. About 90 per cent of the British Chinese community is involved in the catering trade.

# Issues affecting Chinese elders

### State benefits

As we now know, Chinese elders, unlike most other immigrant groups, are more likely to have no entitlement to state benefits. They came to Britain after strict immigration laws were passed that require the sponsoring family to support them. Breaking this bond would mean serious trouble for the family. This is what terrifies Chinese elders into not using any services without paying for them. If their children are working in restaurants, the 'tied' accommodation is usually very inadequate and tensions can run high, but there is little that can be done about the problems. If they lose their jobs, workers also lose their homes.

### Alienation

Many of the elders – perhaps as many as 70 per cent – do not speak or write even very basic English. They are therefore cut off from the world around them. There are newspapers in their languages, but no Chinese radio or television programmes. Many middle-aged Chinese women are also in this situation because, although they may have been here for many years, the circumstances of their lives did not allow them the time to go out and learn English.

**Mrs Tang**, 55, a housewife:

> We were so lonely when we came. The men were working 16 hours a day; we could not speak English, so we also had to find work in the Chinese shops and restaurants. Or we stayed at home. We took our

children to school but we could not understand the system, or help them at all. Our children are successful because they can communicate. For us it was like being blind and deaf and dumb outside.

Some elders lead fulfilling lives within their households, helping to educate the grandchildren in the old ways and giving a sense of continuity to their families. They have their own community centres where they can eat good Chinese food, play Mah Jong and talk about their lives and problems to one another. Other elders feel that their values and lifestyles are no longer shared even within their own families. Their lives feel powerless and at times without meaning. They also have no strongly held belief that they have a right to demand better treatment from society at large. Instead, there is often a heartbreaking stoicism, as if this situation is something that they, as strangers in someone else's country, have to expect.

**Min Lee**, 23, who works in the family takeaway restaurant:

I remember having these arguments with my grandfather. I asked him why the English never behaved so humble in our country, in Hong Kong, even now. They were strangers there. So why did they behave like they had a right to be there? We pay taxes so we should have rights. But my grandfather told me I had too much hot blood and that I should be more patient.

Young Chinese people are among the most highly qualified people in Britain. Many of them are moving into the professions and upper income brackets.

## Illness and death

Many elders have health problems that relate to the amount and kind of work they have had to do during their lives as well as the lives they are leading now. The NHS and social services have largely failed to cater for the health and other needs of this community, especially those who do not speak English. Children are often used as interpreters, which, for a formal people, is acutely distressing. The Chinese have fewer health problems than many other ethnic groups, but ill-health tends to increase substantially after middle age. The 1991 Census revealed: 'Both males and females from the Chinese ethnic group experience lower proportions with long-term illness in each 5-year group up to retirement age, and it is only among the oldest sections of the community that illness rates consistently exceed those for white people.'[3] (The figures also show that the Chinese largely live in rented accommodation and work substantially longer working weeks than white people and many other groups.)

About 20 per cent of Chinese people are hepatitis B carriers. There is high incidence of cancer of the nose, oesophagus (gullet) and stomach in the community. Certain forms of anaemia are also common.

There is anecdotal evidence that arthritic conditions, for example, are quite common among the Chinese population. The highly sophisticated and effective Chinese traditional medicines and treatments are often used – and, these days, by all kinds of people outside the community. There are now community centres and health centres for the Chinese, which care workers should find out about. Health education messages – for example, of the danger of smoking, something that many Chinese men do – are not really understood or accepted. Women prefer female medical and care staff.

Members of the family sit by a dying person. People generally believe in reincarnation. There are no rituals unless the person is a Christian. Some people believe that seeing a dying person will bring them ill fortune, so they may avoid the dying person and their family. It is best to check with a family member what kind of support, if any, would be appropriate from a care worker.

Some families use a special shroud. White is the traditional colour of mourning. Bodies are buried or cremated, and sometimes money is burnt with the body. Some elders keep their own burial gowns and these are often their best clothes. The period of mourning is 49 days. Most people find the need for post-mortems distressing, partly because of their religious beliefs.

## A combination of problems

Alison Norman recognised many years ago how these factors work to create very serious difficulties for Chinese elders:

> There is no doubt that they are quite often in great difficulties . . . suffering not only from culture shock but also from ill-health arising from a lifetime of work in an unhealthy kitchen or on the land. They have experienced overcrowding and rejection by the younger generation, while lack of work documentation and the perennial language and literacy problems make it very difficult for them to find out and claim their welfare rights (if they have any) or to make use of the health service.[4]

The long unsocial hours worked by families mean that people cannot always go with elders to clinics and hospitals. Because they are so widely dispersed around the country, there may not be other Chinese families to help them.

The needs of the Chinese elders remain largely unexplored because of a lack of proper research. They do not speak out and so it is assumed that they have no serious needs or that these are met by their families.

## Inappropriate or inadequate care provision

There are other reasons why elders are not using the services or demanding better treatment.

- The service provided is not culturally appropriate to their needs.
- Language and communication needs are not properly met in social service provision or health care, and there is an urgent need to rectify this. In one Midlands city, an enormous number of Chinese patients registered with a black doctor who spoke Cantonese. Since his retirement, they have lost an essential

facility and many still appear at his doorstep imploring him to look after them.

■ There aren't enough day care centres for Chinese elders, even where there is an established Chinese community, so there are few examples to follow. Those that do exist are not adequately funded.

■ The little research that has been carried out shows that Chinese elders feel the following points need to be noted:
   – they do not drink tea with milk;
   – they believe in the power of food to cure illness and to improve well-being;
   – they are often bored because they cannot understand English television;
   – they are not treated equally;
   – Chinese key workers would help to make their feelings understood.

### INTERNAL DIVISIONS AND RIVALRIES

As in all communities, Chinese people identify with various groups. Many Chinese associations are organised around kinship relationships. Other issues have started to emerge that affect the provision of services. Within the community there are struggles for influence and power, and this creates a vacuum. Social worker Wing Leung Siu found this out the hard way when trying to get the social services department in Birmingham to start a day care centre for Chinese elders:

... the internal divisions of a seemingly homogenous minority Chinese community could also form a formidable barrier which would cause delays and setbacks in communicating the genuine urgency of demands for Chinese elders, who in the meantime were unfortunately and inevitably caught in the struggles between different groups.[5]

FALSE ASSUMPTIONS

Many false assumptions are made about the Chinese community: that they look after their own and that they are a competent, trouble-free and well-off immigrant population who don't need to make any demands on the welfare state. In fact, says Wing Leung Siu, the reality is that the Chinese community does not yet possess the organisational structure and economic resources necessary to deal with the various social needs, such as health, housing and social services, of its elders. Other myths have also been challenged. It was thought for a long time that Chinese people are mentally robust and therefore do not need counselling and other services. It is now clear that mental problems do exist and that appropriate health services should be provided for individual Chinese people in need.

## *Welfare and other unmet needs*

The annual report of a Chinese community centre in London showed clearly that the three major areas for consultation in 1993/4 were housing, translation and benefits. The conclusions were:

> Our main area of work fell within the fields of welfare rights, housing, council tax enquiries and nationality . . . Translating and interpreting are still in great demand . . . the failure of the provision of translated material and the lack of trained interpreters can deny clients access to much-needed services and provisions, and cause them great hardship and difficulty.

Significant areas of work for the centre involved people who were losing their accommodation – tied to their work in restaurants – usually when they reached their mid-50s, and then being unable to get priority on council housing lists. There were also many people needing help with claims for benefits, made late because of their ignorance of the system.

**A Chinese woman**, reminiscing:

> In 1975, my husband died and we were evicted from our flat. I lost my husband, and I had no English. Suddenly I felt life was very miserable.[6]

## *Chinese carers*

Although it is true that many Chinese families look after their own, it is by no means easy for them to do so. Carers are often themselves isolated and unable to get the information they need. Many have serious money problems and do not know how to get financial assistance. The health of the elders they are looking after is often their greatest worry. They may well be looking after people with many long-term problems but don't always know what is important for their care.

### CHANGING ATTITUDES AND PROVIDING INFORMATION

There are other issues that remain untackled. Some Chinese community workers believe that there needs to be an education campaign within the community, to make them more aware of their rights and feel comfortable using the available services instead of feeling ashamed. At present, Chinese elders do not seek help outside or, if they do, they will not admit to it because of the shame they feel.

**Mrs Wong**, a 55-year-old housewife:

> I know people who really need some help because the family has many money problems. But they say 'We don't want to be a burden with our little needs. We should try and save money for the government.' I know one man has used Social Services but he will not admit it.

The Chinese community also needs practical information on how it can influence local authorities. Wing Leung Siu recommends:

> It is the social workers' obligation under the commitment of the social work profession to take the necessary steps to include these neglected

elderly in their services as a target population and to restore dignity to those Chinese elders by providing services which will permit them to lead a full and meaningful life in this country.[7]

In some cities, such as Manchester, there is sheltered accommodation for Chinese people and some classes in basic English for those who never learnt it when they came. There may be such facilities in your area.

# Religions

Some Chinese people from Hong Kong are Christians, mainly Catholic or Baptist. But most Chinese people live by certain principles that are influenced by Buddhism and Confucianism. The values they try to live by are:

- Obligations to the family.
- Respect for the elders.
- Self-reliance.
- Honesty.
- Inner strength and self-control.

Buddhism emphasises the importance of love for all life, charity, and self-denial and discipline. Some Chinese elders wear or carry a religious talisman in order to protect themselves; it is important to ask permission before touching it or removing it for care purposes.

Chinese people have deep beliefs about good and bad luck. They believe in horoscopes based on their own calendar and also on personality types. Personalities depend on the time of birth and also fall into the categories of Yin and Yang. Yin people are considered to be quiet and introverted, and Yang people more outgoing.

The Chinese believe that the soul has to be assisted to Heaven; for example, in the coffin is placed a paper boat for the journey and paper money. Food is offered to ancestors on feast days and incense is burnt.

# Family

Most Chinese people live in extended families. The children do not normally leave home until they are married, so it is quite common for parents, children, grandparents and other elders to live together. Eating together is central to their family life, as is respect across the ages, with a balance struck between the individual needs of family members and the wider demands of the family and community.

Status and relationships within extended families are clearly defined and certain titles and forms of address are used. The main breadwinner is the head of the family; all incomes are pooled and used for the benefit of the whole family. Parental authority is central to family life and even adults in their thirties expect to have parental influences on their lives. Individualism is valued less than obligation to the family, and bad behaviour is seen as bringing shame on the entire family unit. Children are encouraged to take responsibilities at an early age. Elders are accorded respect (and expect it) because of their wisdom and experiences and also because they are a connection to the past.

Divorce is still rare in the Chinese community. Family pressures to remain together are strong; even when separations take place, they are done without recourse to the law.

Traditionally, men are the heads of families, making crucial decisions and taking overall responsibility. Women are expected to look after the home and be dutiful towards their husband's family. This is true of all eastern cultures. Families are also involved in the choices that are made for life partners. These customs and expectations are changing as western values affect younger people.

# Diet

Food for the Chinese is central to their sense of well-being, and most Chinese people are very well informed about the benefits and dangers of eating certain foods. Rice is regarded as the essential source of nourishment and energy, and the diet is generally very healthy. Meat is eaten in small quantities but no dairy produce.

Most food is steamed or quickly fried, which means that vitamins are preserved.

**Mary Lee,** who works for a Chinese herbalist:

> When she went to hospital, my grandmother really suffered with her food, which was either over-cooked and heavy or raw. And they never asked her what she could eat. She just could not digest the food she was given.

There is a whole range of beliefs about the kinds of food one should eat in different situations, and most elders know these. There is a complex system about how food and the body interact, which comes from the Yin/Yang theory of food. All foods are divided into Yin foods (cooling), Yang foods (heating) and Yin Yang for neutral foods. From the western point of view, there is little obvious logic as to why one food is considered Yin and the other Yang. The effect of each food depends on the personality type of the individual. Food can create harmony or discord in the person, both physically and emotionally.

Yang foods include:

| | |
|---|---|
| butter | goose |
| chinese cabbage | onions |
| chocolate | potatoes |
| Coca Cola | red meat |
| coffee | seafood and oily fish |
| fried foods | spiced foods |
| garlic | sugar |
| ginger | yams |

Yin foods include:

| | |
|---|---|
| bean shoots | green leafy vegetables |
| boiled and steamed food | herbs |
| crab | tofu |
| fruit | |

Neutral foods include steamed rice and carrots.

It is important to check on the kinds of food that elders feel they ought to be eating, or, more importantly, which foods would be harmful to them. Because really fresh food is hard to obtain here and there is little or no intake of dairy produce, some Chinese elders may have problems with a lack of calcium.

Other practices differ from what western doctors may prescribe. With fever, for example, the tradition is to wrap up warm and to drink hot liquids, not cool drinks as recommended by western doctors.

## Festivals

The most important festival is the **Chinese New Year**, which is celebrated for up to 15 days. Presents are exchanged and special foods are made. There are many traditional beliefs about what should be done during this time and these are meant to determine what kind of year will lie ahead. There are also remembrance days for those who have died. Autumn celebrations and the **boat festival** in the summer are also important.

## Clothes

Most Chinese elders wear trousers. They do not feel comfortable with hospital gowns and other attire that they are not used to.

## Language, culture and values

The two most common languages are Mandarin and Cantonese, although there are people from Hong Kong who also speak other dialects such as Hakka. The written script, which is the same for all the dialects, is very complex.

Sunday is when Chinese children attend language classes or people shop and visit one another. For many it is the only day they have off work.

After giving birth, Chinese women are expected to rest, avoid cold drinks and not wash their hair for several days. Women elders will take over their roles temporarily.

Formality is important, even between close family members. Eyes, for example, are lowered when someone is speaking to a person of a higher status. It is not considered polite to contradict such a person or to say 'no'. It is regarded as impolite to directly criticise a person or embarrass them in public. 'Losing face' is something that many elders find difficult. Food is offered to all guests (who include care workers) and refusals are seen as rudeness. If care workers 'barge in' on people's lives, touch the objects in the home and seem to take over, it may well be regarded as poor manners and cause offence.

As in the Asian communities, the elders and middle-aged people in the Chinese community are deeply affected by the breakdown of the conventions they value, such as respect for old age; duty to the family is of fundamental importance and formality is strictly observed. The younger generation is influenced by the mores of this country where freedom and individualism are often considered more important than family obligations and older people may be regarded as a burden.

New schemes are starting up in which volunteers from the community befriend elders and provide help, support and friendship. This is something that the Chinese Health Resource Centre in London's Westminster is trying out. Some of the children are rejecting their own language and then finding it hard to talk to their elders. Looking after their younger grandchildren, which so many Chinese elders used to do, becomes more difficult when the children go to school and start learning English.

**Mr Sam,** a Chinese elder:

> I worked for 40 years in a restaurant in Hong Kong. Then I got a problem in my bones. I came here to be with my daughter and her husband, because I have no son. My illness has got worse. I have no

> money and I do not wish to ask my daughter; it would be a big shame. But they are very kind to me and they too have problems with their young growing up in this country where there is no discipline at all.

Because the Chinese community in Britain are scattered around the country, often in remote parts, elders can feel especially isolated. Younger members of the family often work long hours in the restaurants, and the elders' sense of guilt and being useless is made worse.

**Min Lee**, a college student

> My grandparents were miserable before they died. I did feel for them. They felt guilty because they were not doing more to help us – we were working twelve hours a day – the children had grown up so there was nothing to do there, and they just used to sit and stare into the distance. My grandfather even stopped eating, like he shouldn't really eat because he was not contributing anything. He was a proud man. You know, I was happy for them when they died.

Other changes, too, can leave the elders bewildered. Daughters are all meant to get married, but nowadays many Chinese women are choosing to go into higher education and careers.

Although most Chinese elders have no dream of returning home and they see that life in this country has often given their families a decent standard of living, there may be a sadness about them when they are getting to the last years of their lives.

**Mr Yoon**, a worker at a Chinese community centre:

> They often joke about being buried in English soil, saying that then they will have to speak English so they can converse with their English neighbours underground.

The most important thing to understand about the Chinese community – and most of the other non-western communities – is the gap between the world the elders knew best and the world they are in now. As people get older, they often seek the comfort of the known and of routines, so this gap becomes more significant. When that gap is between not just elders and society in general but also the younger members of their family, it must take a person of incredible strength not to feel dislocated and troubled.

Amy Tan, a Chinese-American woman, wrote a moving introduction in her novel *The Joy Luck Club*, which is about the lives of different generations of Chinese women adjusting to new lives and relationships in the West. The introduction has the story of an old woman who had bought a swan in a market in Shanghai because the vendor told her that the bird was once a duck that stretched its neck hoping to become a goose but ended up a swan. When she moved to the States she couldn't take the swan, which she wanted to give to her daughter, so she could understand how a creature 'could become more than what was hoped for . . . Now the woman was old. And she had a daughter who grew up speaking only English and swallowing more Coca Cola than sorrow . . . And she waited year after year for the day she could tell her daughter this in perfect American English . . .'[8]

## Names

The family name comes first, followed by the personal name or names. Women keep their own family names when they marry. Some people have changed the order of their names so that they follow British conventions. Christian Chinese names are in the order given name, middle name and family name. There are only 438 surnames in China. Formality is important, so the title Mr or Miss or Mrs should be given even when using the personal name. Asking someone for their first and last name can be confusing for a Chinese elder because not all of them follow Christian naming traditions.

# THE VIETNAMESE COMMUNITY

The Vietnamese are the last immigrants to be admitted into Britain as a group. They came as refugees. Although many of the issues that affect them are similar to the ones that concern the Chinese community, there are significant differences, mainly because of their painful history and the manner of their arrival.

## History

In 1978/9, the 'boat people' of Viet Nam hit the headlines in the western world. Saigon had fallen in 1975, and the Americans had left after losing the long war in Viet Nam. Many of these boat people were refugees, leaving after the fall of Saigon to the Viet Cong army because they had been closely associated with the USA. Over the next few years nearly 160,000 refugees either left or were 'encouraged' to leave by the Vietnamese government. Hundreds died as they tried to cross the seas in small inadequate boats. Many of them ended up in refugee camps in Hong Kong, where the shortage of space and the large numbers arriving daily were creating a crisis. Two people had to sleep on each tiny bunk, and seven people with their belongings lived in an area 1.8 by 1.2 metres (6 by 4 feet). There was a tiny cooking area outside each dormitory, and communal toilet and washing facilities.

Viet Nam has suffered from war and political upheavals for several decades. There were conflicts not just with outside forces such as France and the USA but also between North and South Viet Nam. Because of this history most Vietnamese are deeply suspicious or even fearful of officials and others from their own country unless they know them. Hostility continues between many of those who supported the USA and those who supported the Communists, and this can flare up among Vietnamese elders living in Britain. This should not surprise anybody: consider how unforgiving some Allied veterans of World War 2 still are of the Japanese.

# Refugees accepted by Britain

In 1980 about 22,000 Vietnamese people were allowed to come and settle in Britain. In many cases families are still waiting to be reunited. The Government policy for these refugees was to 'provide the Vietnamese with survival skills and an initial launch into the community'. But, according to Carol Dalglish, an expert on this history, there was short-term thinking and not much more: there was no long-term strategy for settlement.[9]

It is well known that newcomers, especially those who did not plan to leave their homelands, seek to be with those with whom they can share experiences, cultural norms, religious beliefs and language. This is particularly important because, after they leave their homes, they have to live as stateless people for a long time and they lose a central aspect of their identity. Many may have lost their relatives or have lost track of them.

**Miss Ho,** a patient at a therapy centre:

> I know I'm going mad. I don't eat because I don't want to eat. Because I remember that my family is dead and many of them had no food. I feel bad that I am here and I am not dead.

## Resettlement and issues that affect Vietnamese elders

The refugees went into camps for up to six months but only a tiny minority became competent in English during this period. Those in the older age group, suffering from emotional distress, found it very difficult to pick up English.

One of the problems was that only three months were allotted to give these refugees what they needed in terms of language training and basic survival skills. After that, further settlement work was put in the hands of different voluntary agencies. Rivalry and disagreements arose, and none of the agencies was really equipped to handle the task.

The other strategy used by the Government was the dispersal policy, by which the Vietnamese were settled in small groups throughout Britain. It was intended to 'spread the burden' and also discourage 'ghettos' but the result was disastrous. It is hard to imagine what it must have felt like to be a group of seven boat people stuck out in some small village with very different customs and culture.

**Miss Saigon,** the name a student has called herself:

> I was nine years old, and with my parents and brother and one aunt we were in this village where for weeks they just stared at us and turned their heads away if we smiled. In school the teachers were kinder. But we felt like monsters. My mother used to cry every evening. But not in front of them. We are proud people. So, as soon as we could, we moved to London and there it was much better.

Many Vietnamese elders are illiterate in their own language. A large number have never been able to find work, either because of their language problems or because their skills have not matched the jobs available. Moreover, unlike the Chinese, there was no financial base with which to start up small businesses.

Even people who had skills to offer received little or no help to make the most of their talents in the resettlement process. This has left many of them, as they approach old age, feeling inadequate and lacking in the self-respect that they hold so dear. Extraordinarily, the resettlement policy did not include finding employment for the Vietnamese. In time they would be treated as scroungers, but they were discriminated against and so could not find work or training schemes. It is important to remember that most of these people were farmers or skilled craftspeople or professionals back home; it is very sad that their talents have been wasted.

**Mr Xinh,** 53, unemployed:

> I was a navy engineer but I have no work for ten years. We are not lazy people but it is so hard to find the work when you are a refugee. You are treated like a child. I am very grateful to Britain, but now I am

getting old I feel terrible. I make these pictures of my country. I know we cannot go back; maybe in the next life our country will be more lucky.

## Key issues

■ After such traumas as they have gone through, survival and safety for themselves and their loved ones are their priorities.

■ They seek freedom from further persecution, and do not want to be treated like second-class citizens.

■ As with the Chinese, there is a reluctance to depend on the state, partly because of their culture and partly because they are very conscious that they are 'only refugees' who should not demand any rights.

■ They want and need confirmation of their personal and cultural identity, and acceptance as human beings.

■ Some have still not had their basic needs met – health, housing, economic security, etc.

Even where physical needs have been catered for, there is still much work to be done to rebuild lives psychologically. The hardest thing for refugees to acquire is what they all want: to be treated as individuals with specific needs and abilities, not as part of some mass 'lost' people. Most do not wish to return to their country but want to remain in Britain.

Some of them have faced racial abuse and attack, and this has affected their sense of well-being. Most walk away from verbal abuse; others are too frightened to retaliate even when physically attacked.

There are hardly any facilities available for the elders, and many need to get out and mix with their own people, especially as space in the home tends to be restricted. When families are experiencing tensions, the elders will not talk about it or say if they would like to move out.

# Religions

Three main religions underpin the values that most Vietnamese live by: Buddhism, Confucianism and Taoism. Even among Christian converts, there is a tendency to incorporate some of the following principles.

## Buddhism

- Existence is hard and often taxing.
- Desire and craving that cause anguish should be controlled and overcome.
- There is no hell and heaven but individuals are responsible for their actions.

## Confucianism

- As with the Chinese people, Confucianism spells out social and family relationships, respect for elders and also one's ancestors.

## Taoism

- Taoism teaches the balance between human beings and their environment.
- There is a strong belief in reincarnation and the belief that everyone is responsible for their destiny.

Care workers can get confused if they don't understand that Vietnamese (and Chinese) people can describe themselves as having two or even three religions. There is less emphasis in these religions on a personal relationship with God or the after-life. There is more concern with how an individual lives and controls his or her own daily life. Some Vietnamese people find it difficult to talk about religion because of persecution back home.

The Vietnamese lunar month of July is when most people pray for their ancestors to be safe and happy in the next world, under the protection of Buddha, or to be forgiven by Buddha for any sins or wrongs they have done.

# Diet

The food is similar to Chinese food. Soup and rice are eaten at every meal. Fish sauce rather than soy sauce is often used and chillis are added to make food pungent. Some Vietnamese are vegetarians; others don't eat meat for the whole of July, when they have something to pray for (eg for illness to be cured or a lost relative found) or as a way to thank God/Buddha.

# Festivals

A number of festivals are the same as those celebrated by the Chinese. **Tet Nguyen Dam,** the New Year celebration, usually lasts for three days; traditionally, in the country, it could last all of the Vietnamese lunar month of January and people would leave their work on the land to rest and 'recharge' themselves in preparation for the seasons to come. There is also **Tet Thanh Minh** in March when people visit their ancestors' graves, **Tet Doan Ngo** (the early May festival to kill germs, snakes etc) and a special festival for children, called **Tet Nhi Dong** or **Tet Trung Thu** (mid-autumn festival).

# Language, culture and values

The vast majority of refugees from Viet Nam speak Vietnamese, which is very different from Chinese. However, about 5 per cent of people from Viet Nam are ethnic Chinese who speak different dialects of the Chinese language as well as Vietnamese (which they adapt to be able to communicate or to do business with others). This means that, in terms of translation, it may be possible to use a Cantonese speaker from the Chinese community if no Vietnamese interpreter is available.

The people believe in education, hard work and betterment for its own sake rather than for wealth. There is an enormous sense of unity within and obligation to members of the extended family, but almost no tradition of helping anyone outside this network. The concept of voluntary work, for example, is non-existent. Research among a group of 50 Vietnamese elders in Coventry found them all living with their families. But, although these traditions have survived so far, there are fears that the young are changing and will forget them in due course. An article in The *Sunday Times* described how one family lives:

> Kien Dan Tran's 78-year-old mother, Dung Thu Huynh, and his 71-year-old uncle, Hoa Mai Huynh, share the modern house near Crystal Place . . . Dung, the eldest male child, will when he marries accept looking after his parents in old age.[10]

Friendships and family relationships are central to the sense of belonging. The Vietnamese writer Thuy Vuong says in his book:

> The Vietnamese family has been so indispensable for the existence and survival of Vietnamese society and of the nation that, if any one wishes to destroy that society or nation, he must first destroy the Vietnamese family.[11]

This, in a sense, has happened to the refugees. Some have not yet managed to gather even their immediate families around them. For elders this is a source of great pain. The family is actively involved in births, deaths, adoption, settling disputes, welfare, medical care, education and providing financial support. Without this framework, therefore, the sense of isolation can be extreme. As Carol Dalglish writes:

> The separation of families, the anxiety for family reunions and the grieving for those lost has to be borne in mind in all dealings with those recently settled, as these experiences are likely to colour their reactions to their new environment and the opportunities offered.[12]

Many of the family structures and obligations are similar to those for the Chinese (see p 137). Divorce is still a rare occurrence in Vietnamese families.

## Carers

Many Vietnamese families care for their own when they are ill or elderly; family members who are at home will take up this caring role. In many cases elders are cared for by their grandchildren. The care is often all hours, and this is what is expected by the family and the person being cared for.

In a study in south London, the researchers found that these young carers were not well informed about available services and were therefore coping on their own without any help, often in very difficult circumstances. There were problems of financial and other hardships. For example, carers in some poor families found it hard to provide adequate heating for Vietnamese elders, who felt the cold acutely, and to wash soiled linen without washing machines. Many are still adjusting to life in this country.

The report included a description of Chinh, a 19-year-old Vietnamese woman, who was caring for her grandparents. Her grandmother was bedridden after a stroke and the family had had no care from social services in spite of countless requests for help. The study concluded:

> The Vietnamese/Chinese carers received more family help and support than the other groups . . . This does not mean that they are a self-sufficient group with no need of services. When services give few welcoming messages to people recently arrived in this country, it is natural for them to turn to their own communities for support . . . since they receive no services, they continue to care with hardly any help.[13]

## Illness and death

Hepatitis B is carried by 20 per cent of the Vietnamese population. Tooth decay is a problem, but in this group it is the emotional pain of the war and its aftermath that is worst. In both the Chinese and Vietnamese communities 'chi' or vital energy is very important. It is believed to be the life force, and illness is related to how much this is blocked and needs correcting.

Dying patients usually prefer to die at home because they believe that, otherwise, the spirit will not find peace. If this is not possible, tact and understanding will be needed to explain to the family.

Loud crying and wailing is traditional. In hospitals, a separate room for this would be advisable. Photographs are sometimes taken of family gatherings at funerals. White is the colour of mourning.

Much belief revolves around the spirit of the dead and the formal rites of the funeral. There can be some anxiety that, unless correct rituals are followed, the soul of the dead will not rest in peace. In Buddhism, the date for a funeral is chosen by consulting the dead person's horoscope. Sometimes the bodies are cremated, sometimes buried. If cremated, the ashes are returned home and placed in a jar in a temple. If the person is buried, ritual offerings of food and incense are left at the grave. Paper money and candles are burnt as offerings for Buddhists, and special remembrance days are marked in the first year.

Grief is openly expressed and shared. Support is usually provided by close relatives, both emotional and material if needed. Sometimes, however, superstition about death bringing bad luck means that relatives may keep their distance from the bereaved. So support cannot be assumed.

## Names

The family name appears first, followed by a middle name and then a personal name. A woman keeps her surname after marriage. Male titles include Ong, Anh, Chu and Bac. Van is normally used as a middle name. Female titles include Ba, Chi and Co. Thi is usually used as a middle name.

The personal name is usually used only by family members. These days, Vietnamese people are changing the order of their names to fit in with British conventions. Asking for first and last names, though, can be confusing for Vietnamese elders because they don't all follow Christian naming traditions

The needs of the Vietnamese community are summarised by one elder. He used to be a naval officer, then took to the seas with his wife and three children, watched people he knew die and has ended up an enormously sad man in an east London housing estate where racial abuse and assault are commonplace:

> I don't mind about the food, the weather or even these stupid people who insult you. I am very happy that my children are in this country and are going to the university and I am very grateful. But my life has been wasted because I could not work and could not get the respect from the society. That is more important to me than my life.

# 6 The Jewish, Polish and Turkish communities

In this chapter we look at three groups of elders whose original homes were on the European mainland. They are from ethnic minority communities that are often left out of relevant studies and surveys. Their inclusion here is extremely important, not only because there are issues that care workers and providers need to be aware of but also because they illustrate both the commonality of experience for immigrants to this country and key differences.

## THE JEWISH COMMUNITY

### Key issues

- Jewish people have been in Britain for many centuries, but the main Jewish immigration occurred during and after World War 2, following Nazi attempts to exterminate the entire population from mainland Europe.
- Regarded as one of the most successful communities in this country, Jewish people have had a tremendous influence on the arts, business, the law, politics, academia and the world of finance.
- They have a history of looking after their own, and this tradition certainly applies to the facilities they have set up for their elders.
- Many Jewish people have assimilated into British society. This was possible because physically they are not as easily distinguishable as other ethnic groups and also because this is what they wanted for themselves and their children. Other communities would find this impossible or undesirable.

- In terms of religious belief there are enormous differences between various British groups and individuals. They go from strictly orthodox Jews who live within their own community to non-religious Jews who nevertheless feel culturally Jewish. In between you get a range of people with varying degrees of religious observance.

- Most Jewish people have a shared sense of history and collective memories. When there are signs of anti-semitism as we have had recently in Europe, it deeply affects the survivors of the holocaust and their descendants. Nazi rule and the genocide of millions of Jewish people have understandably left a mark.

- The Jewish community is regarded as a religious and also an ethnic community. Like Arabs and other Middle Eastern people, they are Semites. Arabic and Hebrew are Semitic languages. Jews whose origins lie in eastern and central Europe are called Ashkenazi Jews, and those from the Middle East, North Africa and Spain are known as Sephardic Jews.

## History

The one element that defines many of the elders of the Jewish community in Britain is their awareness of a long history of persecution. Anti-semitism has been a feature of western history for hundreds of years and it does not take much even now for it to surface. Many of the European Jews will have personally experienced terror and loss of people they knew in concentration camps. In the 1980s a young Jewish woman was killed by an elder who had been in one of the camps and who had never recovered mentally or emotionally. The irony is that the young woman was a photographer taking pictures of just such Jewish elders.

While this is a powerful collective memory for all Jewish people, and a reminder to them of how vulnerable they were and can still be, it is important to remember that there are differences between individual Jewish people when it comes to how vulnerable they feel. Those who were born in this country, for example, are the descendants of early Jewish migrants in the eighteenth and nineteenth centuries. Some of them were Russian Jews who had fled the official persecution against them following the assassination of Tsar Alexander II. This was between 1881 and 1914. Their children, who are now themselves elders, retain many of the cultural practices of this first wave of Jewish refugees.

These elders feel a sense of persecution much less acutely than the European Jews because, on the whole, the level and manifestation of anti-semitism in Britain have been much less pervasive and appalling than almost anywhere else on the European continent.

**Julia**, a Jewish academic who retired five years ago from her university job:

> I can honestly say that I have never experienced any antipathy or antagonism towards me during the course of my entire life. Perhaps because I was an academic. Being an English Jew has been a completely different experience for me from those who came here from Germany. Sometimes when I was younger, I almost used to feel a sense of guilt and envy that I didn't have that anguish to offer and that I felt boringly safe and secure. But it is important for people to know that not all Jewish elders are traumatised.

Contrast this with the thoughts of Hugh, another Jewish elder, also an academic, now retired.

**Hugh**:

> As you get older and nearer the end of your life, you remember these times even more sharply than you did when you were younger. I get nightmares now and I cry in my sleep. But it is very difficult, because time is moving on and people expect not to go on about the past. The only person who understands is my grandson. The one thing you know as a Jew is that history and all the persecution for centuries before that.

**Esther**, his wife, who lost her family in the concentration camps in Germany, adds:

> Our most vivid memories always concern Germany. How we decided to leave it, how fortunate we were to escape it – yet how so much of ourselves we left behind. So much that you can't ever forget.

Whatever happened in the years afterwards, it seems that, for many Jewish people who went through the pain and terror of Nazism, much of this comes back as they grow older and they need to talk about it.

**Hugh** again:

> I think you have to understand something else, too. For so many years we did not talk about these things, and there are many reasons for this. There was a lot of hidden hostility here which we did not want to provoke. So I remember when our children went to school, we taught them not to talk too much about their Jewishness. It was in order to protect them. Then of course there is the terrible pain of recall, for some mingled with guilt and shame. There are such complex emotions tied in with this history that even now people cannot really come to terms with what happened and why. And then there is that even deeper sense that it has always been thus for us, throughout history.

Hostile attitudes towards Jewish refugees were seen in Britain even when people began to find out what was happening to Jews in Germany. There has always been a contradiction between the self-image of this country as warm and welcoming to those in need and the reality. As one study on refugees observed:

> 'Throughout the 1930s most countries stuck rigidly to their immigration policies and quotas despite the rumours emanating from Germany . . . all countries, including Britain and the United States, stood adamant in refusing government assistance to the refugees, insisting that this was Germany's responsibility.'[1]

In the 1930s the British Medical Association, in an urgent report to the government, opposed the entry of Jewish refugee doctors to Britain. They argued that they were biologically and culturally so distinct that they could never become a part of this country.

Between 1933 and 1939 every refugee had to be sponsored, either privately or by an organisation that undertook that they would not be a burden to the country. In 1938 a central committee was set up – the joint Consultative Committee on Refugees – to collectively provide such guarantees. It is estimated that 56,000 refugees came over in this period from Germany and East European countries. This then set a pattern, which may in part be responsible for the highly impressive self-help tradition that has evolved in the British Jewish community.

**Hugh** again:

> You have to understand why we are so good at this kind of thing. It is not because we are special but because our history has prepared us for such terrible betrayals. For us to help ourselves has become one more survival issue. This does not mean we are better immigrants or refugees at all. All our organisations use private funds and also state resources that are at our disposal, but this is more possible for us than other groups because we have gained influence in many spheres of life.

The refugees who came here in the 1930s were less traditional in many ways than the previous arrivals. Many were highly qualified and had made names for themselves in the professions, arts and other fields. Like the Afro-Caribbean and Chinese peoples who had had earlier experiences of life in this country that percolated down to the post-war immigrants, the newer groups of Jewish refugees learnt from the experiences of previous generations and then made their own contributions to the collective memories.

## Origins and dispersal

The Jewish community in Britain is made up of people whose origins lie in disparate places such as Poland, Russia, the Ukraine, Czechoslovakia, Rumania and Germany.

It is estimated that there are now over 400,000 people of Jewish origin living in Britain. Strictly accurate numbers are hard to find because many Jewish people feel intensely suspicious of any kind of ethnic monitoring after what happened in Germany and also because some have assimilated so entirely into the mainstream society that they do not see any point in describing themselves solely on the basis of their religious or ethnic roots. More controversially, there is a minority who wish to dissociate themselves from other ethnic minorities whom they feel are perceived as troublemakers and a burden.

**Daniel**, a 55-year-old businessman:

> It really is not in our interests to be in a book with other ethnic minority groups. We are people who have given more to this state than we have ever taken out of it. We don't need other people to look after our needs and we certainly don't wish to be like those immigrants who never ever get up on their own two feet.

These are therefore general figures, which need to be treated with caution. About 20 per cent of British Jews are over retirement age. Most live in London or the outskirts, but there are other communities around the country. In Leeds you can find the descendants of the early refugees from Russia; they once made up 12 per cent of the population of this city.

**Joshua**, a Jewish elder at a synagogue in Coventry:

> There are about 40 families living here. This synagogue was established 120 years ago. But Jewish people have been living here for hundreds of years. They were involved in ribbon weaving and later in the industrial revolution and the service sector.

Many inter-war and post-war arrivals settled initially in the east end of London, where they worked in the 'rag' trade and found cheap housing. With education a high priority, the children of many of these original east end Jews have become phenomenally successful and have moved out into more affluent areas. What often tends to happen is that the children move, leaving ageing communities in parts of inner London. In some of these inner city areas, most of the Jewish population are elders. In Tower Hamlets there is a growing problem of isolation and immobility, which means that the essentials such as kosher food are harder to acquire. These needs are not catered for by most relevant authorities.

# Religion

Practising Jews believe in one God. Orthodox Jews live strictly according to the Torah, the five books of Moses that detail codes of law and behaviour which govern every aspect of life. These are Genesis, Exodus, Leviticus, Numbers and Deuteronomy (as in the Old Testament of the Christian Bible). Jewish people believe that God requires them to live a good life – that they must achieve holiness in this world rather than the after-life. How you treat your fellow human beings is just as important as praying to God.

Whilst Orthodox Jews follow these rules strictly, Progressive, Reform and Liberal Jews (who have their own synagogues) have adapted their religious observance to suit their modern lifestyles. There can be much disagreement between the factions. Sabbath is observed by many but not all Jewish people. It begins on Friday evening and ends on Saturday evening. No work is done. In some homes no baths are run or lights switched on. Candles are lit and prayers said. Special food may also be cooked. This is an important break from routine and a time for the family to renew itself.

Jewish boys are circumcised eight days after birth, usually by a recognised person called a mohel. At the age of 13, boys are accepted into the community in a ceremony called the Bar Mitzvah; for girls it is called the Bat Chayil.

There are many Jewish people who are not religious and who live secular lives.

## *Prayers*

Prayers are said three times a day. Some Jewish men carry leather bags containing sacred texts and some wear prayer shawls. All such texts and prayer books should be regarded with respect and not touched. Synagogues are found all over the country and they are a focal point for the community as well as places to pray.

## Diet

Practising Jews observe some kind of dietary regulations. These include the following:

- No pork products are eaten, and shellfish of all kinds is forbidden; both these are considered unclean.
- Other meat can be eaten if it is kosher – killed according to Jewish regulations. This is mainly in order to kill animals as quickly and painlessly as possible. The blood is drained out and the meat is salted and washed to remove all traces of blood.
- No meat from an animal that has died naturally or from a disease can be eaten.
- Meat from the hindquarters of an animal is not eaten.
- Strict observers don't eat meat and dairy products at the same meal (some hours must pass between eating the two types of food).
- Meat and milk products are not cooked together. They are kept apart and cooked in separate utensils; separate sets of plates are used for meat and for milk products.
- Kosher wines, margarines and oils are available.
- Food prepared by non-Jews (gentiles) may be a problem for devout Jews. If such a situation arises and there is no alternative, you will have to explain tactfully that, although you respect this, sometimes, because the system is under pressure, these preferences cannot always be catered for. It is important not to feel insulted by such requests.
- Kosher food is served in separate dishes from non-kosher food.

## Festivals

Among the many festivals are the following.

**Rosh Hashanah**, the New Year, starts the Jewish new year with the Ten Days of Penitence. It is a day for reflection and prayer, and a time when people realise their sins and unite in God.

**Yom Kippur**, the Day of Atonement, is the tenth day of Penitence, and the holiest day in the Jewish calendar. Many devout people fast for 24 hours leading up to sunset on Yom Kippur itself.

**Passover** is the Jewish festival of eight days that commemorates the Exodus of the Jews from Egypt and the redemption of the Israelites. During Passover all foods containing yeast are prohibited. Symbolic dishes such as unleavened bread are prepared to remind the Jewish people of their struggles and to celebrate their freedom. It is a family occasion.

**Hanukkah** is an eight-day event in December when candles are lit to remember the re-possession of the Jewish temple in Jerusalem from the Greeks. Children get presents throughout this period.

## Ablutions

People wash before they pray. Most Jewish elders wash their hands before they eat.

## Clothes

Religious Jews dress modestly; in the Orthodox community, women cover their hair with either a scarf or a wig. Men sometimes wear a skull cap and a special undergarment. The particular clothes worn by this group defines them and in some ways makes them a target for attacks and abuse. There is evidence that Orthodox Jews face overt abuse and sometimes violence in the streets.

## Language, culture and values

Most Jewish people speak English, although in the Orthodox community Yiddish is spoken as the first language and many elders also speak other European languages.

The family is very important to most Jewish people. The mother is particularly important because the Jewish line is passed on through the woman rather than the man.

**Jacob**, a middle-aged deeply religious man:

> In many ways we are like the Asian people. Our identity is strong and our values are family oriented. We take care of everything in our community. I don't know any family that uses Social Services. If the family cannot do it, we have welfare boards. We try to look after our own.

This has happened in part to respond to the specific requirements of Jewish elders. It shows how, even where a community has assimilated successfully (and not all elders approve of this) and there aren't radically different value systems or language problems, the distinct needs of minority groups remain significant and important to them. Where they exist, such services provided from within clearly work very well indeed; Jewish Care is a model for many in how this can be done. As Pam Schweitzer has said:

> The Jewish community is often held up as a model of how a minority can accept its responsibilities and care for its own elderly and infirm population. Certainly the excellent organisation and varied programme of activities in the Jewish day centres was impressive, and there was plenty of evidence of a continuing link with Yiddish culture as well as religious observance.[2]

Some Jewish people feel strongly that these links must be kept alive in order to prevent the Jewish identity from fading away.

**Jacob** again:

> Just because we can disappear into the society and many of us are liberals and live like anyone else, does not take away the identity that is Jewish at its heart, at its core. And I don't want people to assume that my Jewishness in not an issue. I want them to ask me what I eat, whether I keep Sabbath or not. The problem is, these days, they just think it cannot matter.

The following are some issues that the Jewish community is now having to deal with.

## Assimilation

Like Jacob, there are some in the community, especially among the young, who are beginning to question the way Jewish people have assimilated into mainstream British society. With the large numbers of mixed marriages and because it is not easy to convert to Judaism, there are fears among the elders – and the young – that the community will simply die out. The Jewish line is passed on through the mother, not the father, which limits the families in mixed marriages who can pass on the Jewish faith to their children.

**David,** a university student:

> I think we went too far and we gave up too much of our identity. With that and the number of people who are marrying out of the community, our religion will die in a hundred years' time.

## Turning back to the religion

Some people who gave up almost entirely on their religion and their cultural practices seem to seek their place within the community when they are old or dying. This is causing some controversy.

**A rabbi** in the Midlands:

> You do not see these people contributing in any way to our way of life for their entire lives and then at the end they seek us. The people we bury in our cemetery must be seen as active Jews, but on the other hand you cannot deny people their wishes when they are dying or after they have died. But it is difficult.

There is also increasing recognition of the needs of Jewish elders who survived the holocaust and who for decades have bottled up their feelings and fears. New residential homes were set up in the late 1990s for these people. To make the homes culturally sensitive, there are no video cameras or uniformed security guards, so people are not reminded of their time in the camps. All Jewish rituals are kept up for residents, and volunteers – including young German students – are brought in to work and learn. Residents are not forced to remember; great care is taken not to push this, as the results could be very damaging. Most of all, no assumptions are made about how the individuals have dealt with this history.

## Illness and death

Orthodox Jews have strict beliefs about some kinds of medical intervention (eg transplants). During Passover, some medicines may also be a problem. It is important to contact the relevant rabbi to check this out. Among some Orthodox Jews, a diet that is low in fresh fruit and vegetables may cause health problems. Some children of Jews originating from eastern and central Europe suffer from a genetic disorder called Tay–Sachs disease.

When there is a death or someone is dying, prayers are said by close contacts. Different rabbis serve different Jewish groups and this should be checked with the family of someone who is dying. After death the body is washed by people of the community and burial takes place as soon as possible. Post-mortems are not permitted unless it is for legal reasons. The community is, where possible, supportive to those grieving. For eight days people mourn and pray; this continues within the family for up to eleven months.

Men and women are buried in separate areas. In some cases now, among less orthodox Jews, cremation is chosen.

As in most ethnic communities, when death occurs enormous support is given by those from the same community; you need to work with family members and others to provide appropriate support. If there is no community and family support, you should find out what you can do by talking to someone at Jewish Care or a synagogue.

## Useful terms

**kappel** small skullcap worn by some Jewish men

**kosher** food that meets Jewish requirements; the term is also used
generally to mean acceptable or correct

**rabbi** Jewish priest

**scheitel** scarf or wig worn by orthodox Jewish women

**Shabbat** sabbath

# THE POLISH COMMUNITY

Here we look in the main at the non-Jewish Polish community,
which arrived here after World War 2. It is important to distinguish
between the two groups who have settled here from Poland and
also to understand the relationship between them. Polish Jews
would usually see themselves as Jewish rather than Polish.

## Key issues

- Most Polish people arrived' here during World War 2 and its
  aftermath.
- Some immigrants from Poland are Jewish but most are Roman
  Catholics.
- They have settled well in Britain but most, even third-generation
  British Poles, have not lost their connections with their Polish
  heritage.

## History

The first major immigration from Poland to Britain was of Jewish
people at the end of the nineteenth and beginning of the twentieth
centuries. They were fleeing from anti-semitism and persecution,
which were rife at the time. Anti-semitism still exists in Poland.

The second influx of refugees from Poland took place after 1939.
When Communists took over the country, many who considered
themselves to be an army and government in exile came to Britain.

Other Polish people who had fought with the Allies and liberated Polish prisoners of war also came to this country. By the 1950s, 135,000 Polish people had settled here. Many had been stationed here during the war and they moved into those same areas. Camps and hostels were used to provide them with accommodation, and small Polish enclaves established their communities here. In time, these enclaves and hostels broke up and by the 1960s most people had moved into private accommodation. They still, however, tended to live in clusters in major cities across the country.

The community was close and organised as a state with military and social organisations and even special commemoration ceremonies. The British government looked favourably on these exiles, and restrictions on other groups did not apply to Polish people. But there was resistance from others affected by immigration policies restricting entry, although the Poles had arrived here not out of choice but of necessity.

The trade unions rejected Polish workers and there was also a degree of prejudice against Polish exiles; this pushed Poles into building up a strong in-group solidarity. Academic studies of the period argue that other factors were responsible for the attitudes towards Polish migrants:

> . . . many of the migrants spoke little English and did not possess relevant skills . . . The civil rights of these minorities were restricted . . . and their access to social rights limited. This was because of a reluctance, felt perhaps most strongly in the Trade Union movement, to accept that the newcomers might be included in the circle of those to whom benefits might be conferred within the new welfare state.[3]

This is probably why the Polish people, like the Jewish community, put all their energies into self-supporting networks and sponsorship to overcome the animosity of the society in which they found themselves.

# Dispersal

Most of the settlements of Catholic Polish people are in London, Manchester, Bradford, the Midlands and Slough. It is common to find Polish churches, social centres and clubs there. They provide mutual help and support, especially for the immigrants who are getting older. However, as the group becomes more dispersed and widespread, and as the children marry outside the Polish community, the elders may find it more difficult to keep their traditions going.

**Peter,** a Polish elder in his 80s who lost one leg in the war:

> When my comrades in war die one by one these days, I want to cry – not only because they were my friends and family in this country but because all those things that kept us going, our optimism, the way we celebrate Christmas, who we are as Polish people, is also going with them. We are lucky that we kept our language to continue with the younger generations. My grandchildren can talk to me in Polish, but they are changing the way they think and their world is also changing. And of course our country is changing even faster. So it feels as if inside my head is the only world I am comfortable with and outside I feel cold and strange and alone.

**Eva,** Peter's wife:

> Right from the beginning we sought out each other. We felt such a terrible sense of loss. We had left behind a country with so many memories and unfulfilled dreams, and there was so much that we could not understand over here. The language and the way of life. Some things were also wonderful as the country rebuilt; it was like watching a miracle. And we had good friends among the English.

A large number of Polish people who came here were deskilled. Many professionals took up manual work because there was no real choice, so there was a loss of confidence. But there was also burning ambition to make sure that their children grasped the opportunities that were available to make good.

# Religion

The main religion of this group of Poles is Catholicism; it is practised actively, and not just by the older generation. The Polish churches in Britain – mostly in inner city areas – are well attended by young and old, who share a deep faith, language and cultural bonds.

**Catherine**, a frail 80-year-old:

> My eyes are not so good so I bring my Polish newspaper and somebody reads it to me after mass.

# Diet

The Polish diet is somewhat similar to English food although there are of course special dishes and differences in the foods that are cooked for Christmas, for example. No meat is eaten at Christmas. Fish is eaten on Christmas Eve. Potato dumplings, cabbage, spiced sausages and meatballs cooked in particular ways are common foods. Polish baking is famous and in Polish cafes around Britain you can still find authentic cakes, doughnuts and biscuits.

# Festivals

The (non-Jewish) Polish people follow the Christian calendar and observe the many festivals throughout the year. **Easter** is particularly important, and it is usually **Christmas Eve** that is celebrated with a feast rather than **Christmas Day**, which tends to be a quieter time. All this is changing after half a century in Britain, where children are growing up with mixed identities.

# Language, culture and values

Almost all Polish people in this country speak their own language. Most also speak English now, although when they first came the language barrier was their biggest problem.

**Yvonne,** a British-born Polish woman working in adult education:

> My parents, who are both now dead, used to tell me how awful it was for them when they first came. They could not speak a word of English and had left behind a country they deeply loved. The humiliation of not being able to communicate and feeling like helpless children was what really got them.

### Family relationships

Luckily this community does not seem to suffer inter-generational conflicts as acutely as many others. The language, traditions and rituals have been maintained by having Saturday schools. Most Polish children are taught only their own language in the early years. They pick up English when they start school. This means that they can communicate with the elders in the community and ancestral links can continue.

**Yvonne** again:

> Our families are much more important to us all our lives, much more than the English people. We don't go out without them or go to pubs . We spend time together, always talking. So you can imagine what happens when an old person is left alone, or has no children. It is worse for him than death.

**Peter** and **Eva** again:

> Family life is very important to us. We try to stay very close and that has not changed as much as in other groups, but of course it is happening slowly.

There is a communal sense of pride and obligation that the elders in the community should be looked after by their families.

**Tomasz,** a veteran:

> I read about this old lady who was taken to hospital and they were trying to find out somebody in the family to come and see her. That I hope would never happen in our community. Many of these people are getting very old and vulnerable.

Until recently much pastoral care was provided by the priest and members of the community. Most people had hardly any contact with social services departments. But as the inevitable changes take place in this group, there is now an increased awareness that there will be more need for community workers who can communicate in Polish. There is still, however, a reluctance to 'trouble' anybody and a feeling that people just have to make do. This is how history is played out in people's lives. Their reception when they arrived in Britain has made the Polish population, just like the Vietnamese refugees, insecure about their rights in this society.

**Mr Kanski,** a 70-year-old retired plumber:

> We are very proud and also worried that if we ask for too much, like some of the other immigrants, British people will start hating us also. We try not to trouble them, to be independent if we can and even if we can't. Some of these immigrants are just looking for trouble. We are not discriminated against. We try and organise from inside our groups. And we all work very hard when we are younger. We don't take holidays every year or just spend. We save all the time.

## Identity, memories and longings

Not many Polish elders feel the need to return home, although those who visit their original country say that their health improves because it is not as damp as Britain. The war still holds painful memories, and Poland has gone through so many shifts and changes that it is not what it once was. Economic problems continue even after the fall of communism, which makes return an unrealistic goal because life is still so hard there.

Their children feel British in ways that are more meaningful, and their emotional feelings about Poland are weaker than those of their parents and grandparents. A major aspect for many East European elders is the enormous political changes they have witnessed in their homelands in the past decade.

**Catherine** again:

> It seems in some ways like a dream because, from here, it is difficult to imagine how things have changed in Poland. I am too ill to travel, so I talk to the young Polish people who arrive here these days just to find out.

### Religious differences

A very important fact that is often not recognised by people providing social services is the divisions that exist within and between groups who have come from the same country. Someone from Poland could be a Polish Catholic or a Polish Jew, and the latter might in fact have experienced anti-semitism from Polish Christians. There is also the delicate issue of Polish people and Jewish people (in general) feeling that their suffering in the hands of the Nazis is not properly acknowledged by the other group.

**Mr Rose**, a Jewish pensioner from Poland:

> Even today in Poland there are people who hate us or who think that we deserved it or that we have had all the attention while they too suffered under the Nazis. And among Jewish people there are those who do not think that the Polish suffering under Hitler was as bad as ours. Human beings are so complicated and destructive, aren't they? So just because we both fled Poland means nothing.

# Death

Many older people in the Polish communities find it difficult to discuss with friends their fears of dying or going into care homes, and some like Peter do seem to be suffering from a sense of terror. One thing that does sustain them in a very real way is their faith in their religion. Most stick closely to the Catholic rites when someone is dying. And the church is very supportive to the bereaved as well as to the dying. It is important for care workers to understand how important religion is to most Polish people, especially during stressful times.

## THE TURKISH COMMUNITY

In Britain we have Turkish people from the mainland as well as from Cyprus. Although there are differences between the two groups, on the whole they have enough in common to be regarded as one community.

The information in this section can also apply to the many Kurdish people who have taken refuge here in recent years because of the way some of them have been treated by the Turkish authorities. So, although they may be enemies, they are very similar people.

## Key issues

- Greek Cypriots and Turkish Cypriots have had a turbulent history in the past two decades. Getting their religious identity wrong – which is easy enough to do because they look alike – would be extremely offensive.
- Turks are mostly Muslims but have their own culture and particular history, which makes them unlike Muslims from Pakistan and other parts of the world. There are strong traditions that immigration has not eroded.

Getting the benefits they are entitled to is one of the most difficult problems for Turkish elders. A project serving the needs of Turkish Cypriot elders in Harringay found:

A large majority don't speak English and are experiencing a language barrier when attempting to access statutory services. Many of the elderly people are further disadvantaged because they cannot read or write Turkish and are therefore unaware of the services available to them even when translated information is available. Some pensioners have been in Britain, living in Harringay, for many years, and there is still a very low up-take of home care, health screening, occupational therapy and other clinical services.[4]

Beyond the usual problems of getting information in their language and finding out about changes that have been or are taking place, some Turkish Cypriots are becoming caught up in specific immigration regulations. Since 1994, for example, a 'Residency Test' has been established which says that you have to be a habitual resident in this country to qualify for state benefits. A number of Turkish elders have spent time back home and then returned to Britain, and they are being denied Income Support and other benefits. Kurdish asylum seekers from Turkey are likely to be affected by the new asylum laws and the denial of benefits for many seeking refuge. There is a lot of anxiety in the community about all this.

# History

Turkish people from the mainland arrived in Britain in the 1950s, 1960s and early 1970s. They came mainly because manufacturers in the clothing industry needed them and offered them work. They were given work permits by the government of the time because of the need for labour in this sector. Some also came to work in catering.

Turkey was modernised and secularised this century. It was felt by political leaders, particularly Kemal Atatürk, the Turkish president until the 1930s, that the country's future lay with Europe. Therefore, although their religion is central to the life of Turkish people, Turkey has not been an Islamic state for many decades. Part of the modernisation process included an emphasis on female rights and education and on personal freedom. This is what many British Turkish elders grew up with.

Turkish Cypriots also came to Britain during the 1950s and took up work in the clothing trade. Many became very successful and in turn employed other Turkish workers. It would probably be true to say that Turkish Cypriots have a stronger historical connection with Britain than those from Turkey itself, because Cyprus was a colony.

By the mid-1960s there were about 90,000 Cypriots in this country. This included Greek and Turkish Cypriots who, though many have become enemies, have much more in common in terms of their values than you might expect. Cyprus has a different history and in many ways its history made the island cosmopolitan: Egypt, Rome, Greece and Turkey have all made their mark. The wars in 1963 and then in 1974 marked an end to an integrated society and created not just a divided country but also new enmities and uncompromising brands of nationalism. Cyprus has changed radically from what it used to be, but some elders from the community are locked in their minds in that pre-war period.

**Mr Mehmet,** a retired cook:

> Before, you never saw so many armymen in our country. It was beautiful, it was peaceful. Like in Lebanon, it was easy to live with Greek people. We had the same thoughts, about our children and even the food. Then the wars destroyed all the peace and we all become hard people. I feel very much about that.

There were therefore economic and political reasons why people came to Britain and why they have never returned.

# Dispersal

Most Turkish people live in the Greater London area, with some in the home counties, Birmingham and Manchester. It is difficult to get accurate statistics because figures are based on geographical areas that group Greek and Turkish Cypriots together, people from mainland Turkey forming a separate group.

Most Turks work in the catering trade or in the clothing industry. The tendency is for Turkish workers to work for Turkish employers or to be self-employed in some small business. The Turkish enclaves that exist are entirely self-sufficient in terms of the commercial services people need.

## Religion

Turkish people are, with very few exceptions, Muslims; there are Turkish mosques in many cities, which are well attended. Because the Turks are culturally so distinct from Pakistanis and Bangladeshis, the mosques are usually separate although, technically, any Muslim can pray in any mosque.

## Diet

Turkish people follow all the directives on food that their religion dictates, in common with other Muslims. But culturally their diet is different from, say, the Pakistanis. They eat more salads and food that is less pungent than south Asian food. In many ways, as for other groups, food is normally not a problem for Turkish elders because it is relatively easy to get what they need. Like the Greeks, Turks eat yoghurt, feta and haloumi cheese, olives, lamb, tomatoes and pitta bread. Honey is very important and rice is a staple food.

It is when they are in hospital or they need meals-on-wheels that food becomes a serious problem. In areas where their numbers are not significant, most local authorities do not cater specially for the needs of Turkish people.

## Clothes

Unlike in many other Muslim communities, Turkish women do not generally wear body cloaks. Some cover their heads, others dress in western clothes. Recently, however, greater numbers of women have taken to wearing the hijab head covering.

# Language, culture and values

Turkish is not related to any other eastern language. Some Arabic has entered the language, mainly because most Turkish people are Muslims who would read the Qu'ran.

In Turkey over the past few years, a more fervent form of Islam has been asserting itself. This astonishes many Turkish elders because it is beginning to infiltrate political and social life as never before. Some elders react negatively to this and see it as an insult to Atatürk. Others are more orthodox and see this as something desirable. Nevertheless, there is little doubt that some traditional values and strict codes of behaviour that Turkish immigrants brought with them when they left have been eroded, at least in urban areas of Turkey and Cyprus.

**Leila,** a middle-aged woman from Turkey, who has three young daughters:

> It is very difficult for me to understand the world. My children they do not go out at night after nine o'clock. That is the rule; I have made it. But in my country, my brother's children they are going to the nightclubs. But I don't want my children to become the fanatic like the Islamic party in Turkey. So we are very worried. And my father, he is very confused about the meaning of Turkish life.

Loneliness is a major problem for Turkish elders because, as in Asian families, relationships are changing and people no longer have the extended family and other networks to sustain them. Younger people have to work hard to keep up their standards of living and many simply do not have the time they once might have had to spend with their elders. Some sons have moved away from the parents, which restricts their ability to provide even quite basic support.

## Family life

The Turkish community has undergone many of the inevitable changes that immigration brings into family life. Although there are strict moral codes, many of these are being relaxed by the young. Sex only within marriage, respect for parents and other elders and notions of social shame are being affected by alternative values seen in the media and other sources of influence.

**Aydin**, a community worker:

> There was always a stigma attached to young people, men or women, getting a flat of their own. You are supposed to live with your parents and siblings until you get married. Now there are youngsters who are breaking out of that. And, like it or not, there is sexual experimenta-tion, changes in aspirations – many girls had no role models of profes-sional women before; now they want to study and get a qualification and not just get married at 19. Gender roles are also changing. And if parents have a hard time coping with this, can you imagine what it feels like to be a powerless elder watching things changing and know-ing that there is much more going on than they can ever discover?

On the other hand, many young people in the community find the elders of their community more accommodating and understand-ing than their own parents.

**Aydin** again:

> My grandfather has been my friend when I have had terrible times. You don't know how hard it can be for a young ambitious girl in our community. There is so little faith, and so much fear of education. He has supported me to do my A levels. He has told my parents that I should go to university. He even gave me some of his savings. There are many Turkish girls who are running away from parents because they restrict them so much. At least in our home, my father respects my grandfather, so I have an easier life.

In terms of educational achievements, Turkish children have not done as well as some of the other immigrant groups. In part this was because language problems and the need to work long hours when they first moved here made it very difficult for Turkish par-ents to be involved in the education of their children. They did not know how to challenge the system. In some families, education was not a priority; survival and manpower were.

The expectation is that the elders will be looked after by their families. Most would feel deeply ashamed if an elder had to go into a care home or sheltered accommodation. This means that there has been little demand for such facilities, despite the many problems faced by Turkish elders.

In part the anxieties that Turkish families feel arise from the fact that they have experienced racism and have had to struggle to earn a decent income. Some have indeed made good. Others have bettered their lives a little, but at great cost to their health and well-being. Others are just managing to get by.

## Death

Elders, worried about what will happen to them when they die, often scrimp and save in order to have money that can be used to take their bodies back home. Many don't want to be buried in Britain.

**Husseyn**, 60, a widower:

> We came here and it was a good life. I did everything for my family and I worked very hard. But my heart is in Cyprus. I want my grave there, in the sun. Where my father, uncles, grandfathers all are lying.

# REFERENCES

## Chapter 1

1 Karl Atkin, Ethnic minority elders, *Nursing the Elderly*, March/April 1992, p 1

2 See Yasmin Alibhai-Brown, *Equal Value, Equal Care: Promoting best practice in care delivery*, National Extension College, 1994

3 Joy Anne McCalman, *The Forgotten People: Carers in three minority ethnic communities in Southwark*, Kings Fund Centre, 1990, Foreword

4 Dr Lynda Eribo, *The Support You Need*, Kings Fund, 1991, Foreword

5 Shabira Moledina, *Great Expectations: A review of services for Asian elderly in Brent*, Age Concern Brent, 1989, p 17

6 *Age and Race: Double Discrimination*, Commission for Racial Equality/Age Concern, 1995

7 Naina Patel, *A Race Against Time*, Runnymede Trust, 1990, p 63

## Chapter 2

1 *Social Trends 28*, Office for National Statistics, 1998

2 Quoted by Mark Johnson in his unpublished lecture, Age, Migration and Discrimination, Centre for Research in Ethnic Relations, University of Warwick, 1995

3 Ibid

4 See, for example, Colin Brown, *Black and White in Britain: The third PSI survey*, Heinemann, 1984

**5** See *Racial Attacks and Harassment*, Report of the UK House of Commons Select Committee, 1994

**6** Alison Norman, *Triple Jeopardy: Growing old in a second homeland*, Centre for Policy on Ageing, 1985, p 1

**7** Ranjit Sondhi, ex-Deputy Chairman for the Commission for Racial Equality, Speech made to the Standing Conference of Ethnic Minority Citizens, AGM, 1994

**8** Department of the Environment, English House Condition Survey, HMSO, 1991

**9** Lena Dominelli, *Anti-Racist Social Work*, Macmillan Education, 1988, p 118

**10** *Labour Force Survey 1995*, Office for National Statistics

**11** Mark Johnson, op cit

**12** Ranjit Sondhi, op cit

**13** Vivienne Coombe, Ethnic minority elders, In *Race and Social Work: A guide to training*, Vivienne Coombe and Alan Little (eds), Tavistock Publications, p 219

**14** Reg Walker and Waquar Ahmad, Asian and Black elders and community care, *New Community*, July 1994, pp 635–646

**15** Shabira Moledina, *Great Expectations: A review of services for Asian elderly in Brent*, Age Concern Brent, 1989

**16** Ranjit Sondhi, op cit

**17** See Naina Patel, *A Race Against Time: Social service provision to black elders*, Runnymede Trust, 1990

**18** Josephine Kwahali, Hear their words, *Community Care*, 31 March 1994

**19** Naina Patel, op cit, pp 19–20

## Chapter 3

1 Jeff Crawford, Harringay Community Relations Council Report, 1978

2 Peter Fryer, *The History of Black People in Britain*, Pluto, 1984, p 10

3 Sir Harry Johnston, *The Black Man's Part in the War*, quoted by Fryer, op cit, p 296

4 *The Liverpool Courier*, 11 June 1919, quoted by Fryer, op cit, p 302

5 These coloured 'intruders', *John Bull*, 26 Jan 1946, quoted in Fryer, op cit, p 363

6 Steve Fenton, Health, work and growing old: the Afro-Caribbean experience, *New Community*, vol 14, no 3, Spring 1988

7 R Glass and H Pollins, *Newcomers: The West Indians in London*, Centre for Urban Studies, University of London, 1960, p 120

8 See Naina Patel, *A Race Against Time: Social service provision to black elders*, Runnymede Trust, 1990, pp 19–20

## Chapter 4

1 Rozina Visram, *Ayahs, Lascars and Princes*, Pluto, p 13

2 *Tatler*, February 1709, quoted by Visram, op cit, p 14

3 Caroline Adams, *Across the Seven Seas and Thirteen Rivers*, Thap Books, 1987, pp 95–96

4 Rozina Visram, op cit, p 47

5 Alison Norman, *Triple Jeopardy: Growing old in a second homeland*, Centre for Policy on Ageing, 1985, p 31

6 See A Jones, *The Numbers Game*, Anchor Housing Association, 1994

7 Quoted by Colin Brown, 'Same difference': the persistence of racial disadvantage in the British employment market, In *Racism and Antiracism*, Peter Braham, Ali Rattansi and Richard Skellington (eds), Open University, 1992, p 48

8 Ibid, pp 48–49

**9** Jean Ellis, *Breaking New Ground: Community development with Asian communities*, Bedford Square Press, 1989, p 3

**10** Karl Atkin, Elaine Cameron, Francis Badger and Helen Evers, Asian elders' knowledge and future use of community, social and health services, *New Community*, vol 15, no 3, April 1989, pp 439–445

**11** Shabira Moledina, *Great Expectations: A review of services for Asian elders in Brent*, Age Concern Brent, 1989

## Chapter 5

**1** Yuen Tse, *Organising Chinese Women in Black Feminist Groups: Developing a working proposal for organising Chinese women in Town A*, Unpublished dissertation, Department of Applied Social Sciences, Warwick University, 1986

**2** Douglas Jones, The Chinese in Britain: origins and development of a community, *New Community*, vol 7, no 3, Winter 1979, pp 116–132

**3** David Own, *Chinese People and 'other' Ethnic Minorities in Britain: Social and economic circumstances*, National Ethnic Minority Data Archive, 1991 Census Statistical Paper No 8, University of Warwick, December 1994

**4** Alison Norman, *Triple Jeopardy: Growing old in a second homeland*, Centre for Policy on Ageing, 1985, p 40

**5** Wing Leung Siu, *What About the Needs of Dispersed and Isolated Minorities? The experience of setting up a Chinese day care centre within a social services department in Birmingham*, unpublished practice study, Department of Applied Social Studies, Coventry Polytechnic, 1991

**6** Pam Schweitzer, A place to stay, In *Growing Old Away From Home: Multicultural health care and the rehabilitation of older people*, AJ Squires (ed), Edward Arnold/Age Concern, 1991

**7** Win Leung Siu, op cit

**8** Amy Tan, *The Joy Luck Club*, Minerva, 1989

**9** Carol Dalglish, *Refugees from Viet Nam*, Macmillan, 1989, p 87

**10** Jonathan Margolis, Homes from home?, *The Sunday Times*, 9 October 1994

**11** Thuy Vuong G, *Getting to Know the Vietnamese and Their Culture*, Ungar, 1976, p 21

**12** Carol Dalglish, op cit, p 61

**13** Joy Anne McCalman, *The Forgotten People: Carers in three minority ethnic communities in Southwark*, Kings Fund Centre, 1990, pp 63–68

## *Chapter 6*

**1** Carol Dalgliesh, *Refugees from Viet Nam*, Macmillan, 1989, p 3

**2** Pam Schweitzer, A place to stay, In *Growing Old Away From Home: Multicultural health care and the rehabilitation of older people*, AJ Squires (ed), Edward Arnold/Age Concern, 1991, p 38

**3** EB Rose and Associates, *Colour and Citizenship, A report on British race relations*, Institute of Race Relations/Oxford University Press, 1969, p 20

**4** *Turkish Speaking Elders Project*, Annual Report, Age Concern Harringay, 1994/5, p 1

# USEFUL ADDRESSES

In most urban areas with significant populations of ethnic minority people, you can find Community Relations Councils or Race Equality Councils. Local Age Concern groups, Citizens Advice Bureaux and Help the Aged centres are also a useful source of information. All these organisations are listed in local directories, and they can provide guidance and information.

**African Welfare and Resource Centre**

Bridge Park
Harrow Road
London NW10 0RG
Tel: 0181-961 6881

**All Faiths for One Race (AFFOR)**

173 Lozells Road
Birmingham B19 1RN
Tel: 0121-523 8076

**Asian Elderly Concern**

15 Eastfield Road
London E7 3BA
Tel: 0181-509 2894

**Asian Family Counselling Service**

74 The Avenue
Ealing
London W13 8LB
Tel: 0181-997 5749

**Asian Women's Resource Centre**

134 Minet Avenue
London NW10 8AP
Tel: 0181-961 5701

**Asian Resource Centre**

101 Villa Road
Handsworth
Birmingham B19 1NH
Tel: 0121-523 0580

## Carers National Association

20–25 Glasshouse Yard
London EC1A 4JS
Tel: 0171-490 8818
Adviceline 0171-490 8898 (10–12, 2–4 weekdays)

## Chinese Community Centre

44 Gerrard Street
London W1V 7LP
Tel: 0171-439 3882

## Commission for Racial Equality

Elliott House
10–12 Allington Street
London SW1E 5EH
Tel: 0171-828 7022

## Family Welfare Association

501 Kingsland Road
London E8 4AU
Tel: 0171-254 6251

## Jewish Care

221 Golders Green Road
London NW11 9DW
Tel: 0171-458 3282

## Polish Social and Cultural Association

238 King Street
London W6 0RF
Tel: 0181-741 1940

## Standing Conference of Ethnic Minority Senior Citizens

5 Westminster Bridge Road
London SE1 7XW
Tel: 0171-928 0095

## Turkish Cypriot Cultural Association

14a Graham Road
London E8 1BZ
Tel: 0171-249 7410

## Vietnamese Refugee Community

9 Granville Court
Nynehead Street
London SE14 6JB
Tel: 0181-469 0307

## West Indian Concern

Caribbean House
Bridport Place
London N1 5DS
Tel: 0171-739 0840

## West Indian Ex-Servicemens Association

165 Clapham Manor Street
London SW4 6DB
Tel: 0171-627 0702

# USEFUL PUBLICATIONS

Alibhai-Brown Y, *Equal Value, Equal Care: Promoting best practice in care delivery*, National Extension College, 1994

Bhalla A and Blakemore K, *Elders of the Minority Ethnic Groups*, All Faiths for One Race, 1981 (address on p 184)

Bright Les and Turay Mariama, *More than Black and White: A study of black and ethnic minority elders' concerns about the care services*, Counsel and Care, 1996

Commission for Racial Equality, *The Needs of the Chinese Community in Scotland and the North East*, CRE, 1988

Farrah M, *Black Elders in Leicester*, Leicester Social Services Department Report, 1986.

Fenton S, *Ageing Minorities: Black people as they grow old in Britain*, Commission for Racial Equality, 1987

Glendinning F (ed), *The Elders in Ethnic Minorities*, Beth Johnson Foundation, 1979

Glendinning F and Pearson M, *The Black and Ethnic Minority Elders in Britain*, Working Papers on the Health of Older People, No 6, Health Education Council and Keele University, 1988

Gunaratnam Y, *Call for Care*, Health Education Authority/Kings Fund Centre, 1991

Hall S, *Forty Winters On: Memories of Britain's post-war Caribbean immigrants*, Lambeth Council, 1988, Introduction

Henley Alix, *Asians in Britain – Caring for Muslims and their Families: religious aspects of care*, National Extension College/Department of Health and Social Security/Kings Fund Centre, 1982

Henley Alix, *Caring for Hindus and their Families: religious aspects of care*, National Extension College/Department of Health and Social Security/Kings Fund Centre, 1983

Henley Alix, *Caring for Sikhs and their Families: religious aspects of care*, National Extension College/Department of Health and Social Security/Kings Fund Centre, 1983

Jones A, *The Numbers Game*, Anchor Housing Association, 1994

Mares P, *The Vietnamese in Britain: A handbook for health workers*, Health Education Council/National Extension College, 1982

Mares P, Henley A and Baxter C, *Health Care in Multiracial Britain*, Health Education Council/National Extension College, 1985

Neuberger J, *Caring for Dying People of Different Faiths*, Austen Cornish, 1987

The 1990 Trust, *Black Elders: A forgotten minority*, The 1990 Trust, 1995

Shang A, The seeds of Chinatown: the Chinese in Britain, in *Race and Social Work*, Vivienne Coombs and Alan Little (eds), Tavistock, 1986

Ward Sue, *Ethnic Elders' Benefits Handbook*, Age Concern Books, 1997

Wilson R (ed), *Age in Exile*, British Refugee Council, 1988

Wing Kroong L and Kerrie PK Lin, *Working with Chinese Carers*, Health Education Council/Kings Fund Centre, 1992

## Other publications

Find out about newspapers, radio and television programmes in relevant languages for different minority groups. Community centres will advise you on these.

# ABOUT AGE CONCERN

*Caring for Ethnic Minority Elders: A guide* is one of a wide range of publications produced by Age Concern England, the National Council on Ageing. Age Concern cares about all older people and believes that later life should be fulfilling and enjoyable. For too many this is impossible. As the leading charitable movement in the UK concerned with ageing and older people, Age Concern finds effective ways to change that situation.

Where possible, we enable older people to solve problems themselves, providing as much or as little support as they need. Our network of 1,400 local groups, supported by 250,000 volunteers, provides community-based services such as lunch clubs, day centres and home visiting.

Nationally, we take a lead role in campaigning, parliamentary work, policy analysis, research, specialist information and advice provision, and publishing. Innovative programmes promote healthier lifestyles and provide older people with opportunities to give the experience of a lifetime back to their communities.

Age Concern is dependent on donations, covenants and legacies.

**Age Concern England**
1268 London Road
London SW16 4ER
Tel: 0181-765 7200

**Age Concern Scotland**
113 Rose Street
Edinburgh EH2 3DT
Tel: 0131-220 3345

**Age Concern Cymru**
4th Floor
1 Cathedral Road
Cardiff CF1 9SD
Tel: 01222 371566

**Age Concern Northern Ireland**
3 Lower Crescent
Belfast BT7 1NR
Tel: 01232 245729

# PUBLICATIONS FROM AGE CONCERN BOOKS

## Health and care

**Know Your Medicines 3rd edition**
Pat Blair

This revised and updated edition of the popular guide explains many of the common questions older people – and those who care for them – may have about the medicines they use and how these may affect them. Written in a clear and concise way, topics include: what medicines actually do; using medicines effectively; common ailments; medicines and your body systems. This new edition will prove to be a valuable source of advice and guidance.

£7.99   0–86242–226–4

**Taking Good Care: A handbook for care assistants**
Jenyth Worsley

Written for professional carers of older people, this book covers such vital issues as the role of the care assistant in a residential home, communication skills, the medical and social problems encountered by carers, the resident's viewpoint, and activities and group work.

£7.50   0–86242–072–5

**CareFully: A handbook for home care assistants 2nd edition**
Lesley Bell

Comprehensive and informative, this new edition of a highly acclaimed guide provides key advice for home care workers in promoting independence. Packed with practical guidance, detailed information on good practice and recent developments in home care provision, all chapters are related to S/NVQ level 2 revised units in care. Topics covered in full include:

- basic skills of home care assistants
- the health of older people
- receiving home care – the user's perspective
- the importance of core values
- providing a service for the new millennium
- taking care of yourself

Complete with case studies, checklists and a unique new section on users' perspectives, this is a book to enable all home care workers to face their job with confidence and enthusiasm.

£12.99   0–86242–285–X

### The Nutrition of Older Adults
Dr Geoffrey Webb and June Copeman

This book offers a wide-ranging review of the nutritional needs, priorities and problems experienced by older people. Fully referenced, and including a readable introduction for non-specialists, this text also explores the social, demographic and economic factors affecting diet and nutrition in later life.

Co-published with Arnold

£13.99   0–340–60156–6

# Money matters

### Ethnic Elders' Benefits Handbook
Sue Ward

For many older members of ethnic minority groups, the rights to Social Security benefits will be no different from those of anyone else, if you have full UK citizenship or have spent all your working life in Britain. But for many others there are special rules to cope with an already complex system. Written in clear and concise English, this handbook is intended to help anyone from an ethnic minority understand how the system works, what their rights are and how they can claim a Social

Security benefit to which they may be entitled. Topics covered include: nationality law for older people; immigration law and older people; health and social care; social security and people from other countries.

This book aims to help people through the maze of legal issues covering immigration and citizenship, and on related Social Security rights for those at or near pension are. It is full of advice and includes an explanation of terminology, useful publications and organisations, and relevant DSS leaflets.

£9.99   0–86242–229–9

If you would like to order any of these titles, please write to the address below, enclosing a cheque or money order for the appropriate amount made payable to Age Concern England. Credit card orders may be made on 0181-765 7200.

**Mail Order Unit**
Age Concern England
1268 London Road
London SW16 4ER

# Information line

Age Concern produces over 40 comprehensive factsheets designed to answer many of the questions older people – or those advising them – may have, on topics such as:

- finding and paying for residential and nursing home care
- money benefits
- finding help at home
- legal affairs
- making a Will
- help with heating
- raising income from your home
- transfer of assets

Age Concern offers a factsheet subscription service that presents all the factsheets in a folder, together with regular updates throughout the year. The first year's subscription currently costs £50; an annual renewal thereafter is £25.

To order your FREE factsheet list, phone 0800 00 99 66 (a free call) or write to:
**Age Concern**
FREEPOST (SWB 30375)
Ashburton
Devon TQ13 7ZZ

# INDEX